Nigel Cawthorne is the author of *Military Commanders* and *Vietnam – A War Lost and Won*. His writing has appeared in over a hundred and fifty newspapers, magazines and part-works – from the *Sun* to the *Financial Times*, and from *Flatbush Life* to *The New York Tribune*.

D1328834

П4О О2Ɔ О/4 4

Recent titles in the series

A Brief Guide to the Supernatural
Leo Ruickbie

A Brief Guide to Star Trek
Brian J. Robb

A Brief Guide to James Bond
Nigel Cawthorne

A Brief Guide to Jane Austen
Charles Jennings

A Brief Guide to Secret Religions
David Barrett

A Brief History of Angels and Demons
Sarah Bartlett

A Brief History of Bad Medicine
Robert Youngston

A Brief History of France
Cecil Jenkins

A Brief History of Slavery
Jeremy Black

A Brief History of Sherlock Holmes
Nigel Cawthorne

A Brief History of King Arthur
Mike Ashley

A Brief History of the Universe
J. P. McEvoy

A Brief History of Roman Britain
Joan P. Alcock

A Brief History of the Private Life of Elizabeth II
Michael Patterson

A BRIEF GUIDE TO

JEEVES AND WOOSTER

NIGEL CAWTHORNE

RUNNING PRESS
PHILADELPHIA · LONDON

ROBINSON

Constable & Robinson Ltd
55–56 Russell Square
London WC1B 4HP
www.constablerobinson.com

First published in the UK by Robinson,
An imprint of Constable & Robinson, 2013

Copyright © Nigel Cawthorne 2013

The right of Nigel Cawthorne to be identified as the
author of this work has been asserted by him in accordance
with the Copyright, Designs and Patents Act 1988

All rights reserved. This book is sold subject to the condition
that it shall not be reproduced in whole or in part, in any form or by any means, electronic or
mechanical, including photocopying, recording, or by any information storage and retrieval system
now known or hereafter invented, without written permission from the publisher and
without a similar condition, including this condition, being imposed on the subsequent purchaser.

A copy of the British Library Cataloguing in
Publication data is available from the British Library

ISBN 978-1-78033-824-8 (paperback)
ISBN 978-1-78033-825-5 (ebook)

1 3 5 7 9 10 8 6 4 2

First published in the United States in 2013 by Running Press Book Publishers,
A Member of the Perseus Books Group

All rights reserved under the Pan-American and International Copyright Conventions

Books published by Running Press are available at special discounts for bulk purchases in the United
States by corporations, institutions, and other organizations. For more information, please contact the
Special Markets Department at the Perseus Books Group, 2300 Chestnut Street, Suite 200,
Philadelphia, PA 19103, or call (800) 810-4145, ext. 5000, or email
special.markets@perseusbooks.com.

US ISBN 978-0-7624-4805-0
US Library of Congress Control Number: 2012942956

9 8 7 6 5 4 3 2 1
Digit on the right indicates the number of this printing

Running Press Book Publishers
2300 Chestnut Street
Philadelphia, PA 19103-4371

Visit us on the web!
www.runningpress.com

Typeset by TW Typesetting, Plymouth, Devon

Printed and bound in the UK

CONTENTS

Introduction   *vii*

Chapter 1   P. G. Wodehouse   1

Chapter 2   The Birth of Jeeves and Wooster   15

Chapter 3   The Short Stories   42

Chapter 4   The Novels   92

Chapter 5   Bertram Wilberforce Wooster   153

Chapter 6   Jeeves   169

Chapter 7   Aunts and Uncles   177

Chapter 8   Fiancées and Sweethearts   188

Chapter 9   Drones and Other Acquaintances   209

Chapter 10 Old Hardened Arteries and Rozzers   221

Chapter 11 Stage and Screen   231

Bibliography   *235*

Index   *237*

INTRODUCTION

What ho! And welcome to the world of Jeeves and Wooster. It is a world of sunshine, country houses and champagne, somehow permanently stuck in the Edwardian era before the slaughter of the First World War.

Although the Jeeves and Wooster stories seem quintessentially English, they were largely conceived and written in America by a man who spent more than half his adult life in the United States, eventually becoming a citizen in 1955. Indeed, the first Jeeves and Wooster stories were set in New York. However, most of the stories are located in an England contrived to appeal to an American audience.

The stories were first published in the *Saturday Evening Post* and later in *Cosmopolitan Magazine*, beginning in September 1915, before being published in the *Strand Magazine* in the UK. The novels and collections of short stories have since been published on both sides of the Atlantic and worldwide. In the 1990s, the ITV television series and subsequent DVDs, starring Stephen Fry and Hugh Laurie, found a new following. There are over twenty chapters of the Wodehouse Society in North America. They also flourish in the Netherlands, Russia, Finland and Italy. There are two as far away as India and one in New South Wales, Australia.

P. G. Wodehouse first visited the United States in 1904 and lived there on and off after 1909. He had his first bestseller there with the novel *Something New* (entitled *Something Fresh* in the UK) in 1915 and achieved fame on Broadway as a lyricist with Jerome Kern and Guy Bolton in 1917. He then moved to Hollywood. After returning to Britain and living in France, he settled in the United States permanently after the Second World War.

Jeeves and Wooster are Wodehouse's best-known characters. They appear in thirty-five short stories and eleven novels. They first featured in the short story 'Extricating Young Gussie', which appeared in the collection *The Man with Two Left Feet*. Their last novel, *Aunts Aren't Gentlemen*, was published in October 1974, four months before Wodehouse's death.

The master–servant relationship provides the framework for comedy. The cunning servant and foolish master combination has been used since classical times. While Bertie Wooster is good-hearted but weak-willed, 'mentally negligible', as Jeeves described him, and almost guaranteed to make a hash of any scheme he takes in hand, Jeeves is omniscient, efficient and, above all, loyal.

The writing, of course, is of the highest standard. Evelyn Waugh said of Wodehouse: 'One has to regard a man as a master who can produce on average three uniquely brilliant and entirely original similes on every page.'

The plots are strong and beautifully crafted. These usually involve Bertie getting engaged to someone he hates and his subsequent attempts to disentangle himself, while simultaneously involved in some morally dubious enterprise. The plot of 'The Great Sermon Handicap', for example, revolves around betting on which local vicar will preach the longest sermon. The stories are studded with vivid characters – Aunt Agatha, who 'eats broken bottles and wears barbed wire next to the skin'; Aunt Dahlia, formerly a stalwart of the Quorn and Pytchley Hunts; Gussie Fink-Nottle, newt-fancier and orange-juice addict; Madeline Bassett, the glutinously soupy girl, who thinks stars are God's daisy chain; Roderick Spode, would-be British dictator, leader of the Black Shorts, whose piercing eyes can open an oyster at sixty paces and whose shameful secret is that he is the proprietor of the ladies' lingerie shop; and the dog Bartholomew, an opinionated and irascible Aberdeen terrier, whose growling and snapping once kept Bertie and Jeeves marooned on top of a wardrobe.

It is refreshing to pass time in the company of such creations and visit a world where there is no credit crunch or weapons of mass destruction, where no one works because they are so wealthy and any temporary shortage of funds can be cured by a well-timed inheritance.

However, it would be nice to think that Britain had moved on from the world of rigid class distinction portrayed by Wodehouse. Sadly, this is not the case. In jolly old England these days, the Cabinet is stuffed full of old Etonians once more. There is a surfeit of Bertie Woosters, but not a single sage-brained Jeeves in sight. Pip-pip.

Nigel Cawthorne

I

P. G. WODEHOUSE

Jeeves and Wooster – as much as they existed at all – inhabit a comic version of the class-ridden England in which P. G. Wodehouse was born and brought up. However, he came from neither the upper classes in which Wooster dwelt nor the servant class where Jeeves was tethered, but from somewhere in between.

Wodehouse was from the landed gentry. Like Bertie Wooster, he could trace his family's ancestry back to the Norman Conquest in 1066. Sir Constantine de Wodehouse was knighted by William the Conqueror's son, Henry I, and a Sir Bertram de Wodehouse accompanied Edward I on the invasion of Scotland in 1296.

Over the years, the Wodehouse family accumulated eighteen knighthoods, a baronetcy, a barony and an earldom – all grist to Wodehouse's fictional mill. However, P. G. came from a cadet or junior branch of the family, far removed from titles or even the prospect of one. His father, Henry Wodehouse, worked as a magistrate in Hong Kong from 1867 until he retired in 1895 and seems to have been the source of much of the colourful colonial vocabulary that appears in Wodehouse's books. Otherwise, as Wodehouse put it in his memoirs, his father was 'as normal as rice pudding'.

Wodehouse's mother, Eleanor, was the daughter of the Reverend John Bathurst Deane, an amateur genealogist who could also trace his family back to Norman times. A formidable woman like those depicted in Wodehouse's fiction, Eleanor was rooted in the country life of England. However, the family was of a slightly bohemian bent. One sister was a painter, trained in Paris, who exhibited at the Royal Academy in London; another, Mary, wrote poetry and romantic novels.

In the 1870s, Eleanor joined the so-called 'fishing fleet' of single women who went out to the colonies in the hope of snaring a husband. She married in 1877 and set about producing a family of eccentrically named sons. There was Philip Peveril born in 1877, Ernest Armine in 1879 and Richard Lancelot in 1892; all were known by their more peculiar second names.

Pelham Grenville was born on 15 October 1881, the same year as Picasso and Bartók, and just a few months before Virginia Woolf and James Joyce, though his effect on contemporary literature would be markedly different from Woolf's or Joyce's. He was named after his godfather Colonel Pelham von Donop. He did not like his forenames, calling them a 'frightful label', as he says in the introduction to *Something Fresh*. Fortunately, his own childish rendition of Pelham, 'Plum', stuck, while throughout his professional life he used P. G.

Wodehouse was born prematurely. At the time, his mother was visiting one of her sisters at 1 Vale Place, 50 Epsom Road, Guildford, Surrey, around 30 miles south-west of London. She then took the infant back to Hong Kong where he was handed to the care of a Chinese maid. At the age of two, he was returned to England with his two older brothers. Eleanor rented a house in her hometown of Bath and engaged Miss Roper as a governess to look after them. Miss Roper was first of a series of strict 'aunts' who looked after the children, while Eleanor returned to Hong Kong.

Indeed, Plum had eight actual aunts in England who played a part in his upbringing. One of them, Mary, was a quarrelsome spinster whom he described as 'the scourge of my childhood'. She is thought to have been the model for Bertie's fearsome Aunt Agatha, while Eleanor's oldest sister, Louise 'Looly' Deane, is thought to have inspired the genial Aunt Dahlia. He saw so little of his mother – Wodehouse was with his parents for barely six months between the ages of three and fifteen – that she could almost be considered an aunt as well. Among his uncles there were four clergymen, the inspiration, perhaps, for 'The Great Sermon Handicap'.

In 1885, Wodehouse's parents returned to England so his father could collect his Companion of the Order of St Michael and St George (CMG), an order of chivalry for British subjects to recognise non-military service. They took the opportunity to pack the children off to a small boarding school in Croydon on the south-east edge of London, run by Cissie and Florrie Prince – two more 'aunts', perhaps. Holidays were spent with real aunts in country houses.

At school, Wodehouse once hid behind the sofa when Florrie was proposed to by George Hardie Scott in a scene in which Bertie Wooster himself would not have been out of place. Wodehouse also remembered stealing a turnip from a nearby field. Food was scarce and the regimen strict. Nevertheless, Wodehouse later described his childhood as 'a breeze from start to finish with everyone I met understanding me perfectly'.

Wodehouse was a voracious reader and knew he wanted to be a writer from an early age, recounting in *Over Seventy* that

'I started turning out the stuff at the age of five.'

At six he read Alexander Pope's translation of the *Iliad*. Around that time his widowed grandmother and her four unmarried daughters moved to an Elizabethan house named Cheney Court in the village of Box, five miles from Bath in the west of England. The ménage there inspired the scene in *The Mating Season* in which Bertie goes to stay with Esmond Haddock and his five aunts at Deverill Hall in King's Deverill. There were, of course, servants and, as a child, Wodehouse got to know downstairs life intimately.

For the sake of Peveril's health, the three boys were sent to Elizabeth College on Guernsey in the Channel Islands. Life there, again, was 'very pleasant'. At the age of ten, Wodehouse was sent to Malvern House, a preparatory school in Kent that specialized in preparing boys for the Royal Navy, the career his father had picked out for him. However, this hardly suited a bookish boy like Wodehouse. He was unhappy there and took his revenge in his fiction. Malvern House became the ghastly prep school where Bertie Wooster and Reginald 'Kipper' Herring did 'a stretch' before Eton, as he relates in *Jeeves in the Offing*.

Wodehouse's poor eyesight disqualified him from active service in the Royal Navy and in 1894 he won a scholarship to Dulwich College in south London where elder brother Armine was already happily ensconced.

'My schooldays at Dulwich were just six years of unbroken bliss,' said Wodehouse in *Over Seventy*, which he actually found rather disappointing. To be a writer, he thought, you needed 'an eccentric father, a miserable misunderstood childhood and a hell of a time at public school'.

At Dulwich, the young Wodehouse excelled at rugby, cricket, boxing and athletics. He had a fine voice and sang at school concerts, and succeeded his brother as editor of the school magazine. It was, he said, 'like heaven'. In many ways, both in his heart and in his head, he never left his old school, admitting in *Performing Flea* 'a bad case of arrested mental development . . . I seem not to have progressed a step since I was eighteen'.

He read English literature and the classics, writing as quickly in Latin and Greek as he could in English. His teachers included William Beach Thomas, who went on to become a distinguished journalist, and Philip Hope, who taught composition in prose and verse and delighted the boys with his ability to translate a sentence into Latin or Greek in version after version.

Although Dulwich College was not Eton or Harrow, it was imbued with the class system that is such a feature of Wodehouse's work. At first he was a boarder. Then, in 1895, his parents returned to England. They took a house in Dulwich and Armine and Plum became day boys. This experiment in family life was both painful and short-lived. His parents were strangers to him and he was used to living around his contemporaries. At the end of the school year, the family moved out to Stableford in Shropshire, near the Welsh border, and Plum became a boarder again.

In 1897 Wodehouse won a senior classical scholarship and joined the Classical Sixth. He shared a study with Bill Townend, a lifelong friend who himself went on to become a writer, though not as successful as Wodehouse. The two of them talked incessantly about books and Townend recalled his friend writing a series of plays after the pattern of the Greek tragedies, which were outrageously funny and dealt with masters and boys of the school.

A fan of W. S. Gilbert, Wodehouse played Guildenstern in Gilbert's farce *Rosencrantz and Guildenstern*. In the Upper Sixth, he was in the cricket first eleven and the rugby first fifteen. He seemed all set to go up to Oxford like Bertie.

While Peveril had stayed on at Elizabeth College and went

on to join the Hong Kong police force, Armine went to Oxford, where he was awarded the Newdigate Prize for poetry and graduated with a double first. Then he went to India where he became tutor to Jiddu Krishnamurti, the messiah of the Theosophical Movement.

Plum expected to follow in his brother's footsteps but his father then had to break some bad news to him. As his pension was paid in rupees, whose value was dropping, he could not afford to send another son to university. Instead, Plum was to go to work in the City. Through his father's connections, he got a job in the Hongkong and Shanghai Banking Corporation (today's HSBC).

Even before he left school Wodehouse began making money out of writing, keeping an accounts book entitled 'Money Received from Literary Work'. The first entry was a half-guinea (52½p) for an essay called 'Some Aspects of Game Captaincy' published in *Public School Magazine*.

At first he found himself like a fish out of water at the bank, but it was not in Wodehouse's nature to be downcast. His colleagues were a nice crowd and he enjoyed the companionship. He later put experience in the bank to good use in his book *Psmith in the City*. The rhetoric of the nine-to-fivers also enhanced his vocabulary. He spent his evenings writing or out on the streets trying to find material, sometimes long into the night. He was regularly late to work and sometimes arrived with his pyjamas peeping out from under his business suit. His home at that time was a bedsit in Markham Square, Chelsea, later the home of the impecunious Stanley Featherstonehaugh Ukridge, protagonist in nineteen short stories and one novel.

Though he was generally fit, Wodehouse came down with mumps while at the bank. In rare cases, this affects the testes, causing infertility and even impotence. Sex is notable by its absence from the works of Wodehouse and there is speculation that this might have been the cause.

Wodehouse played for both the bank's rugby and cricket teams and, during his lunch hour, would shoot across the river to the Oval cricket ground to watch play there. His prowess as a sportsman did not make up for his shortcomings as a clerk, however. At work he wrote a story called 'The Formal Opening of a New Ledger' on the front page of a ledger in the hope of amusing the head cashier. At the last moment his nerve failed him and he removed the offending page. This then provoked a row between the head casher and bank's stationer, who concluded that only an imbecile would remove the front page of a ledger. 'Have you an imbecile in your department?' asked the stationer.

'Why yes,' said the head cashier, '... P. G. Wodehouse.'

In later life, Wodehouse implied that this incident got him the sack from the bank, though this was untrue. There was also an apocryphal tale that he once became so tired of reconciling figures that he walked to London Bridge and the river. However, that did not get him fired either. He quit of his own volition after two years. By then his work was appearing regularly in *Tit-Bits*, *Pearson's Weekly*, *Answers*, *Captain* and *Globe and Traveller*.

'I wrote everything in those days,' he told biographer David Jasen 'verses, short stories, articles for the lowest type of weekly paper.'

He avoided humorous stories, even though that was where his inclination lay. Instead, he went in for sentiment, thinking that was the type of thing for which editors were most likely to pay. However, in November 1900, his first comic article was published in *Tit-Bits*. It was called 'Men Who Have Missed Their Own Weddings'. This was just a small portion of his output.

'Worse bilge than mine may have been submitted to editors in 1901 and 1902,' said Wodehouse in *Over Seventy*, 'but I should think it unlikely.'

Nevertheless, during his two years at the bank, some eighty of his articles and stories were published.

In August 1902, he was approached by his old schoolmaster William Beach Thomas. Beach Thomas was then working on the *Globe and Traveller*, a daily evening broadsheet, one of the eight that London supported at the time. He asked Wodehouse to take over the daily 'By The Way' column while he went on holiday. The job consisted of scanning the morning papers and writing short humorous takes on items of news for a midday deadline. It was an opportunity not to be missed. So on 9 September 1902 Wodehouse quit the bank to go freelance. The following year, Beach Thomas quit the *Globe* and Wodehouse became a full-time member of staff.

The offices of the *Globe* were in the Strand, then the centre of London's nightlife. There he would have been surrounded by 'Gaiety girls' from the Gaiety Theatre and silly young men of the Wooster stamp on their way to the Savoy or Romano's. Both places get a mention in the Jeeves and Wooster stories.

Just nine days after quitting the bank, the twenty-year-old Wodehouse published his first book, *The Pothunters*, which had originally run as a serial in *Public School Magazine*. It concerns the theft of sporting trophies – or 'pots' – from a public school. It was dedicated to Joan, Effie and Ernestine Bowes-Lyon. The cousins of Elizabeth Bowes-Lyon, who went on to become Queen Elizabeth, wife of George VI and The Queen Mother, they were just the sort of girls who also inhabited Bertie's world.

He was soon making enough money to move out of Markham Square and into upmarket Walpole Street, spending the weekends in the country, often in Emsworth House in Hampshire, courtesy of his friend and fellow freelance writer Herbert Westbrook. This, he found, was the perfect place to work.

In 1903, Wodehouse published forty-seven stories and

poems in *Punch* magazine alone. He also contributed to the *Daily Chronicle*, *Vanity Fair*, *Illustrated Sporting and Dramatic News*, *Windsor Magazine* and *Royal Magazine*. He interviewed his literary hero Sir Arthur Conan Doyle for *VC Magazine* and lunched with W. S. Gilbert.

Wodehouse followed *The Pothunters* with a series of books set in fictional public schools. By then he had already made his mark as a comic writer with the poem 'The Parrot', which appeared on the front page of the *Daily Express* on 30 September 1903 and satirized the position of the Liberal Party on 'imperial preference'. It was a huge success and, although published anonymously, it made his reputation among those in the know. By the end of the year, he had saved enough money to set sail for the United States of America.

Sailing on the SS *St Louis*, he arrived in New York on 25 April 1904.

'Being there was like being in heaven,' he wrote in *America, I Like You*, 'without going to all the bother and expense of dying.'

His intention had been to move on to Philadelphia, the home of the *Saturday Evening Post*, and to meet the former heavyweight champion 'Gentleman Jim' Corbett, who was out of town. Nevertheless he immersed himself in the world of boxing, leading to a series of stories featuring a boxer named 'Kid' Brady. He returned to England on 20 May, where he found his work very much in demand.

'In 1904 anyone in the London writing world who had been to America was regarded with awe,' he said in *Over Seventy*. 'My income rose like a rocking pheasant.'

For the summer issue of *Punch* he wrote 'Society Whispers from the States' and in August he was made full-time editor of the 'By the Way' column, employing both Bill Townend and Herbert Westbrook. That did not stop him rattling out another couple of books. After a brief sojourn at Mrs Tickell's school of dramatic art in Victoria Street, he contributed a song to the West End musical *Sergeant Brue*. According to his notebooks, he also spent much time conversing with waitresses, another staple in the world of Wooster.

In 1906, Wodehouse published his first comic novel, *Love Among the Chickens*. It featured a struggling freelance writer, Jeremy Garnet, and introduced Ukridge. Both ex-public schoolboys, naturally, they epitomized the type of young Edwardian who inhabits all his fiction. The deal was handled by J. B. Pinker, the literary agent who also represented such luminaries as Oscar Wilde, Joseph Conrad, Henry James and H. G. Wells. The novel was reprinted within a year. Even Wodehouse's cricketing took on a literary bent. He played for the *Punch* XI with A. A. Milne and for J. M. Barrie's Allahakbarries whose team included Sir Arthur Conan Doyle and Jerome K. Jerome.

Signed up by actor-manager Seymour Hicks, Wodehouse was put to work supplying topical lyrics for musical comedy *The Beauty of Bath*. For the first time, he collaborated with the American composer Jerome Kern who had come over from New York to work on the show. Together they had a hit with 'Oh, Mr Chamberlain!' He would spend weeks in the country with Hicks and his wife, who called him 'the Hermit' because of his devotion to his work. Soon he had enough money to buy a car, but within a week, this ended up in a ditch.

Working for the theatre had a profound effect on his writing. To Wodehouse, Jeeves and Wooster, and his other stock characters, became like highly paid actors who could be summoned to the stage and were guaranteed to put in a worthwhile performance. Indeed, he rewrote novels as plays and plays as novels.

While producing lyrics for more of Hicks's musicals, he wrote a novel with Herbert Westbrook, kept his day job on the *Globe* and turned out freelance contributions for numerous other publications. He also continued to produce serials and, in *Jackson Junior*, he introduced Rupert (later Ronald) Eustace Psmith – 'the "P" is silent as in pshrimp,' he explained. A monocle-wearing Old Etonian, Psmith, nominally at least, embraces socialism. Inspired by Rupert D'Oyly Carte, son of the Savoy Theatre impresario Richard D'Oyly Carte, he was one of Wodehouse's most popular comic characters and, with his upper-class airs and humorous circumlocution, he might be seen as a prototype Bertie Wooster.

Jackson Junior and its follow-up *The Lost Lambs*, both serialized in the *Captain*, were published together in book form as *Mike* in 1909. With a cover-price of six shillings (25p), this was seen as Wodehouse's first novel for adults. Psmith went on to appear in *Psmith in the City* and *Psmith, Journalist*, both serialized in the *Captain*, followed by *Leave it to Psmith*, serialized in the *Saturday Evening Post* in 1923.

However, Wodehouse's journalistic career in London was faltering. The *Globe* had been sold, though he had been commissioned to compile *The Globe By the Way Book*, an anthology of extracts, with Herbert Westbrook. In response to the anti-German fever stirred up by *The Invasion of 1910*, principally written by William Le Queux and serialized in the *Daily Mail*, Wodehouse wrote the satirical novella *The Swoop*, in which Germany, Russia, China, Morocco, Monaco, the Swiss Navy and the inhabitants of the island of Bollygolla all invade England. But as it is August everyone is on holiday and only the Boy Scouts resist. Eventually, the leaders of the invasion are offered lucrative engagements on the music-hall stage. The book did badly, but a New York literary agent had placed *Love Among the Chickens* with an American publisher for an advance of $1,000, so Wodehouse decided to try his luck on the other side of the Atlantic again.

Once again, he planned just a short trip but once in Manhattan, he sold two short stories to *Collier's* and

Cosmopolitan, netting himself $500. It was, he said in *Over Seventy*, 'like suddenly finding a rich uncle from Australia. This, I said to myself, is the place to be.'

He sent a resignation telegram to the *Globe*, and moved into the Hotel Earle in Washington Square, not far from Wooster Street in Greenwich Village. This was the home of other young writers who nicknamed him 'Chickens' after his success with that book. With his new found wealth, he bought himself a second-hand Monarch typewriter. However, he found commissions hard to come by and began to write for the pulps. But he still had an outlet in England where he got another series off the ground. This was *Psmith, Journalist* – originally *Psmith USA* – chronicling his eponymous hero's life as a freelance in America. The first episode in the *Captain* was accompanied by an interview with the author.

Wodehouse returned to England. Although he had found a ready market in the United States, he did not know enough about life there to write about it effectively. However, it had given him the material for a novel, which was originally about an Englishman in America. This was published as *The Intrusion of Jimmy* in the US and *A Gentleman of Leisure* in the UK. But while the first half of the novel is set in Manhattan, the second is in a country house in Shropshire.

In England, he went back to work on the *Globe* and wrote 'The Man Upstairs' for the *Strand Magazine*. However, a producer in New York wanted *The Intrusion of Jimmy* adapted for the stage, so Wodehouse returned to New York in April 1910. Back in London later that year, he moved into the Constitutional Club on Northumberland Avenue. He found that life in clubs and hotels and on ocean liners, where everything was laid on, helped him maintain his astonishing work rate.

After completing *The Prince and Betty*, he returned to New York in April 1911, sailing on the *Lusitania*, the pride of the

Cunard line. He was back in England that June to catch the height of the cricket season, so he missed the opening of *A Gentleman of Leisure*, starring Douglas Fairbanks Sr, in New York. It was later revived in 1913 in Chicago as *A Thief in the Night* with John Barrymore. Wodehouse had now made his mark on the theatrical world in the United States. Meanwhile, he pumped out stories in successive issues of the *Strand*, introducing Reggie Pepper, an upper-class twit who has inherited vast sums from a rich uncle. Another Wooster prototype, Reggie was an adaptation of the 'dude' parts Wodehouse had seen on the American stage. The seven Pepper stories were also published in the US in *Collier's* and *Pictorial Review*.

Wodehouse returned to stage work with *After the Show*, a music-hall sketch show featuring the Honourable Aubrey Forde-Rasche and his valet Barlow. Then he returned to New York where he showed off his increasing mastery of the transatlantic market in the novel *The Little Nugget* about the kidnapping of an American kid from a British prep school. This was serialized in *Munsey's Magazine* in the US while simultaneously coming out in book form in the UK.

Back in London, he collaborated with an old colleague from the *Globe* named Charles Bovill on the revue *Nuts and Wine* and the series *A Man of Means* published in the *Strand* in the UK and *Pictorial Review* in the US. It featured Roland Bleke, a young man whose financial success is a mixed blessing.

In the summer of 1914, Wodehouse sailed back to New York on a German liner. War was coming. Aged thirty-three, he had tried to join up before setting sail, only to be rejected because of his bad eyesight. Instead, he took a commission from *McClure's Magazine* to interview John Barrymore. He landed on 2 August, two days before Britain declared war on Germany. The following day, he was introduced to Ethel Wayman, a twice-widowed

Englishwoman who was supporting her ten-year-old daughter at boarding school by touring with a repertory company. She was his polar opposite – outgoing, extravagant and highly sexed. She set her cap at him. Their romance blossomed that summer with trips to Long Island where they would eventually settle. Within two months of meeting, they married.

While Ethel socialized and spent Wodehouse's money, she also organized his life so that he could get on with the only thing he wanted to do – write. In the spring of 1915, Ethel's daughter Leonora joined them in New York for a visit. He later adopted his stepdaughter and, once she was an adult, she became his closest confidante.

Wodehouse made a regular income, contributing to *Vanity Fair* under a number of pseudonyms. They moved out to Long Island, where they surrounded themselves with pets and, over the years, made friends with W. C. Fields, Ring Lardner, Robert Benchley, F. Scott Fitzgerald, Enrico Caruso, Isadora Duncan and Rudolph Valentino. Wodehouse also took up playing golf there, since he was denied his normal sporting outlet, cricket.

The war soon began to affect his income from England, so in December 1914 he sat down and began to work on *Something Fresh*, the first of his comic novels set in Blandings Castle. It was as if he was trying to preserve the Edwardian England that the Great War was about to destroy forever. The novel was published as a serial called *Something New* from 26 June to 14 August 1915 in the *Saturday Evening Post* and in volume form on both sides of the Atlantic that summer, using the title *Something Fresh* in the UK. It was Wodehouse's breakthrough novel, garnering $3,500 from the *Post* alone. It featured a certain Algernon Wooster, a minor character who did not make another appearance. Wodehouse quickly followed up with another Anglo-American novel, *Uneasy Money*, which was also serialized in the *Post*.

2

THE BIRTH OF JEEVES AND WOOSTER

Wodehouse had wanted to be published by the *Saturday Evening Post* since his first arrival in America in 1904. The editor, bluff Kentuckian George Horace Lorimer, was no Anglophile, but he had an eye for a good story and had already published Rudyard Kipling, G. K. Chesterton and H. G. Wells. So for Wodehouse the publication of *Something New* in the *Post* was a landmark. While waiting for the serialization of *Uneasy Money* to begin in December 1915, Wodehouse was eager to cement the relationship with some short stories. The week after *Something New* finished, the *Post* published 'At Geisenheimer's', set in a dancehall on Broadway. This appeared in the October issue of the *Strand* as 'This Love-r-ly Silver Cup'.

Four weeks later, on 18 September 1915, the *Post* published 'Extricating Young Gussie'. In it, a young Englishman named Bertie – no surname – is attended by a valet named Jeeves and beset by the monstrous Aunt Agatha, who sends them to New York on an errand. The story appeared in the UK in the *Strand* in January 1916 and then in a volume of short stories called *The Man with Two Left Feet*, published in the UK in 1917 and in the US in 1933.

While Bertie jumps off the page fully formed, Jeeves plays only a minor role.

'I blush to think of the offhand way I treated him at our first encounter,' Wodehouse wrote years later in the introduction to *The World of Jeeves*.

Wodehouse was always on the lookout for characters that would sustain a magazine series, as Conan Doyle had done with Sherlock Holmes and Dr Watson. He had tried with the disreputable Ukridge, the absurdly political Psmith and his cricket-playing buddy Mike Jackson, but they were too limited. Jeeves and his young master showed distinct possibilities, though.

However, there was a distraction. Wodehouse had been appointed dramatic critic of *Vanity Fair*, where he would later be succeeded by Dorothy Parker. In that capacity, he met up with Jerome Kern again, who was now working with an Anglo-American playwright, Guy Bolton. They needed a lyricist, and Wodehouse and Bolton hit it off straightaway. This began a collaboration that revolutionized musical comedy, moving it away from the tired formulas of Viennese operetta, injecting colloquial wit and vigour, and making them rich along the way. Together, Wodehouse, Bolton and Kern were responsible for *Miss Springtime* (1916), *Have a Heart* (1917), *Oh, Boy!* (1917), *Leave it to Jane* (1917), *Oh, Lady! Lady!* (1918), *Sally* (1920) and *Sitting Pretty* (1924). In 1917, they had five shows running simultaneously on Broadway, a feat never equalled before or since. Wodehouse and Bolton also collaborated with George and Ira Gershwin on *Oh, Kay!* (1926) and Cole Porter on *Anything Goes* (1934). Wodehouse contributed the lyrics for the song 'Bill' in *Show Boat* (1927) and worked with Florenz Ziegfeld of *Follies* fame.

'Musical comedy was my dish,' said Wodehouse in *Over Seventy*. 'The musical comedy theatre was my spiritual home. I would rather have written *Oklahoma!* than *Hamlet*.'

He also burnished his craft there.

'In musical comedy you gain so tremendously in Act One if you can give your principal characters a dramatic entrance instead of just walking them on,' he wrote in a letter to Bill Townend.

Correspondingly, in all the Jeeves and Wooster stories there are long passages of dialogue, interrupted only by Bertie's monologues addressed directly to the reader. And in *Oh, Boy!* the character Jim Marvin truncates his words for comic effect, a wheeze Wodehouse would later use in Bertie's soliloquies.

The lure of Broadway did not take him away from his other work. 'Leave it to Jeeves' was published in the *Saturday Evening Post* on 5 February 1916. Here Bertie gets his surname and Jeeves emerges as the Einstein of domestic service. Wodehouse explained later that he had got one of Bertie's friends into a bad tangle and could not think of a way to get him out of it. Having Bertie come up with a solution was totally out of character.

'For a long time I was baffled,' he wrote in a letter to Lawrence Durrell, 'and then I suddenly thought, "Why not make Jeeves a man of brains and ingenuity and have him do it?" After that, of course, it was simple.'

Although 'Leave it to Jeeves' was set in New York, Jeeves and Wooster clearly remain highly stylized Englishmen. For Wodehouse this was another advantage.

'I started writing about Bertie Wooster and comic earls,' he explained later in a letter to lifelong friend Denis Mackail, 'because I was in America and couldn't write American stories and the only English characters the American public would read about were exaggerated dudes.'

Wodehouse followed up with 'The Man with the Two Left Feet', which returns to Geisenheimer's. It is about a New York banker who tries to impress his young wife by trying to learn to dance. Not a Wooster or a comic earl in sight.

On 22 April 1916, Jeeves and Wooster were back in action with 'The Aunt and the Sluggard'. But Wodehouse was only making tentative steps with his new characters, confining them to short stories. In September, the *Saturday Evening Post* began serializing *Piccadilly Jim*, which returns to another staple of Wodehouse's fiction, rich Americans in England. It was an unexpected hit.

When *Piccadilly Jim* finished, the *Saturday Evening Post* followed it immediately on 18 November with 'Jeeves Takes Charge'. 'Jeeves and the Unbidden Guest' followed on 9 December and 'Jeeves and the Hard-Boiled Egg' on 3 March 1917. 'The Aunt and the Sluggard' and these stories were published soon after in the *Strand* and appeared in the collection *My Man Jeeves* in the UK in 1919, accompanied by four Reggie Pepper stories.

'Jeeves and the Chump Cyril' was published in the *Saturday Evening Post* on 8 June 1918 and in the *Strand* on 18 August, amid a swathe of other Wodehouse stories. Then Jeeves and Wooster took a break, while Wodehouse's next serialization in the *Post*, *A Damsel in Distress*, earned him $10,000. Again it features a wealthy American in England – this time a US composer in the country home of a peer.

In 1919, Wodehouse returned to England for the publication of *My Man Jeeves* and the opening of some of his musicals in the West End. His evocation of the now vanished Edwardian era struck a chord with a people exhausted by a devastating war. But Wodehouse could not stay in Britain. His presence was required on Broadway and he found that if he stayed in Britain for more than six months, he was liable to pay income tax on his earnings on both sides of the Atlantic.

While Ethel involved herself in the social round and a number of discreet affairs, Wodehouse would often retire to his club or a hotel with his Monarch and a stack of paper. He continued to produce novels set in the Anglo-American milieu but he devoted much of 1921 and 1922 to Jeeves and Wooster, writing 'Jeeves in the Springtime', 'Scoring off Jeeves', 'Aunt Agatha Takes the Count', 'Comrade Bingo', 'The Great Sermon Handicap', 'The Purity of the Turf', 'Bertie Changes His Mind', 'The Metropolitan Touch', 'The Delayed Exit of Claude and Eustace' and 'Bingo and the Little Woman'. These were all published in the *Strand* in the UK and, simultaneously, in *Cosmopolitan* in the US. In 1923, they were published in volume form as *The Inimitable Jeeves* – with the exception of 'Bertie Changes Mind', which appears in *Carry On, Jeeves!*, and the addition of 'Jeeves and the Chump Cyril'. These stories are firmly set in England, except for 'Jeeves and the Chump Cyril', in which Bertie has been dispatched to New York, and 'Aunt Agatha Takes the Count', in which he sets off to Roville-sur-Mer.

His sojourn in England allowed Wodehouse to visit his stepdaughter Leonora's boarding school with its headmistress Miss Starbuck, who proved so daunting that Wodehouse hid in the shrubbery when collecting the child. This provided the inspiration for 'Bertie Changes His Mind', the only story narrated by Jeeves.

The *Inimitable Jeeves*, published as *Jeeves* in the US, sold over three million copies before the Second World War.

Like many English writers of the 1920s and 1930s – outside the Bloomsbury Group – Wodehouse could no longer abide London; thanks to Prohibition, New York had also lost its appeal. After years of transatlantic commuting, in 1924, Wodehouse began to put down roots in Le Touquet, a French seaside resort popular with the rich.

His dizzying output did not slacken. He was never happy

if he was not facing a deadline. That year, the publication of *Ukridge*, a collection of stories featuring the protagonist of *Love Among the Chickens*, and *Bill the Conqueror*, a novel about an American in England, marked Wodehouse out as England's top comic writer.

He visited England regularly, often staying at ivy-clad Hunstanton Hall in Norfolk, the home of a distant cousin and model for Aunt Agatha's house at Woollam Chersey, in Hertfordshire, not far north of London. Wodehouse could be seen working on a punt on the moat with his typewriter perched precariously on a small bed-table.

Jeeves and Wooster returned to the *Saturday Evening Post* with 'The Rummy Affair of Old Biffy', 'Clustering Round Young Biffy' and 'Without the Option'. Along with the four Jeeves and Wooster stories from *My Man Jeeves*, 'Bertie Changes His Mind' and 'Fixing it for Freddie' (a rewrite of the Reggie Pepper story 'Helping Freddie' from that volume), these new stories were published as *Carry On, Jeeves!* in the UK in 1925 and in the US in 1927.

Wodehouse then broke temporarily with the *Saturday Evening Post*, striking a deal with *Liberty*. He returned to the *Post* in 1929. In the meantime, *Liberty* only got three Jeeves and Wooster stories – 'The Inferiority Complex of Old Sippy', 'Jeeves and the Impending Doom' and 'Jeeves and the Yuletide Spirit'. Another seven – 'Jeeves and the Song of Songs', 'Jeeves and the Dog McIntosh', 'Jeeves and the Love that Purifies', 'Jeeves and the Spot of Art', 'Jeeves and the Kid Clementina', 'Jeeves and the Old School Chum', 'Indian Summer of an Uncle' and 'The Ordeal of Young Tuppy' – went to *Cosmopolitan*. They were published simultaneously in the *Strand* and, together, they were published as *Very Good, Jeeves* on both sides of the Atlantic in 1930, though the titles of the stories vary slightly. At the same time, Wodehouse began adapting the work of foreign playwrights with some success in London and New York.

As a respite from his relentless travelling, Wodehouse took the lease on a sixteen-roomed mansion at 17 Norfolk Street, Mayfair, just off Park Lane, London, where he had a butler, uniformed footmen, parlour maids and two secretaries, though these were for Ethel. Though he was not given a title until the last year of his life, he had a Rolls-Royce with the Wodehouse crest on its doors. He even treated himself to a second Monarch typewriter, which sat on a plain deal table in the upstairs bedroom where he worked. But he did not work at home much. When he was in London there were constant interruptions and too much call on his time, so he would take himself off to the Hotel Impney near Droitwich where he could work undisturbed. In the summer of 1928, he took Rogate Lodge, near Petersfield in Hampshire, south-west of London, where he played the role of country gentleman and hosted house parties, a staple of Jeeves and Wooster. Wodehouse now travelled in high literary circles. John Galsworthy, winner of the Noble Prize for Literature, came to lunch. In 1926, Wodehouse was elected a Fellow of the Royal Society of Literature and, in 1939, was made a Doctor of Letters by Oxford University.

While Jeeves and Wooster took the backseat in the early 1930s, Wodehouse continued to write other series, with stories set at the Drones and at Blandings Castle. Then there were the recollections of pub raconteur Mr Mulliner. He produced a series of novels and there were his regular stints on Broadway. He was, he told Bill Townend, conducting a 'vast campaign', at one point writing six stories simultaneously.

With the advent of talking pictures, writers were suddenly in demand in Hollywood. Wodehouse paid his first visit there in 1929. Winston Churchill was also visiting California at the time and William Randolph Hearst held a lunch for him. Hearst's mistress, Marion Davies, knew Wodehouse having appeared in *Oh, Boy!* on Broadway. She smuggled him on to the guest list and the two great Englishmen were introduced. Wodehouse returned to the West Coast the following year, this time under contract, and took a house in Beverly Hills. He wrote later in *Over Seventy*: 'It was an era when only a man of exceptional ability and determination could keep from getting signed up by a studio in some capacity.'

Wodehouse had form. He had sold the film rights of 'The Man Upstairs' in 1914 and *A Gentleman of Leisure* had been filmed as a silent movie in 1915. His novel *A Damsel in Distress* had been made into a movie in 1919, while *Oh, Boy!* and *Oh, Lady! Lady!* had hit the screen in 1919 and 1920. There had also been a talkie version of his play *Her Cardboard Lover*, adapted from the French original by Jacques Deval, in 1929. He was set to work producing dialogue for otherwise undistinguished movies.

On *Those Three French Girls*, he employed a tried and tested formula.

'I altered all the characters to earls and butlers, with such success that, when I had finished, they called a conference and changed the entire plot, starring the earl and the butler,' he explained in a letter to Denis Mackail.

Pocketing $1,700 a week, he drove over to the studio when required. Otherwise he mixed with the Hollywood glitterati, particularly writers he had known from New York and English expats, so he would have someone with whom to play cricket. Together, Wodehouse and Charles Aubrey Smith founded the Hollywood Cricket Club. Thanks to Marion Davis he was also a guest at Hearst's San Simeon estate. He found the endless sunshine in California 'jolly' and swam three times a day. But that did not mean he abandoned his gruelling work schedule, boasting in a letter to Bill Townend that he had 'a new plot for a short story every day for a week'.

At MGM, Wodehouse worked for Irving Thalberg who told him that *Leave It to Psmith* was his favourite book, though he fell silent when Wodehouse suggested that the studio might like to acquire the film rights. MGM also passed on Jeeves after Thalberg's chauffeur said he thought that 'Jeeves' was the name of his wife's butcher. Twentieth Century Fox made two Jeeves movies in the 1930s with little success.

Wodehouse worked on the script for *Candle-Light*, his own adaptation of Siegfried Geyer's *Kleine Komödie*. But he seems to have spent most of his time producing new serializations and novels including *Big Money*, *If I Were You*, *A Prince for Hire* and *Hot Water*. In May 1931, the studio did not renew his contract, but his stay in Hollywood had given him plenty of material for future work. Otherwise, Hollywood, he told the *Los Angeles Times*, had paid him '$104,000 for loafing'. He had used the time 'to write a novel and nine short stories, besides brushing up my golf, getting an attractive suntan and perfecting my Australian crawl'.

American Magazine, which had just serialized *If I Were You*, asked him to write some stories about American characters, to which Wodehouse replied: 'Americans aren't funny. If they were, there would be more than about three American humorous writers.'

However, he did include Hollywood grotesques in the five Mulliner stories that appear in *Blandings Castle* and in the novel *Laughing Gas*.

After spending the rest of the summer in California, Wodehouse was planning to return to England. However, London was bleak and, on top of his losses from the stock-market crash, he faced a large tax bill, so he minimized his liability by taking up residence in France, taking a large house near Cannes with a German butler, an Alsatian footman, a Serbian cook, a French chauffeur, an Italian maid and an English odd-job man. It was there that he began the first Jeeves and Wooster novel, *Thank You, Jeeves*. He took time to the learn French and to visit H. G. Wells who was staying nearby. But the need for money was pressing and he wrote sixty-four pages of *Thank You, Jeeves* in seventeen days – a personal best. That included three rewrites because he 'went off the rails', he said in a letter to Bill Townend. 'That is the curse of my type of story. Unless I get the construction absolutely smooth, it bores the reader.'

It was completed in May 1932, and the serialization began in the *Strand* in August 1933. American serialization rights were sold to *Cosmopolitan* for a record $50,000. Though the book was written in Cannes, following a long sojourn in Hollywood, most of the action takes place in and around Chuffnell Hall in Somerset.

'I don't believe I could ever write a Cannes story or a real Hollywood story,' he told Bill Townend. 'Anything in a country house seems real to me, however fantastic – I suppose because the atmosphere is so definite.'

Still in Cannes, he returned to Blandings Castle with *Heavy Weather*.

While Wodehouse had been in tune with the frivolity of the Jazz Age, almost as much as he had been with the leisured life of the upper classes in the Edwardian era, he was out of step with the Great Depression in America, hunger marches in Britain and the rise of fascism on the Continent. Other English writers turned to communism. Wodehouse makes fun of it in 'Comrade Bingo', in which Bertie is denounced as: 'A prowler, a trifler, and a bloodsucker.'

'Has he ever done an honest day's work in his life?' asks Comrade Little. 'And I bet he still owes his tailor for those trousers.'

In *Thank You, Jeeves*, Bertie briefly hires a replacement for Jeeves named Brinkley, of whom he has his suspicions.

'Outwardly he was all respectfulness,' says Bertie, 'but inwardly you could see that he was a man who was musing on the coming Social Revolution and looked on Bertram as a tyrant and an oppressor.'

Later Bertie says: 'I hadn't the slightest objection to his spending his time planning massacres for the bourgeoisie, but I was dashed if I could see why he couldn't do it with a bright and cheerful smile.'

Brinkley was also compared, unfavourably, to Stalin and Al Capone. These are not the words of a man leaning to the left. On the other hand, Roderick Spode and his Black Shorts are clearly a satire on Oswald Mosley and his Blackshirts. Even Mussolini gets a backhanded namecheck. Wodehouse was a conservative. Although not a committed appeaser, he was nevertheless for peace.

In the 1930s, he wanted to return to England, but he could not face paying tax there. His pet dogs would also face six months in quarantine. So Wodehouse moved back to Le Touquet, which was close enough to England to allow regular trips home.

In the summer of 1933, he spent a few weeks at Hunstanton Hall writing *Right Ho, Jeeves*, having worked out the plot beforehand. This followed the serialization of *Heavy Weather* in the *Saturday Evening Post*. The British edition of the book was dedicated to Raymond Needham KC, the barrister who had convinced the British authorities that, for tax purposes, Wodehouse was only resident in Britain for two years between 1927 and 1933. In the United States, the book came out in volume form under the title *Brinkley Manor*.

Wodehouse had decided to return permanently to the US, but he still had tax problems there, too. So Wodehouse and his household moved temporarily into the Dorchester Hotel while he got on with his next novel, *The Luck of the Bodkins*. They then moved on to the Hôtel Prince de Galles in Paris. But when he started on the book for a new musical for Cole Porter he moved back to Le Touquet, which was just across the Channel from Guy Bolton's cottage in Sussex, and they worked from a room in the Hôtel Royal Picardie. Once the book was finished that July, Porter, who had been gadding around in Europe, turned up and ran through the music on a piano in the casino nearby. The end result was *Anything Goes*, though Wodehouse insisted that only two lines of his original dialogue survived.

Wodehouse leased, then bought, Low Wood, a house in Le Touquet that he had considered buying ten years earlier. He continued his output of short stories and his play, *The Inside Stand*, a stage version of his 1932 novel *Hot Water*, was produced in Glasgow.

With his tax problems in the United States now sorted too, Wodehouse was surprised to receive an invitation to return to Hollywood. On the way, he stopped off in Philadelphia to see George Horace Lorimer, who was retiring from the *Saturday Evening Post*, and collect $2,000 he was owed. By the time he arrived in Hollywood, his old friend Thalberg was dead and so Wodehouse went back to work on *Rosalie*, a screenplay he had been working on when he had left Hollywood five years earlier. Again MGM did not renew his contract, but Wodehouse had used his time to write the novel *Summer Moonshine*, which was sold to the *Saturday Evening Post* for $40,000. However, RKO Pictures were interested in making a new musical version of his novel *A Damsel in Distress* and so he went to work there.

Wodehouse then became embroiled in a row between the left-wing Screen Writers Guild and the conservative Screen Playwrights, recognized by the studios, which he had joined. As a result of this he packed up and returned to Le Touquet, by this time the world was on the brink of war once more. Wodehouse's reaction was to write *The Code of the Woosters*. It could hardly be described as a political work but, with Roderick Spode and his Black Shorts making their appearance, it did making a passing nod to the issues of the day. And again, the *Saturday Evening Post* was prepared to cough up $40,000 for it.

In 1935, Wodehouse had invented a new stock character in Uncle Fred, who first saw the light of day in the short story 'Uncle Fred Flits By'. Directly after finishing *The Code of the Woosters*, Wodehouse began the novel *Uncle Fred in Springtime*, which dispatches him to Blandings.

Although Wodehouse knew the names of Hitler, Mussolini and Stalin, he saw them as players in some sort of international rugby game and ignored the possibility of a new war in Europe. He was more concerned with the fact that, forty years after being denied the chance to go to university, Oxford had decided to confer on him an honorary Doctor of Letters degree at a special ceremony on 21 June 1939. At a formal dinner at Christ Church afterwards, not only was Wodehouse ignorant of the dress code, when he was called upon to make a speech – and on written form the gathering was expecting a funny one – he was taken completely unawares, rose to his feet, said 'Thank you', and sat down again.

The following month, he and Bill Townend watched a cricket match at Dulwich. It would be the last time they would meet. Wodehouse was back in Low Wood, putting the finishing touches to his next novel, *Quick Service*, when on 3 September 1939 Neville Chamberlain came on the radio to announce that Britain had declared war on Germany.

To start with, Wodehouse was a little worried about the war. Would he be able to get typewriter ribbons? Would there be problems getting his manuscripts to the United States? But after this initial concern, nothing much seemed to happen and he had already plotted a new Jeeves and Wooster novel.

That winter he thought of returning to the United States, but only because it was bitterly cold in Europe. There was no apparent danger. The English newspapers began turning up late and he had two French medical officers billeted in his house, while Ethel begin inviting young British soldiers and airmen she found in the area home to dine. Once visitors were comfortable, Wodehouse would return to work or take the dogs out for a walk.

The manuscript of *Quick Service* reached the US safely to be serialized by the *Saturday Evening Post* and a collection of Drones Club stories, *Eggs, Beans and Crumpets*, was readied for publication.

Wodehouse began work on the Jeeves and Wooster novel *Joy in the Morning*. He still intended to travel to the United States at some point, via the port of Genoa, which was only closed on 10 June 1940 when Italy declared war on France.

As the German Army sped through the Low Countries in the spring of 1940, Ethel burnt any papers or notes that might be considered anti-German. For instance, Mulliner makes reference to Hitler at the beginning of 'Buried Treasure' and Wodehouse had written a satirical short story called 'The Big Push', which appeared in *Punch* on 13 December 1939, in which Hitler, Hess, Göring, Goebbels, Himmler, von Ribbentrop and others discuss the destruction of Britain, making as much sense as if they were members of the Drones Club.

As the Germans entered France, friends begged the Wodehouses to leave, but two things stood in P. G.'s way. If he left for England, their dogs would be quarantined and he would have to break off writing *Joy in the Morning*. Plainly, Jeeves and Wooster had to come first.

On 21 May 1940, the Wodehouses made an attempt to flee but their car broke down. They made another attempt with friends, but amid the chaos of roads clogged with fleeing refugees their vehicle packed up too. They returned to Low Wood for the night. By the morning the German Army had reached Boulogne and they were cut off from the Channel ports.

A few days later, they were out shopping for vegetables when they ran into a German patrol. Wodehouse's account naturally makes light of the incident. He exhibited the stiff upper lip expected of him, describing the encounter in his unpublished 'Apologia' merely as 'embarrassing'.

Soon a nine o'clock curfew was established and German soldiers came to requisition their cars and Wodehouse's bicycle. Germans bathed in the bathroom at Low Wood and used the other facilities. Despite being surrounded by the enemy, Wodehouse continued to work as usual.

Then all expatriate males were required to report each morning to the Kommandant in the Hôtel de Ville, a two-mile walk. Wodehouse's literary agent in New York wrote, asking whether Wodehouse could write a magazine piece about the experience. He also got up a petition, asking the German ambassador in the United States to arrange for the Wodehouses release. This served to alert the Germans to the propaganda value of their captive.

In July 1940, all enemy aliens under sixty were interned. Wodehouse was fifty-eight. Under guard, he was given ten minutes to pack. He left behind the manuscript of *Joy in the Morning*, which was finished except for the last four chapters, taking instead *The Complete Works of Shakespeare*. Then he was taken, along with other Brits from Le Touquet, to a prison in Loos, some sixty miles away in Belgium. Low Wood was requisitioned and Ethel had to move to a room in a local trout farm.

Wodehouse shared a cell with two other men where he slept on the floor. They were fed thin soup and given half-an-hour's exercise a day. But Wodehouse was not one to get down-hearted and kept notes of his experiences for use later. After a week, the three were transferred to an Army barracks in Liège further east. But before they were moved a German soldier came up to Wodehouse, shook his hand and said: 'Thank you for Jeeves' – as Wodehouse recorded in his camp note book.

After that he spent five weeks in a Napoleonic fortress at Huy on the Meuse river. There he wrote an appeal to the Red

Cross on behalf of the other internees, asking to be allowed to communicate with their families. A Gestapo officer tore it up in front of his face.

He was then transferred to a converted lunatic asylum in Tost, a small town in Upper Silesia, formerly part of Poland but now annexed by Greater Germany. The American consul in Paris tried to keep up with Wodehouse's movements. He was hampered by the fact that, in the German records, 'Wodehouse' was variously rendered as 'Widhorse' and 'Whitehouse'.

Unable to continue with *Joy in the Morning*, Wodehouse began *Money in the Bank*, a book about Lord Uffenham, thought to be have been inspired by fellow internee Max Enke. Although Wodehouse had recorded the horrors he had seen travelling across Nazi Germany for journalistic purposes, his new novel was set in the unruffled England of country houses where people dress for dinner, though some of the coarser language of the all-male internment camp does peep through.

While other inmates found their new surroundings difficult to cope with, Wodehouse quipped that it was only appropriate that the Nazis had sent him to a lunatic asylum and that the whole experience of captivity was all too familiar from boarding school. He was, however, excused the strenuous duties assigned to the younger men at Tost. He said he even enjoyed his time there because, without women, men become boys again.

The camp commander, the *Lagerführer*, who had been interned in England in the First World War, organized a library and a camp newspaper. Wodehouse contributed an abridged story based on 'All's Well with Bingo' for the internee's paper, the *Tost Times*. There was also a German-run newspaper, *Camp*, with which Wodehouse had nothing to do. It published a parody of Jeeves and Wooster, with Bertie as a military man, written by a 'P. G. Roadhouse'.

Wodehouse was found a typewriter and given a padded cell in which to work. Not only was it reminiscent of public school, it also reminded him of Hollywood where he had often worked alongside German expatriates. Indeed, he said that he never found an English-speaking German he did not like.

Others did not share Wodehouse's sunny disposition. As the winter closed in, some men committed suicide. Others died from the harsh conditions and suffered nervous breakdowns.

Wodehouse's situation was alleviated by the access he had to the outside world. With the United States not yet in the war, American journalists were still reporting from inside Germany. An Associated Press reporter came across British Civilian Prisoner 796 – Wodehouse – and got permission to interview him in front of the *Lagerführer* and a Gestapo minder.

The piece was published in the *New York Times* on 27 December 1940, alongside a picture of Wodehouse looking haggard. He had also used the Associated Press reporter as a conduit to sell a piece provisionally called 'Whither Wodehouse' to the *Saturday Evening Post*. It was now impossible for the Nazi authorities to overlook what a powerful propaganda tool they possessed and their attitude towards him changed. They even shipped the manuscript of *Money in the Bank* to the United States for him through official channels.

The *Lagerführer* had read 'Whither Wodehouse?' It was a typically light-hearted piece like those he had written to make his fellow internees laugh. No doubt on instructions from above, he suggested that Wodehouse broadcast to his American fans in a similar vein. In a casual manner, Wodehouse replied, 'I would love to,' or 'There's nothing I should like better,' or words to that effect.

'Whither Wodehouse?' was already on its way to the States, where it was published by the *Saturday Evening Post* under the title 'My War with Germany'. On the afternoon of 21 June 1941, two Gestapo officers turned up at Tost, interrupting a game of cricket. Wodehouse was given ten minutes to pack. Leaving behind the unfinished manuscript of his new Blandings novel, *Full Moon*, he was put on a train for Berlin. This was all very sudden, but he was expecting to be released in another four months anyway, when he turned sixty.

On the day Wodehouse arrived in Berlin, Germany launched its attack on the Soviet Union. He was put up in the luxurious Adlon Hotel, whose lobby was a meeting place for the likes of William Joyce – 'Lord Haw-Haw' – and Nazi sympathizer John Amery, as well as the American propagandists Robert H. Best and Edward Delaney. There, seemingly by chance, he met Baron Raven von Barnikow, whom he knew from New York and Los Angeles. The baron lent Wodehouse 500 marks and promised to bring him some new clothes. Werner Plack, another German whom Wodehouse had known in California, was also there. Ostensibly a wine salesman, Plack had been a German agent in the United States. He mentioned that he might be able to reunite Wodehouse with his wife, and during the conversation, the idea of Wodehouse making a broadcast to the United States also came up. His old *Lagerführer* from Tost then turned up in civilian clothes to congratulate Wodehouse on his release. Still Wodehouse did not smell a rat.

American correspondents were eager to interview Wodehouse at the Adlon. And once he had a typewriter he promised an article to *Cosmopolitan*. He also, rather reluctantly, agreed to make the broadcasts. He wanted to reassure his American readers who had sent fan mail and food parcels he had not been able to acknowledge. He also wanted to tell the British that the small group of British citizens he had been interned with had kept up their spirits despite the difficult conditions. He did not think he was doing anything wrong as, in his own mind at least, he had been released before he had agreed to make the broadcasts.

Before making any broadcasts via German radio, he did an interview with CBS in which he talked about the books he had been writing while interned. The subject matter appeared irredeemably frivolous in a world plunged into the inferno. And now, just after the British people had endured the Blitz, it was reported that Wodehouse was living in a luxury hotel in the middle of the Nazi capital. Even before he had made his broadcasts, he was denounced as a Nazi stooge.

When Wodehouse had made light of internment in Tost, his fellow internees had roared with laughter. On German radio, it made a different impression. With the Soviet Union now in the war, a titanic struggle was going on, but Wodehouse made it sound as inconsequential as a village cricket match. By the time telegrams came from the editor of the *Saturday Evening Post* and his adopted daughter Leonora begging him to stop, he had already recorded two more broadcasts.

Though few people in Britain heard the broadcasts – they were aired in the small hours of the morning on short wave aimed at the United States – Wodehouse was condemned in the press and in Parliament. The government also forced the BBC to broadcast a vituperative piece of polemic condemning Wodehouse, written by William Connor who contributed the 'Cassandra' column to the *Daily Mirror*. Though this broadcast was roundly condemned by those who heard it, some public libraries banned Wodehouse's books as a result. The BBC also banned his stories and his lyrics, though lifted the ban when the war was over.

When Ethel arrived in Berlin, she put paid to any further broadcasts. The Wodehouses then applied to leave German via Palestine, Lisbon or Sweden, but the Germans were loath to let him go. However, von Barnikow arranged for him to stay in the country house of Baroness Anga von Bodenhausen. There he returned to Jeeves and Wooster, finishing *Joy in the Morning* as well as *Full Moon*, several short stories and 'Wodehouse in Wonderland', his account of camp life. The manuscripts were forwarded to New York by the American embassy. He played the recordings of his broadcasts over and over again, in an act of self-castigation.

After returning to the Adlon Hotel Wodehouse tried to get a German barrister to sue the British press for libel. As the war was still going on, there was little hope of success and he was persuaded to drop the case. Ethel was equally unworldly. When a U-Bahn train stopped a little short of a station one night, due to an air-raid, she complained loudly in English. Nobody pointed out that they were only halted because British bombers were flattening the city.

To escape the bombing, the Wodehouses went to stay as paying guests with the Count and Countess von Wolkenstein in Lobris, Upper Silesia in what is now Poland. They had a library full of English books and publications. There Wodehouse began work on a new novel, *Spring Fever*.

A change of editors and a falter in the fortunes of the *Saturday Evening Post* meant the paper would no longer take pieces from Wodehouse. And at this point the US tax authorities pounced again.

When *Spring Fever* was finished, the Wodehouses got permission to move to France, where they stayed in Paris. But they were not quite free of the Nazis yet. Werner Plack organized a room at the Hôtel Bristol, a collaborationists' hotel. As always, Wodehouse kept his head down and began work on a new Uncle Fred novel, *Uncle Dynamite*. When Paris was liberated, Wodehouse knew he must turn himself in. While MI5 were sending their Major Cussen to interrogate him, a young M16 liaison officer named Malcolm Muggeridge

turned up at Hôtel Bristol. He explained the gravity of
Wodehouse's situation – that he had been accused of treason,
the penalty for which was death. But they got to talking about
books and writers, and over a bottle of wine became firm
friends. It was during Wodehouse's first meeting with Muggeridge that he received the shocking news that Leonora was
dead at the age of forty, after a routine gynaecological
operation. The Wodehouses were devastated.

Cussen's interrogation lasted four days. His fifteen-page
report concluded that Wodehouse had been 'unwise'. His
broadcast had in some small way assisted the enemy and
neither Wodehouse nor his wife had conducted themselves
very well while in Germany. Nevertheless, he thought it
unlikely that any jury would convict. The Director of Public
Prosecutions closed the case, but Wodehouse was never told
this. The fact that he was not still facing prosecution was only
made public five years after his death.

He was, however, arrested by the French authorities. While
he was detained he continued work on *Uncle Dynamite*.
Muggeridge did what he could. Churchill eventually stepped
in, saying of Wodehouse: 'His name stinks here, but he would
not be sent to prison.' Eventually Wodehouse was released. In
the meantime, Muggeridge, among others, helped persuade
him to shelve "Wodehouse in Wonderland" as it was bound to
bring up the matter of the wartime broadcasts all over again.
Besides, a writer of Wodehouse's comic talent would perhaps
never be able get the tone right for such a serious book.

Wodehouse had finished *Uncle Dynamite* while moving
around France in the bitter winter of 1944–5. Herbert Jenkins
printed an unprecedented 20,000 copies of *Money in the Bank*
and the reaction from the book trade seemed to be good. It did
not seem to matter that the world in which Wodehouse set his
stories was long gone, just as long as they were funny.
Wodehouse realized that Charles Dickens continued to write

about a world where transport was provided by stage coach long after the advent of the railway. So it seemed that there was still life in butlers and country houses.

After the war, Wodehouse's fortunes began to pick up and he and Ethel moved into a luxury apartment two doors from the Duke and Duchess of Windsor. Muggeridge introduced him to George Orwell who was in Paris on an assignment for the *Observer*. Both from a public school background, they hit it off famously and Orwell became one of Wodehouse's stoutest defenders.

When Doubleday in New York chose to publish *Joy in the Morning* in 1946, Wodehouse decided that his future lay in the United States and lobbied for a visa. He was in two minds though. The America of the 1920s and 1930s where he had flourished were long gone. He delayed, but was persuaded to return to the United States when he received an unexpected tax refund from the American government. By then he had almost completed his next Jeeves and Wooster novel, *The Mating Season*, aiming to finish the final chapter on the boat.

The Wodehouses sailed from Cherbourg on the SS *America*. The shipping line immediately upgraded him to a stateroom appropriate for a famous author. When the *America* docked in Lower Manhattan, reporters surged on board to be quickly disarmed by Wodehouse. There were no awkward questions there or at a formal press conference organized by Doubleday which was followed by a cocktail party for literary journalists. Then he appeared on the syndicated radio show *Luncheon at Sardi's*. It was a public relations triumph. Suddenly it seemed that everyone wanted to put the war behind them.

The initial euphoria wore off fast. Wodehouse soon found that editors did not want stories set in upper-class England at a time when a bankrupt Britain was suffering rationing and had a socialist government. But curiously, back in austerity Britain, Wodehouse's books proved to be just the tonic readers wanted. The problem was, due to currency controls, he could not get the money out of Britain.

He found a little work, adapting foreign plays and script doctoring on Broadway. The worked picked up, however, after Guy Bolton returned to New York following a long stay in Europe.

The Mating Season received good reviews when it came out in 1949. That year, Wodehouse swapped his visitor's visa for a 'quota visa', granting him residency once he had re-entered the country via Canada. The following year, his British bank account was redesignated an American account, giving him access to his accumulated royalties. Nevertheless, he was advised not to travel to the UK to get them and to remain outside the jurisdiction of the British courts.

Although he was now nearly seventy, Wodehouse still needed to write. But he had no plot. Desperate, he paid his friend George Kaufman $2,700 for the rights to adapt his 1925 screwball comedy, *The Butter and Egg Man*. Initially, Wodehouse thought of turning it into a Jeeves and Wooster story. Instead, he sends expatriate Drone Cyril 'Barmy' Fotheringay-Phipps to Broadway. Several attempts at serialization failed, but Herbert Jenkins in London published it as *Barmy in Wonderland*. There followed a new Blandings novel, *Pigs Have Wings*.

In 1952, Wodehouse moved out to Remsenburg, Long Island, just two miles from Guy Bolton's house. Bolton 'borrowed' Jeeves for the farce *Come On, Jeeves*, which Wodehouse adapted as the novel *Ring for Jeeves*. They also collaborated on *Bring on the Girls!*, subtitled *The Improbable Story of Our Life in Musical Comedy*.

Wodehouse also published *Performing Flea*, a collection of his letters written to Bill Townend. The title comes from Sean O'Casey who said, after Wodehouse's wartime broadcasts: 'If England has any dignity left in the way of literature, she will forget for ever the pitiful antics of English literature's performing flea.' However, at proof stage he cut all reference to his wartime broadcasts, leaving only George Orwell's defence and sympathetic comments by a former prisoner of war. He was once again what he had always been – the writer of inspired light fiction. The British critics were enthusiastic, calling it 'witty' and 'delightful'. It seems that all was forgiven. Wodehouse even made up with William Connor, inviting him to lunch when he was in New York. They became 'bosom pals'. With Malcolm Muggeridge now editor of *Punch*, Wodehouse further rehabilitated himself in Britain by contributing regular pieces. And, as a final gesture, he let his broadcasts be published in *Encounter* magazine, so that everyone could see how harmless they had been.

Despite the success of *Pigs Have Wings*, Doubleday tried to cut both the advance and the royalties on his next contract. Consequently, both *Ring for Jeeves* and *Bring on the Girls!* went to Simon & Schuster. His editor there, Peter Schwed, had a much more hands-on approach to Wodehouse's work, retitling *Jeeves and the Feudal Spirit* as *Bertie Wooster Sees it Through*, *Jeeves in the Offing* as *How Right You Are, Jeeves*, *Much Obliged, Jeeves* as *Jeeves and the Tie that Binds*, *Aunts Aren't Gentlemen* as *The Cat-Nappers* and *A Pelican at Blandings* as *No Nudes Is Good Nudes*. He also reworked the ending in *Jeeves and the Tie that Binds* to justify the title change.

In the US sales were small but steady. In the UK, though, Penguin republished *The Inimitable Jeeves*, *Right Ho, Jeeves*, *The Code of the Woosters*, *Leave It to Psmith* and *Big Money* in paperback. The combined print run was one million copies. Wodehouse had found a whole new audience in Britain. Dealing with his fan mail was a daily chore as he insisted on answering every letter.

In 1955, Wodehouse finally took the plunge and became an

American citizen. He took the step with a certain trepidation, fearing it might hurt his sales in Britain. However, as he explained to Bill Townend in a letter dated 7 October 1956: 'I have always had the idea that there may be trouble if I went to England . . . but I imagine they would hardly dare arrest an American citizen!' This was not without good reason. According to his biographer Frances Donaldson, after the change of government in 1951, discreet enquiries had been made of the new attorney general, Sir David Maxwell-Fyfe, whether he could return to England without risk of legal proceedings. The reply came that 'this could not be guaranteed'. His friend Frank Sullivan, who wrote for the *New Yorker*, said that Wodehouse's naturalization 'made up for the loss of T. S. Eliot and Henry James combined'. Wodehouse returned the compliment with the publication *America, I Like You*, published as *Over Seventy* in the UK.

He continued writing including: *French Leave*, based on a plot by Guy Bolton; *Service with a Smile* (which was originally planned as a Jeeves and Wooster novel entitled *Very Foxy, Jeeves*); *Ice in the Bedroom*; *Stiff Upper Lip, Jeeves*; *Galahad at Blandings*; *A Few Quick Ones*; *Plum Pie*; *Something Fishy*; and *Cocktail Time*. Wodehouse also found himself written about. In 1958, American admirer David A. Jasen began the first authorized biography, *P. G. Wodehouse: Portrait of a Master*. In England, Richard Usborne set to work on *Wodehouse at Work*. When he sent it to Remsenburg for approval, Wodehouse simply removed the chapter on the broadcasts and his internment and destroyed them. Usborne had not kept a copy.

In the run up to his eightieth birthday, the greatest British and American writers of the day took out a newspaper advertisement to honour Wodehouse as a master of the literary art. His own assessment was: 'I suppose my work is pretty juvenile. When you've written about eighty books and they're always exactly the same Edwardian stuff, it's sometimes difficult to churn them out,' he told the *New Yorker*.

In July 1961, twenty years to the day after it aired the attack by Cassandra, the BBC made amends by allowing Wodehouse's friend Evelyn Waugh to broadcast a salute. Wodehouse entreated Waugh not to attack Connor, as he had since become a friend.

By this time, Wodehouse's work had been translated into countless languages, though he could not understand what people in alien cultures made of it. But still he kept on writing a thousand words a day – though his daily output had been more than double that when he was younger. He downed his Martinis, walked the dog, dozed in his chair, watched soap operas – and kept on producing a book a year, though he found it increasingly difficult to write about an England that he had not visited for many decades.

The success of *The World of Wooster* on BBC television in Britain in the 1960s brought him a new readership. There was talk of putting Jeeves back on the stage, but it came to nothing. He maintained a curious celebrity in the United States too. In March 1972, President Richard Nixon, as yet untainted by the Watergate scandal, invited him to a Sunday service. Wodehouse turned down the invitation on the grounds that it would be 'too much of a strain,' he told the *New York Times*. In fact, he was a tenacious agnostic.

More plaudits accompanied his ninetieth birthday. He went on to finish one more Jeeves and Wooster book, *Aunts Aren't Gentlemen*, also known as *The Cat-Nappers*. In the summer of 1974, Madame Tussaud's sent a sculptor so that he could sit in London's famous waxworks. Then in the New Year's Honours list of 1975, he was given a knighthood.

In February 1975, he went into Southampton Hospital for tests, taking the unfinished manuscript of *Sunset at Blandings* with him. The publishers were expecting the completed work by the end of the month. He died on the evening of 14 February, leaving sixteen chapters of its planned twenty-two. For the first time in his life, he had missed a deadline.

3
THE SHORT STORIES

Wodehouse was already an experienced short-story writer on both sides of the Atlantic when he submitted his first Jeeves and Wooster story to the *Saturday Evening Post* in 1915. He published thirty-two short stories before deciding to tackle a full-length Jeeves and Wooster novel. Towards the end of his career, Wodehouse returned to writing short stories featuring Jeeves and Wooster, more than fifty years after they made their first appearance.

'Extricating Young Gussie'
Published in the Saturday Evening Post *with illustrations by Martin Justice on 18 September 1915, 'Extricating Young Gussie' went on to appear in the January 1916 issue of the* Strand Magazine *in the UK, illustrated by Alfred Leete. It then appeared in volume form with thirteen other Wodehouse stories in* The Man with Two Left Feet, *published by Methuen in London on 8 March 1917 and by the A. L. Burt Company on 1 February 1933.*

Somewhere in the small hours – about half past eleven – Bertie is woken by Jeeves with the words: 'Mrs Gregson to see you, sir.'

This is the dreaded Aunt Agatha who starts by telling Bertie that he looks 'perfectly dissipated'. Bertie bleats weakly to Jeeves to bring him some tea. Aunt Agatha has an urgent assignment for him. He is to go to New York to rescue her nephew and Bertie's cousin, Gussie Mannering-Phipps, who has 'lost his head over a creature' – a young vaudivillian named Ray Denison.

Bertie puts Gussie's interest in show girls down to heredity. Gussie's late father, Bertie's Uncle Cuthbert, had met Gussie's mother, Aunt Julia, when she was in pantomime at Drury Lane. Nevertheless, Aunt Agatha commands Bertie to go New York and put an end to the affair. Jeeves is instructed to pack.

When they arrive in New York, Bertie leaves Jeeves to deal with the baggage while he heads for Gussie's hotel – only to find that no Augustus Mannering-Phipps is registered there. Wondering what to do next, Bertie has recourse to a couple of cocktails. Out in the street, he bumps into Gussie outside the offices of a vaudeville agent. It emerges that Gussie has changed his name to George Wilson to go on the stage. It transpires that Ray's father, Joe Danby, an old vaudevillian from London, will not let his daughter marry anyone who is not in the profession. Gussie now has a booking as a singer.

Bertie decides against cabling Aunt Agatha. Instead he cables Gussie's mother, Aunt Julia, asking her to sail to New York.

While Gussie rehearses, Bertie hopes that his first appearance will be such a catastrophe that he will never dare to perform again, putting paid to the marriage. Gussie's first number is a two-hander with the pianist; the second a ballad.

Bertie is dragooned into coming along to Gussie's debut to provide moral support. He sits next to a very pretty girl. Gussie's first song is indeed a disaster. But when he starts the second, the girl beside Bertie gets up and joins in. From a faltering start, their duet turns into a triumph. The girl, it turns out, is Gussie's love-interest, Ray.

The following Wednesday, Aunt Julia arrives in New York. While she is not as formidable as Aunt Agatha, she has the airs of a duchess. First Bertie takes her to see Ray performing at the Auditorium. Then he takes her to see Gussie, who Bertie finds has improved immeasurably.

To complete the picture, Bertie takes Aunt Julia to meet Ray's father. She recognizes Joe Danby immediately: they had been on the stage together. Indeed, Joe had been in love with Julia, but then she had gone off to marry the aristocratic Cuthbert Mannering-Phipps. That's why he would not let his daughter marry out of the profession.

Later Gussie informs Bertie that his mother and Mr Danby are going to marry and, perhaps, go back on the stage together. Gussie and Ray are going to marry, too. A cable arrives from Aunt Agatha and Bertie decides that he had better avoid England for 'about ten years'.

'Leave it to Jeeves' ('The Artistic Career of Corky')

Published in the Saturday Evening Post *with illustrations by Tony Sarg on 5 February 1916, 'Leave it to Jeeves' appeared in the June 1916 issue of the* Strand Magazine, *illustrated by Alfred Leete. It then appeared in the collection* My Man Jeeves, *published in the UK by George Newnes in May 1919. Later it appeared, slightly reworked, as 'The Artistic Career of Corky' in the collection* Carry On, Jeeves!, *published in the UK by Herbert Jenkins on 9 October 1925 but did not appear in a US book until the 1988 American publication by Harper and Row of the omnibus volume* The World of Jeeves.

Although this introductory passage was cut when the re-written story, re-titled 'The Artistic Career of Corky' was collected in *Carry On, Jeeves!*, the original *My Man Jeeves* version begins with Bertie introducing Jeeves as 'my man, you know'. Bertie then goes on to compare him to those 'chappies' at the inquiries desk at Pennsylvania Station who know, without thinking, the times and platforms of all the trains going to every destination.

When the story gets started Bertie explains that they are exiled in New York after being sent over by Aunt Agatha to prevent Gussie marrying a girl on the vaudeville stage. Afraid to return to England for 'long cosy chats' with the aunt, so he sent Jeeves out to find them an apartment.

Bertie has got to know an artist named Corky – Bruce Corcoran, an aspiring portrait painter. In the meantime, Corky sometimes gets drawings in the comic papers and does illustrations for advertisements. However, he is supported by his wealthy uncle, Alexander Worple, who wants his nephew to join him in the jute business, though Bertie has no clear idea what jute is.

One day, Corky arrives as Bertie's apartment with his fiancée, a chorus girl named Muriel Singer. However, his uncle would cause trouble if he knew that Corky had got engaged without consulting him first.

Jeeves comes up with a scheme to introduce Miss Singer to Mr Worple without Worple knowing that Corky has already met her. Worple is an amateur ornithologist who has written a book called *American Birds*. Jeeves suggests that Miss Singer should write a book called *The Children's Book of American Birds* – and as a fellow ornithologist, make the old man's acqaintance. A ghostwriter is hired to supply the text. The ruse works and Mr Worple asks Muriel to call.

Bertie has to go out of town. When he returns, he bumps into Muriel sitting alone in a restaurant. Bertie assumes she is waiting for Corky. In fact, she is waiting for her husband – who turns out to be, not Corky, but his Uncle Alexander.

A few months later, Bertie reads in the paper that Mrs Worple has given birth to a son and heir, dashing Corky's prospects of inheriting his uncle's wealth. Visiting Corky in his studio, Bertie finds him hard at work painting a portrait of a baby in the arms of its nanny. It is his first commission – and it has come from his uncle, who wants him to paint a portrait of his baby son as a surprise for his new wife.

However, Corky cannot help but let his resentment of the child show through in his work. His uncle is furious at the result. Corky's allowance is to be stopped and he is to report for work at his uncle's office. But Jeeves has a solution. He suggests that the painting could be used as the foundation of a cartoon strip. He even has a title for the series: 'The Adventures of Baby Blobbs'.

Published in the *Sunday Star*, it is an instant hit.

'The Aunt and the Sluggard'

Published in the Saturday Evening Post *with illustrations by Tony Sarg on 22 April 1916, 'The Aunt and the Sluggard' appeared in the August 1916 issue of the* Strand Magazine, *illustrated by Alfred Leete. It then appeared in the collection* My Man Jeeves, *published in the UK by George Newnes in May 1919, and later in the collection* Carry On, Jeeves!, *published in the UK by Herbert Jenkins on 9 October 1925.*

The story begins with Bertie in bed. He is woken by Rockmetteller 'Rocky' Todd, a poet who lives out on Long Island. This is a surprise as Rocky is 'the laziest young devil in America' – the sluggard of the title. He has a wealthy aunt named Isabel Rockmetteller in Illinois and hopes to inherit. But Aunt Isabel has written saying that she will pay him a substantial sum each month, provided he plunges himself into the life of New York and writes once a week to tell her what's going on there.

Rocky explains that he hates New York and does not want to live there. Jeeves suggests that Mr Todd gets someone to draft the letters for him. Jeeves himself is delegated and the letters are then sent out from Bertie's address.

Then Aunt Isabel turns up to stay at Bertie's apartment, thinking it is Rocky's. Bertie has to move into a hotel. Jeeves's letters are so persuasive that Aunt Isabel has come to sample the delights of New York herself. As a consequence, she is stopping Rocky's allowance.

Bertie sees Rocky and his aunt out all over town. Then one night, Rocky is alone. He and Bertie head back to the flat for a drink. Just as Rocky is about to pour one, his aunt appears and cries 'Stop!'.

Jeeves had taken her to a revival meeting where the evangelist condemned drinking. She has now seen the light and urges Rocky to leave New York. Rocky agrees and returns to his cottage on Long Island.

'Jeeves Takes Charge'
Published in the Saturday Evening Post *with illustrations by Henry Raleigh on 18 November 1916, 'Jeeves Takes Charge' appeared in the April 1923 issue of the* Strand Magazine, *illustrated by A. Wallis Mills. It then appeared in the collection* Carry On, Jeeves!, *published in the UK by Herbert Jenkins on 9 October 1925 and in the US by the George H. Doran Company on 7 October 1927.*

The story begins with Bertie recalling how he had first hired Jeeves. His previous valet had been stealing his silk socks and Jeeves was sent by an agency. Noticing that Bertie is the worse for wear, Jeeves prepares his version of a prairie oyster – a concoction of raw egg, Worcestershire sauce and red pepper. The pick-me-up works wonders and Bertie hires him immediately.

Bertie is engaged to Lady Florence Craye. She has given

him a book called *Types of Ethical Theory* to read before he returns to Easeby Hall, the Shropshire home of Bertie's Uncle Willoughby. Jeeves had once been in the employ of Lady Florence's father, Lord Worplesdon, and gives the impression that he is not impressed by Bertie's choice of fiancée.

Bertie receives a telegram from Florence urging him to return to Easeby immediately. She is upset. Before he left, Bertie had told Florence to be pleasant to his Uncle Willoughby, on whom Bertie is dependent. Bertie had suggested that Florence ask Uncle Willoughby if she could read a history of the family he was working on. This turned out to be his own racy reminiscences, including the scandalous tales concerning her own father who Bertie's Uncle Willoughby has known since university. Florence is shocked and tells Bertie that he must destroy the manuscript before it goes off to the publisher the following day, otherwise she will not marry him. However, if Uncle Willoughby catches him, Bertie risks being cut off without a penny.

The following day Bertie seizes the parcel containing the manuscript from the hall table where it has been put ready for the butler to take it to the post in the village. He nips upstairs to hide it in his room, only to find Edwin, Florence's younger brother, there. Edwin has just become a Boy Scout and was tidying Bertie's room as an 'act of kindness'. Once Edwin has gone, Bertie puts the parcel in a drawer, locks it and puts the key in his pocket.

The next day Uncle Willoughby phones the publisher and discovers that his manuscript has not arrived. The butler says he did not see it when he took the other mail to the village. Uncle Willoughby concludes that it has been stolen.

That evening, Bertie is walking past the library window when he hears Edwin tell Uncle Willoughby that Bertie had brought a parcel into the bedroom when he was tidying.

Bertie races back to his room to remove the manuscript, but

finds he does not have the key to the drawer. It is in his evening suit that Jeeves has taken way to brush. Uncle Willoughby arrives and finds the locked drawer. Then Jeeves turns up with the key. But the drawer is empty. Jeeves has already removed the manuscript. Bertie tells him to get rid of it.

When Florence is asking Bertie if he has destroyed the manuscript, Uncle Willoughby bursts in to say he has just had a call from his publishers and the manuscript has arrived. Florence breaks off the engagement. Jeeves admits that he sent the manuscript to the publisher and Bertie sacks him. Now free to speak his mind, Jeeves says that he judged that Bertie and Florence were not suited.

The following morning Bertie attempts to read *Types of Ethical Theory* again and concludes that Jeeves is right, and Bertie re-engages him.

'Jeeves and the Unbidden Guest'
Published in the Saturday Evening Post *with illustrations by Henry Raleigh on 9 December 1916, 'Jeeves and the Unbidden Guest' appeared in the March 1917 issue of the* Strand Magazine, *illustrated by Alfred Leete. It then appeared in the collection* My Man Jeeves, *published in the UK by George Newnes in May 1919, and later in the collection* Carry On, Jeeves!

When 'Jeeves and the Unbidden Guest' begins, Bertie is still in New York. He has already had a couple of wrangles with Jeeves over clothing and has always lost, but he is determined to prevail in the matter of a hat. Jeeves wants him to wear a White House Wonder, as worn by President Coolidge, while Bertie has bought a Broadway Special (respectively a Longacre and Country Gentle in the magazine version as Calvin Coolidge did not become President until 1923).

One morning, Lady Malvern and her son Wilmot, Lord Pershore, arrive unbidden. Bertie recalls that Lady Malvern is a friend of Aunt Agatha. She is writing a book about social conditions in the United States and intends to billet twenty-three-year-old 'Motty' with Bertie for a month while she travels around the country. Eager to get back into Aunt Agatha's good books so he can return to England, Bertie is forced to consent.

Once his mother is out of the way, Wilmot goes out on the town. When he brings a dog home, Bertie takes refuge with Rocky Todd on Long Island. He returns to find that Lord Pershore is in prison for assaulting a policeman. When Lady Malvern returns early, Bertie tells her that Wilmot is in Boston. But she retorts: how, then, can he account for the fact that she had seen him the previous day breaking rocks in a prison she had been visiting to gather material for her book?

Jeeves tells Lady Malvern that Mr Wooster had been away and that he (Jeeves) had been responsible for telling him that Lord Pershore had gone to Boston, because of the difficulty of explaining that Lord Pershore had in fact gone to jail voluntarily to help research his mother's book.

In gratitude, Bertie purchases a White House Wonder (or Longacre, in the 1917 version). He also finds that he owes Jeeves $50 – money Jeeves had wagered Lord Pershore that he would not hit a policeman – and gives him $100.

'Jeeves and the Hard-Boiled Egg'
Published in the Saturday Evening Post *with illustrations by Henry Raleigh on 3 March 1917, 'Jeeves and the Hard-Boiled Egg' appeared in the August 1917 issue of the* Strand Magazine, *illustrated by Alfred Leete. It then appeared in the collection* My Man Jeeves, *published in the UK by George Newnes in May 1919, and later in the collection* Carry On, Jeeves!

'Jeeves and the Hard-Boiled Egg' is also set in New York. Things are a little strained with Jeeves as Bertie has decided to grow a moustache. Jeeves does not approve. Bertie's friend Francis 'Bicky' Bickersteth turns up. His uncle, the Duke of Chiswick, is about to arrive in town expecting to find his nephew involved in a lucrative business venture which he has written home about. Instead, Bicky has been living off the small allowance his uncle sent him. Though wealthy, the Duke is a notoriously prudent spender – what the Americans would call a hard-boiled egg.

Jeeves suggests that Mr Bickersteth borrows Wooster's flat, giving his uncle the impression that he is doing well. Impressed, the Duke cancels Bicky's allowance.

To raise money, Jeeves suggests that Bickersteth charge people a modest fee for an introduction to the Duke of Chiswick. When Bickersteth fails miserably at selling introductions, Jeeves arranges for eighty-seven gentlemen who are on a convention from Birdsburg, Missouri, to pay $150 to shake hands with the Duke. However, the first delegates begin to question whether the Duke is really a Duke. Consequently the Duke refuses to meet any more of them and cuts Bickersteth off without a penny.

Jeeves then suggests that, if Mr Bickersteth wants ready money, he could sell the story to the newspapers. Chiswick is terrified of bad publicity. He is forced to take his nephew on at a salary of $500 a year. In gratitude to Jeeves, Bertie shaves off his moustache.

'Jeeves and the Chump Cyril' ('A Letter of Introduction'/ 'Startling Dressiness of a Lift Attendant')

Published in the Saturday Evening Post *with illustrations by Grant T. Reynard on 8 June 1918, 'Jeeves and the Chump Cyril' appeared in the August 1918 issue of the* Strand Magazine, *illustrated by Alfred Leete. It then appeared as two parts, 'A Letter of Introduction' and 'Startling Dressiness of a Lift Attendant', in the collection* The Inimitable Jeeves, *published in the UK by Herbert Jenkins on 17 May 1923 and in the US as* Jeeves *by the George H. Doran Company on 28 September 1923.*

'A Letter of Introduction'

Bertie Wooster has been in America three weeks when Cyril Bassington-Bassington delivers a letter of introduction from Aunt Agatha. Bassington-Bassington is heading for Washington, hoping to enter the diplomatic service.

Before Bertie gets to meet him in person, Bassington-Bassington has been arrested and Bertie has to go and bail him out. He takes with him his friend, American playwright George Caffyn, who takes Bassington-Bassington to see a rehearsal of his new musical comedy, *Ask Dad*. Bertie then receives a telegram from Aunt Agatha telling him, on no account, to introduce Cyril into theatrical circles. When Bassington-Bassington arrives home he announces that Caffyn has given him a small part in *Ask Dad*. He had always wanted to go on the stage but his father would not allow it.

Bertie realizes that Aunt Agatha will blame him and asks Jeeves to come to his rescue, although realtions in the flat had been strained for some days over a pair of bright purple socks Jeeves disapproves of.

'Startling Dressiness of a Lift Attendant'

When Bertie goes to consult Jeeves again about the matter, he finds he has company – another valet, who is a friend, and a boy in a Norfolk suit. The boy calls Cyril 'fish-face'. A fight ensues. It transpires that Jeeves gave the boy a dollar to say it.

A week later Caffyn asks Bertie to come and see a run-through of the show. Caffyn is on stage with Blumenfeld, the manager. The boy is there. He is Blumenfeld's son and

Blumenfeld takes note of his opinion. When Cyril appears, the boy again says he has a face like a fish. Cyril takes exception to this and Blumenfeld fires him.

The following morning Bassington-Bassington is on his way to Washington and Bertie notices that the lift attendant is wearing the pair of his purple socks that Jeeves had taken exception to.

'Jeeves in the Springtime' ('Jeeves Exerts the Old Cerebellum'/'No Wedding Bells for Bingo')

Published in the December 1921 issue of the Strand Magazine *with illustrations by A. Wallis Mills, 'Jeeves in the Springtime' appeared in the December 1921 issue of* Cosmopolitan, *illustrated by T. D. Skidmore. In* The Inimitable Jeeves, *it became 'Jeeves Exerts the Old Celebellum' and 'No Wedding Bells for Bingo'.*

'Jeeves Exerts the Old Cerebellum'
In the park, Bertie meets his old schoolfriend Bingo Little who is always falling in love. This time the object of his affection is a waitress named Mabel. Bingo takes Bertie to the tea-and-bun shop where she works. They had met at a dance in Camberwell to which Jeeves was selling tickets. Bingo wants to marry Mabel and now has the problem of introducing her to his Uncle Mortimer, a retired businessman upon whom Bingo is dependent. Jeeves is to be consulted. It transpires that he is engaged to Mortimer Little's cook, Miss Watson.

As Uncle Mortimer is laid up in bed with gout, Jeeves suggests that Bingo takes over the chore of reading to his uncle in the evening. To further his cause, Jeeves furnishes Bingo with the works of Rosie M. Banks, in which marriage between the classes feature.

'No Wedding Bells for Bingo'
Uncle Mortimer invites Bertie to lunch after Bingo has told him that 'Rosie M. Banks' is Bertie's pen-name. He has taken the theme of Rosie M. Banks's books to heart and when Bertie mentions that Bingo wants to marry a waitress, Uncle Mortimer is delighted. Indeed he, himself, is about to marry Miss Watson – relieving Jeeves of his engagement as he now has an 'understanding' with Mabel.

'Scoring off Jeeves' ('The Pride of the Woosters Is Wounded'/'The Hero's Reward')
Published in the February 1922 issue of the Strand Magazine *with illustrations by A. Wallis Mills, 'Scoring off Jeeves' appeared in* Cosmopolitan *as 'Bertie Gets Even' in March 1922, illustrated by T. D. Skidmore. In* The Inimitable Jeeves, *it became 'The Pride of the Woosters Is Wounded' and 'The Hero's Reward'.*

'The Pride of the Woosters Is Wounded'
While Jeeves is preparing to take his annual holiday, Bertie goes out for a walk and bumps into Bingo Little. He has lost his month's allowance on a horse and has been hired as a tutor to Oswald Glossop at Ditteridge Hall. He has now fallen in love with the daughter of the house, Honoria Glossop, though he does not dare tell her.

Bertie lunches with Aunt Agatha who tells him that she has found a wife for him – Honoria Glossop – and has arranged for him to stay at Ditteridge Hall.

When he arrives at Ditteridge Hall, Honoria is away staying with a family named Braythwayt. Bingo introduces Bertie to Oswald who is fishing from a bridge.

Bertie then comes up with a plan to get Bingo and Honoria together. When she returns, Bertie will lure her to the bridge, then push young Oswald into the lake and Bingo will dive in and save him.

'The Hero's Reward'
Honoria returns the following day with Daphne Braythwayt.
Bertie steers Honoria out to the bridge where he tells her that
a friend of his is 'frightfully in love' with her. Honoria
assumes the friend is Bertie himself. Bertie then pushes
Oswald in. However, Bingo does not emerge from the bushes
to save him as planned, so Bertie has to jump in. Oswald can
swim, however, and reaches the shore before Bertie can rescue
him. Honoria now assumes that Bertie was trying to propose
to her and pushed Oswald into the lake so he could rescue him
to impress her.

Back at the house, Bingo tells Bertie that he was hiding in
the bushes as planned, but then he caught sight of Daphne
Braythwayt and fell in love with her instead. Downstairs in
the drawing room, Honoria is waiting to read the work of
John Ruskin to Bertie.

'Sir Roderick Comes to Lunch' ('Introducing Claude and Eustace'/'Sir Roderick Comes to Lunch')

Published in the March 1922 issue of the Strand Magazine *with
illustrations by A. Wallis Mills, 'Sir Roderick Comes to Lunch'
appeared in* Cosmopolitan *as 'Jeeves and the Blighter' in April
1922, illustrated by T. D. Skidmore. In* The Inimitable Jeeves,
*it became 'Introducing Claude and Eustace' and 'Sir Roderick
Comes to Lunch'.*

'Introducing Claude and Eustace'
As well as forcing Bertie to read Ruskin and other heavyweight literature, Honoria takes him to lunch at Aunt
Agatha's where she announces that, when they are married, he
must get rid of Jeeves.

Before they are wed, Bertie must be given the once-over by
Honoria's father, Sir Roderick Glossop, a leading nerve
specialist – or 'janitor of a loony bin', as Bertie puts it. He has

some concerns about Bertie's mental health after hearing that he pushed young Oswald into the lake.

Sir Roderick is coming to lunch at Bertie's flat the following day. He disapproves of gambling, so Bertie is not to mention horse racing. He does not drink or smoke, eats only the simplest food and eschews coffee.

The following morning in Hyde Park, Bertie bumps into his cousins, Claude and Eustace, and their fellow student Lord Rainsby. They are down from Oxford for the day and have just come from Bertie's flat where they were entertained by Jeeves.

'Sir Roderick Comes to Lunch'
When Sir Roderick arrives for lunch, he stiffens, fearing the presence of a cat. Bertie reassures him that he has no cat. The whole world is going mad, rues Sir Roderick. On the way, his hat had been snatched from his head.

They then hear a mewing. Bertie asks Jeeves whether they are any cats in the flat.

'Only the three in your bedroom,' he replies, explaining that the cats may be agitated after finding a fish under Mr Wooster's bed. Sir Roderick concludes that Bertie is insane and makes for the door. Bertie insists on accompanying him so he can offer some explanation and asks Jeeves for his hat. But the hat Jeeves gives him is Sir Roderick's – the one that had been snatched from his head.

Lord Rainsby turns up explains that to get into a club called The Seekers at Oxford you have to pinch something. Claude and Eustace had stolen the cats, which have now escaped, the fish, which the cats have eaten, and the hat, which Sir Roderick has repossessed. Jeeves had allowed them to stash their swag in Bertie's flat until their train left that afternoon. But now everything has gone. Lord Rainsby then asks Bertie to lend him a tenner so he can bail out Claude and Eustace who have been arrested after trying to steal a motor-lorry.

Jeeves confirms that Sir Roderick now thinks that Bertie is a lunatic. His engagement to Honoria Glossop off, Bertie decides to put 3,000 miles between himself and Aunt Agatha and ask Jeeves to book tickets for the next boat to New York. Later, when the story was collected in *The Jeeves Omnibus*, instead of sailing to America, Bertie takes refuge in the south of France, which set the scene for the following story in *The Jeeves Omnibus*, 'Aunt Agatha Takes the Count' in which Aunt Agatha tracks Bertie down and checks into Bertie's French hotel, with the intention of speaking her mind on the subject of Honoria.

'Aunt Agatha Takes the Count' ('Aunt Agatha Speaks Her Mind'/'Pearls Mean Tears')

Published in the April 1922 issue of the Strand Magazine *with illustrations by A. Wallis Mills, 'Aunt Agatha Takes the Count' appeared in* Cosmopolitan *as 'Aunt Agatha Makes a Bloomer' in October 1922, illustrated by T. D. Skidmore. In* The Inimitable Jeeves, *it became 'Aunt Agatha Speaks Her Mind' and 'Pearls Mean Tears'. In the collection, these two stories appear before 'The Pride of the Woosters' as Miss Hemmingway and the incident concerning the pearl are referred to in that story. These references do not appear in the original story in the* Strand Magazine *and were written in later when the stories were reordered in the collection.*

'Aunt Agatha Speaks Her Mind'

A letter arrives from Aunt Agatha demanding Bertie's presence in the French seaside resort of Roville-sur-Mer. At the Hôtel Splendide, she introduces Bertie to Aline Hemmingway and her brother Sidney who is a curate in Dorset. Miss Hemmingway, she says, is the sort of girl Bertie should marry. Bertie is against the idea, but Jeeves, who disapproves of Bertie's bright scarlet cummerbund, has nothing to suggest.

'Pearls Mean Tears'

Miss Hemmingway and her brother visit Bertie's room. Sidney, they say, has lost heavily at the casino. They need Bertie to lend them money. As security, Aline offers her pearls and Bertie gives them a receipt.

After they leave, Jeeves says that when he was in the employ of Lord Frederick Ranelagh, a criminal called Soapy Sid and his female accomplice had pulled the same scam.

But Bertie says he has the pearls, only to open their case to find it empty. However, Jeeves had recognized Sidney Hemingway as Soapy Sid. He had switched the case, but Jeeves had removed it from his pocket when he helped him on with his coat.

In fact, the pearls belong to Aunt Agatha. Bertie goes to return them only to find that Aunt Agatha has accused the chambermaid of stealing them. Bertie then produces the pearls from his pocket. He explains that her friend Miss Hemmingway had stolen them, then seizes the opportunity to upbraid his aunt for accusing the maid without evidence. Bertie removes his cummerbund and hands it to Jeeves.

In this story when it was rewritten for *The Jeeves Omnibus*, Bertie had bolted for France to avoid the wrath of Aunt Agatha and had fallen for Aline without any prompting from his aunt. In fact, he was making good progress with his wooing before Aunt Agatha even arrived at the hotel, eager to discuss the broken engagement with Honoria as described in 'Sir Roderick Comes To Lunch'. Naturally, the discovery that Aline and Sid were thieves cooled Bertie's ardour. Then, while Aunt Agatha was accusing the hotel chambermaid of theft, Bertie pretended to find the missing pearls hidden under a piece of paper in a drawer, leaving Aunt Agatha 'with the demeanour of one who, picking daisies on the railway, has just caught the down-express in the small of the back.'

'Comrade Bingo' ('Comrade Bingo'/'Bingo Has a Bad Goodwood')

Published in the May 1922 issue of the Strand Magazine *with illustrations by A. Wallis Mills, 'Comrade Bingo' appeared in* Cosmopolitan *in the same month, illustrated by T. D. Skidmore. In* The Inimitable Jeeves, *it became 'Comrade Bingo' and 'Bingo Has a Bad Goodwood'.*

'Comrade Bingo'
Bertie visits Speakers' Corner in Hyde Park where he bumps into Bingo Little's Uncle Mortimer. He has also been ennobled as Lord Bittlesham ('that peerage cost the old devil the deuce of a sum' – referring to the Lloyd George cash-for-honours scandal that broke that year) and is the owner of the racehorse Ocean Breeze, which Bertie is backing at Goodwood. The pair are then vilified as examples of the idle rich by a bearded man from a group calling themselves variously the Heralds, or Sons, of the Red Dawn.

The following day Bertie bumps into Bingo, who reveals that he had been the one denouncing them at Speakers' Corner disguised with a false beard. He has joined the Red Dawn because he is in love with a female member with the revolutionary name Charlotte Corday Rowbotham. He is putting money on Ocean Breeze in the hope that his winnings will give him enough to marry her. The group are also holding a meeting outside the paddock at Goodwood.

Bingo brings Charlotte and her father round for tea at Bertie's flat. This will stand Bertie in good stead when the Revolution breaks out. They are joined by Comrade Butt, a rival for Charlotte's hand.

When Rowbotham thanks Bertie for his hospitality, Comrade Butt complains that the eggs, muffins and sardines he has provided were 'wrung from the bleeding lips of the starving poor'.

'Bingo Has a Bad Goodwood'

Lord Bittlesham receives a threatening letter. He suspects it is from the bearded revolutionary who upbraided him in the park.

At Goodwood, Ocean Breeze comes nowhere. Bertie is discussing the matter with Lord Bittlesham when he spots the bearded revolutionary making another inflammatory speech. In it, he blames Bittlesham for encouraging working people to lose money on his horse.

Comrade Butt then takes over. He claims that the revolutionary message is spreading even among the upper classes. Indeed, he says the nephew of Lord Bittlesham has rallied to the cause and he pulls off Bingo's beard. Bittlesham is aghast. Bingo attacks Butt and both are arrested.

The following morning, Jeeves reveals that he told Butt that his bearded comrade was Bittlesham's nephew, thereby scuppering his prospective marriage to Charlotte.

'The Great Sermon Handicap'

Published in the June 1922 issue of the Strand Magazine *with illustrations by A. Wallis Mills, 'The Great Sermon Handicap' appeared in* Cosmopolitan *in the same month, illustrated by T. D. Skidmore. It then appeared in* The Inimitable Jeeves.

Bertie gets a letter from Claude and Eustace inviting him to a 'sporting event' where he can make good his losses from Goodwood. The twins are staying at the vicarage in Twing, Gloucestershire, where they are cramming for a Classics exam. Bingo Little is staying nearby at Twing Hall where he has taken a job as a tutor after his uncle cut his allowance. On the reverse of the letter is a list of the runners in the 'Sermon Handicap': all clergymen. At the bottom are the odds. Intrigued, Jeeves and Wooster set off for Twing Hall.

At dinner, Bertie sits next to Lord Wickhammersley's

youngest daughter, Cynthia. Apart from Bingo, who has already fallen in love with Cynthia, the other dinner guests are clergymen.

A fellow student of Claude and Eustace named Rupert Steggles and has come up with the idea of betting on the length of sermons delivered by local vicars. The Reverend Francis Heppenstall, usually gives very long sermons but, when Steggles was setting the odds, he did not notice that Heppenstall had dropped half a dozen pages from his sermon case. So Bertie puts a tenner on Heppenstall at seven-to-one.

Then comes the news that the Reverend G. Hayward gave a sermon that lasted twenty-six minutes at a wedding. 'What'll he do when he really extends himself?' asks Eustace.

Bertie has heard Heppenstall give a sermon on Brotherly Love that lasted forty-five minutes. He goes to the vicar and persuades him to preach it again. But Heppenstall comes down with hay fever, so Bertie instead puts a fiver on Hayward at four-to-one. Bertie cycles over to Lower Bingley to hear Hayward's sermon, which comes in at thirty-five minutes and fourteen seconds. Then Bertie learns that Jeeves has put a tenner on the Reverend James Bates.

Jeeves delivers a note that had arrived for Bertie earlier. It is from the Reverend Heppenstall, saying that, as Bertie wanted to hear his sermon on Brotherly Love, he has given it to the Reverend Bates who will preach it at Gandle-by-the-Hill that Sunday.

When Bertie complains that preaching another man's sermon is not 'playing the game', Jeeves points out that the Reverend Bates is engaged to Lady Cynthia and needed to impress to secure a headmastership so that they can marry.

'The Purity of the Turf'

Published in the July 1922 issue of Strand Magazine *with illustrations by A. Wallis Mills, 'The Purity of the Turf' appeared in* Cosmopolitan *in the same month, illustrated by T. D. Skidmore. It then appeared in* The Inimitable Jeeves.

Bertie stays on at Twing Hall and, one morning, Bingo asks him to 'come in on another little flutter'. The village school is holding its sports day in the grounds. Rupert Steggles is running a book on it. Bingo has some inside information on the Mothers' Sack Race. Mrs Penworthy, the tobacconist's wife who has just moved into the area, has won three times at fairs in Worcestershire. Jeeves thinks it is worth risking a tenner each way.

Jeeves fancies Harold, the page boy, for the Choir-Boys' Hundred Yards Handicap, open to all whose voices had not broken by the second Sunday in Epiphany. Though fat, he has a surprising turn of speed. No one knows this because he is not allowed to mix with village lads. However, at evensong, Steggles drops a beetle down the back of Harold's neck. He shrieks and the vicar fires him from the choir, scratching him from the race.

Steggles then nobbles Mrs Penworthy by taking her to the refreshment tent and filling her up with tea and cakes before the race. But Jeeves has persuaded Bingo to put 'a small sum' on Prudence Baxter, the head gardener's daughter and a rank outsider in the Girls' Egg and Spoon Race. She comes fifth. Bingo had bet thirty quid at ten-to-one.

Then the Reverend Heppenstall announces it has come to his attention that the manservant of one of the guests at the hall has confessed to giving several of the contestants five shillings each. By accepting the money the girls have forfeited their amateur status, so the first four were disqualified, leaving Prudence Baxter the winner.

'Bertie Changes His Mind'

Published in the August 1922 issue of the Strand Magazine *with illustrations by A. Wallis Mills, 'Bertie Changes His Mind' appeared in* Cosmopolitan *in the same month, illustrated by T. D. Skidmore. It then appeared in* Carry On, Jeeves! *This is the only Jeeves and Wooster story told from Jeeves's point of view. In it, Jeeves recalls the 'Episode of the School for Young Ladies near Brighton'.*

Bertie is discontented. He has seen a play that makes him want to have a daughter. Jeeves suggests a short stay in Brighton. On their way back to London, they give a girl a lift back to school. Jeeves then informs the headmistress that Mr Wooster is a famous novelist or philosopher. Bertie is then asked to make a speech. Jeeves tells him that there is something wrong with the car so. The substance of Bertie's speech is that you can win money by betting on the fact that, if you stand outside Romano's on the Strand you can see the clock on the wall of the Law Courts in Fleet Street. When he begins to tell a story about a stockbroker and a chorus-girl, the headmistress calls a halt.

Girls have been caught smoking cigarettes from Bertie's cigarette case in the shrubbery. Bertie is blamed. The car now starts. Wooster urges Jeeves to hurry, but Jeeves says he does not want to run over one of the young ladies.

'Well, what's the objection to that?' asks Bertie.

Back at home, he is happy to be back in a firmly bachelor establishment.

'The Metropolitan Touch'

Published in the September 1922 issue of the Strand Magazine *with illustrations by A. Wallis Mills, 'The Metropolitan Touch' appeared in* Cosmopolitan *in the same month, illustrated by T. D. Skidmore. It then appeared in* The Inimitable Jeeves.

Bertie is in London when he gets a telegram from Bingo at Twing Hall announcing that he is in love again. The girl in question is Miss Mary Burgess, the niece of the Reverend Heppenstall, who is staying at the vicarage.

Bingo meets them at the station. While Jeeves goes on to the hall in the car, Bingo takes Bertie on a circuitous route so that they bump into the girl. However, she is walking with the curate, Mr Wingham, a rival for her hand.

Jeeves suggests that, to advance his cause, Bingo make friends with Miss Burgess's young brother, Wilfred. This ends in disaster when Steggles bets Bingo that Master Heppenstall will beat Master Burgess in an eating contest.

However, all is not lost when Wingham comes down with mumps and Bingo has to take over the production of the village school Christmas entertainment. Based on the West End hit *Cuddle Up!* Bingo is calling it *What Ho, Twing*.

Again, Steggles is making book, leading Bertie to believe that he is going to nobble the show.

Some of the numbers Bingo has borrowed from the West End shows are hardly suitable for a children's entertainment. The lights go on and off, and the local squire and his family walk out. The finale is a song from a show at the Palace where chorus-girls shower the audience with oranges made of yellow wool. In Bingo's production, they use real oranges. The audience throw them back.

Less than a week later, the forthcoming wedding of Wingham and Miss Burgess is announced in the *Morning Post*. But Jeeves and Lord Wickhammersley's butler Brookfield had bought Steggles's book, a highly profitable investment.

'The Delayed Exit of Claude and Eustace'
Published in the October 1922 issue of the Strand Magazine *with illustrations by A. Wallis Mills, 'The Delayed Exit of Claude and Eustace' appeared in* Cosmopolitan *with the title*

'The Exit of Claude and Eustace' in November 1922, illustrated by T. D. Skidmore. It then appeared in The Inimitable Jeeves.

Claude and Eustace have been sent down from Oxford and are leaving for South Africa on the *Edinburgh Castle* – or so Aunt Agatha says. They are to be in Bertie's charge for their last night in London. He is to see that they do not miss the boat train in the morning. Naturally, they go out on the town.

Bertie wakes about one in the afternoon, expecting the twins to be long gone. Then Claude walks in. The previous evening at Ciro's he had met and fallen for Marion Wardour, a showgirl from the Apollo; he explains he gave Eustace the slip at Waterloo station.

The moment Claude has gone Eustace breezes in. He too has fallen for Miss Wardour and also did a bunk at Waterloo.

Aunt Agatha arrives to report that, on his way from the Devonshire Club to Boodle's, drunken Uncle George has seen what he believes to the a 'phantasm of Eustace'. There are other near misses.

A few days later Marion Wardour arrives at Bertie's flat at teatime, complaining she is tired of the ceaseless attention of Claude and Eustace. Eventually Claude comes to Bertie and asks Bertie to buy him a new ticket to South Africa. Jeeves tells Bertie that Eustace has also asked him to book a ticket.

Once the twins have gone, Bertie receives a letter from Marion Wardour, enclosing £5 for Jeeves. It transpires that he suggested that Miss Wardour inform them independently that she had a theatrical engagement in South Africa.

'Bingo and the Little Woman' ('Bingo and the Little Woman'/'All's Well')
Published in the November 1922 issue of the Strand Magazine *with illustrations by A. Wallis Mills, 'Bingo and the Little*

Woman' appeared in Cosmopolitan *in December 1922, illustrated by T. D. Skidmore. It appeared in* The Inimitable Jeeves *as 'Bingo and the Little Woman' and 'All's Well'.*

'Bingo and the Little Woman'

While dining with Bertie at the Senior Liberal Club, Bingo falls for a waitress and when the girl accepts Bingo's proposal, Bertie is asked to see Uncle Mortimer to restore Bingo's allowance.

To smooth the way, Bertie is to send Uncle Mortimer a copy of Rosie M. Banks's latest offering, *The Woman Who Braved All*, which he has autographed. A note comes from Uncle Mortimer inviting Bertie to lunch. His heart has been softened by the book – and Bertie's inscription – and he agrees to restore Bingo's allowance. Bingo goes ahead and marries.

'All's Well'

When the newly-weds go to see Uncle Mortimer, Bingo's new wife announces that she is Rosie M. Banks and was only working as a waitress to collect material for her new novel. Uncle Mortimer, convinced that Bertie is the real Rosie M. Banks, does not believe her and there is a huge row.

The following day, Bingo phones to warn Bertie that both Uncle Mortimer and 'the little woman' are coming to demand an explanation. Jeeves suggests that Bertie goes shooting in Norfolk. When he returns everything is sorted. On Jeeves's advice, Bingo told his uncle that Bertie had claimed he was Rosie M. Banks because was a 'loony'– a fact that Sir Roderick Glossop would readily confirm.

'The Rummy Affair of Old Biffy'

Published in the Saturday Evening Post *with illustrations by Arthur William Brown on 27 September 1924, 'The Rummy Affair of Old Biffy' appeared in the October 1924 issue of the*

Strand Magazine, *illustrated by A. Wallis Mills. It then appeared in* Carry on, Jeeves!

Jeeves and Wooster are in Paris, where Bertie bumps into the chronically forgetful Charles Edward 'Biffy' Biffen. He is broken-hearted. After meeting a model named Mabel on a liner to New York and proposing to her, he had forgotten the name of her hotel and her surname, so he could not trace her.

Some days later, Bertie reads in *The Times* of the forthcoming marriage of Mr C. E. Biffen and Miss Honoria Glossop. When Bertie returns to London, Biffy turns up. He wants to know how Bertie got out of his engagement to Honoria Glossop, as he wants to do the same. Bertie consults Jeeves but he refuses to help. So Bertie supplies a bunch of joke-shop flowers with a bulb that squirts water in it, then invites Sir Roderick Glossop to lunch to give Biffy the once over. But Biffy losses his nerve and baulks at giving Sir Roderick a drenching.

For an improving afternoon, Sir Roderick takes Bertie and Biffy to the British Empire Exhibition. Jeeves tags along too but, at Wembley goes his own way. Bertie and Biffy manage to give Sir Roderick the slip and find a bar selling West Indian cocktails.

Biffy then remembers that Jeeves suggested they visit the Palace of Beauty. Behind plate glass are girls dressed as famous women throughout the ages. Suddenly Biffy cries: 'Mabel!'

He smashes the glass with his walking stick. This leads Sir Roderick to think that he too is a 'loony' and he breaks off the engagement.

The reason that Jeeves was not willing to help Biffy to start with was because, when Biffy got engaged to Honoria Glossop, he assumed that he was trifling with Mabel's affections. Mabel is Jeeves's niece.

'Clustering Round Young Bingo'

Published in the Saturday Evening Post *with illustrations by H. J. Mowat on 21 February 1925, 'Clustering Round Young Bingo' appeared in the April 1925 issue of the* Strand Magazine, *illustrated by A. Wallis Mills. It then appeared in* Carry on, Jeeves!

Bertie is writing an article about 'What the Well-Dressed Man is Wearing' for Aunt Dahlia's magazine, *Milady's Boudoir*. Jeeves generally approves of what Bertie has written, but they fall out over wearing soft silk shirts with evening dress. Putting that to one side, Bertie wants to know if Jeeves knows any housemaids who might be gentle with the china, as Bingo's current maid keeps breaking things.

Outside the Covent Garden offices of *Milady's Boudoir*, Bertie bumps into Mrs Little who invites him to dinner the following evening. His Aunt Dahlia is coming with Uncle Tom.

Aunt Dahlia tells Bertie that their cook's food is so bad that it puts Uncle Tom in a bad mood and she fears that he will refuse to go on paying the printer's bills for the magazine. However, the Littles have a great cook, the legendary Anatole.

The following day, Bingo comes to the flat and asks Bertie to 'cluster round'. His Aunt Dahlia has commissioned Mrs Little to write a piece called 'How I Keep the Love of My Husband-Baby'. This will make him a laughing stock at his clubs.

Bingo gets Bertie to steal the manuscript of the article, but Bertie bungles it and legs it.

To avoid further trouble, Bertie accompanies his Uncle George to Harrogate.

When Bertie returns to London, Jeeves reveals that he persuaded Mrs Travers's housemaid to work for the Littles, replacing their current maid who smashes everything. She was previously been engaged to Anatole, who had unceremoniously dumped her. Fearful of living under the same roof as his aggrieved former lover, Anatole quits and goes to work for the Travers. Bingo, Mrs Travers, Aunt Dahlia, Uncle Tom and, finally, Bertie all pay Jeeves for his ministrations. As an added bonus, Bertie tells Jeeves to send back the silk evening shirts he had ordered.

'Without the Option'
Published in the Saturday Evening Post *with illustrations by George Wright on 27 June 1925, 'Without the Option' appeared in the July 1925 issue of the* Strand Magazine, *illustrated by A. Wallis Mills. It then appeared in* Carry On, Jeeves!

The story begins with Bertie in the dock. On Boat-Race night, he had bumped into Oliver Randolph 'Sippy' Sipperley who is depressed because his Aunt Vera, on whom he is financially dependent, has arranged for him to go and spend three weeks with her friends, the Pringles. To get out of this, Bertie recommended that he should steal a policeman's helmet and they were both arrested. Bertie gets off with a fine, which Jeeves delivers. Sippy, who gives his name as Leon Trotzky (spelled Trotsky in the original *Strand* magazine publication, but changed to Trotzky for the book publication in the UK and US), is sentenced to thirty days without the option of a fine.

However, Bertie has not solved a problem, he has created one. If Sippy does not go to stay with the Pringles, Aunt Vera will want to know why. Jeeves suggests that Bertie go and stay with the Pringles in Mr Sipperley's place: he has discovered that Professor and Mrs Pringle have not seen Sippy since he was ten. Bertie dismisses this plan as 'drivel'. Then Jeeves tells him that Mrs Spencer – the dreaded Aunt Agatha – has been phoning. She has read about his court appearance in the newspaper. Jeeves has already called a taxi for Bertie to make his escape. Presumably when Wodehouse wrote the story he had forgotten that in earlier stories Aunt Agatha's name had been Mrs Gregson and her first husband's first name was Spencer (later Spenser). When the story appeared in its US book, Aunt Agatha's name was changed to Mrs Spenser Gregson.

Bertie arrives with the Pringles in time for dinner. Professor Pringle introduces him to his mother and aged Aunt Jane, who remembers Oliver as a nasty boy who teased her cat. Then the Professor's daughter Heloise enters. She is Honoria Glossop's cousin and won't leave Bertie alone.

To avoid Heloise, he climbs down a drainpipe from his bedroom window so that he can pass an hour alone, reading in the summer house. But she pops up there, too. She picks up the novel he is reading, *The Trail of Blood*, and notices his name scrawled across the title page. She asks if he knows 'Bertie Wooster'. She has heard about him from her cousin Honoria and Sir Roderick, and she has recently read about him in the newspaper. She tells him that he is a bad influence and he should drop him as a friend.

Bertie manages to avoid Heloise for a couple of days. Then Sir Roderick Glossop arrives and upbraids Bertie for impersonating the nephew of his old friend: plainly he is insane. Aunt Jane concurs – she has seen him climbing down drainpipes.

Jeeves advises Bertie to go and see Sippy's Aunt Vera. Bertie explains that Sippy is in chokey for assaulting a policeman and that it was all his fault.

Aunt Vera is not upset. She is proud of her nephew. Jeeves explains later that Miss Sipperley had been having trouble recently with the local constable – who turns out to be Jeeves's cousin.

'Fixing it for Freddie' ('Helping Freddie'/'Lines and Business')

Originally this was a Reggie Pepper story called 'Helping Freddie', which appeared in the September 1911 issue of the Strand Magazine *with illustrations by H. M. Brock, and as 'Lines and Business' in the March 1912 issue of* Pictorial Review *in the US with illustrations by Phillips Ward. It was rewritten as 'Fixing it for Freddie' for* Carry On, Jeeves! *with its first magazine appearance being in the September 1928 issue of the* Canadian Home Journal. *This plot was then rewritten a second time as a Drones Club story entitled 'Unpleasantness at Kozy Kot' collected in the American edition of* A Few Quick Ones *with an appearance in the 1 August 1959 issue of the Canadian magazine* Star Weekly, *with illustrations by Jack Bush.*

Bertie's friend Freddie Bullivant has announced his engagement to Miss Elizabeth Vickers, who now refuses to speak to him. So Bertie is going to take Freddie down to Marvis Bay in Dorset for a change of scenery. Elizabeth Vickers is at Marvis Bay, too, but cuts Freddie dead.

Bertie sees Miss Vickers on the beach. She is with her aunt and a child, whom Bertie assumes is her cousin. Bertie snatches the child, figuring that if Freddie turns up saying that he has found the infant, Elizabeth would warm to him.

Freddie tries to return the child, but the child is not Elizabeth's cousin. He is a perfect stranger. When Bertie tracks down the father, the entire family has mumps. As he is a relative of Aunt Agatha, Bertie has to look after this long-lost relation for a couple of days.

Jeeves comes up with an idea to reconcile Mr Bullivant and Miss Vickers. He has just seen a film called *Tiny Hands* in which a child brings its parents back together after they have drifted apart. The idea is to get the couple in proximity and have the child say to Elizabeth: 'Kiss Freddie.'

They begin rehearsing the child. Elizabeth comes by and the child shouts: 'Kiss Fweddie!'

Soon, Freddie and Elizabeth are in each other's arms.

'The Inferiority Complex of Old Sippy'

Published in the April 1926 issue of the Strand Magazine *with illustrations by Charles Crombie, 'The Inferiority Complex of Old Sippy' appeared in* Liberty *magazine on 17 April 1926 with illustrations by Wallace Morgan. It then appeared in the collection* Very Good, Jeeves *published by Doubleday, Doran & Company in the US on 20 June 1930 and by Herbert Jenkins in the UK on 4 July 1930.*

Bertie has bought a vase that Jeeves does not like. Later he heads off to the offices of the *Mayfair Gazette* where Sippy is now editor. Sippy is in love with one of the contributors, Miss Gwendolen Moon, but cannot bring himself to tell her.

Sippy's old headmaster Mr Waterbury arrives with an article that Sippy does not want to publish, but he is too intimidated to reject it. Bertie goes home to consult Jeeves. They decide that Sippy is suffering from an inferiority complex.

After a good night's sleep, Bertie comes to believe that Sippy will only overcome his inferiority complex if he sees Waterbury in an undignified position. He therefore intends to balance a bag of flour on top of the office door so that it falls on Waterbury.

Jeeves think that, first, Mr Sipperley must be induced to propose to Miss Moon. As she is a poetess – and thus of a romantic nature – Jeeves thinks it would be a good idea if she heard that Mr Sipperley had met with a serious injury.

After a lunch fortified with alcohol, Bertie goes to the offices of the *Mayfair Gazette* and places the bag of flour on the top of the door. But Waterbury barges straight into Sippy's private office, avoiding the door with the bag of flour on it.

Sippy promptly rejects Waterbury's article on Elizabethan dramatists – emboldened because he has just got engaged. Jeeves explains that he invited Mr Sipperley round to Bertie's flat. He then called Miss Moon and informed her that Mr Sipperley had met with a nasty accident. Before she arrived, Jeeves hit Mr Sipperley over the head with one of Bertie's golf clubs. When Mr Sipperley came round, Jeeves told him that Bertie's new vase had fallen on him – and had smashed.

Bertie then opens the booby-trapped door and the flour falls on his head.

'Jeeves and the Impending Doom'
Published in the December 1926 issue of the Strand Magazine *with illustrations by Charles Crombie, 'Jeeves and the Impending Doom' appeared in* Liberty *magazine on 8 January 1927 with illustrations by Wallace Morgan. It then appeared in the collection* Very Good, Jeeves.

Aunt Agatha has invited Bertie down to her home at Woollam Chersey in Hertfordshire in the home counties. A telegram then arrives that reads: 'Remember when you come here absolutely vital meet perfect strangers.'

When Bertie arrives at Woollam Chersey, Aunt Agatha tells him that he must make a good impression on the Right Honourable A. B. Filmer, a Cabinet minister, who is staying there. He is not to drink or smoke.

Bertie meets Bingo Little in the garden and Bingo reminds him of the telegram. Bingo is tutoring Aunt Agatha's son, Thomas, and, if Aunt Agatha knew Bingo was a pal of Bertie's, she would sack him immediately. Things are not going well. Filmer, who is president of the Anti-Tobacco League, has caught Thomas smoking. Thomas is planning a hideous revenge and Bingo is sure to be sacked. Jeeves has nothing to suggest apart from 'ceaseless vigilance'. As Bertie dresses for dinner, he senses impending doom.

The following day, while Bingo and Bertie are playing tennis, Thomas disappears. Then the tennis is interrupted by rain. Filmer is nowhere to be seen. Aunt Agatha sends Bertie out with a raincoat to find him.

Filmer is marooned on an island in the middle of the lake. Jeeves and Wooster make for the boathouse. As they approach the island, they see Filmer on the top of the small octagonal building on the island, rather than taking shelter from the rain inside. When Bertie reaches the building, he is attacked by a swan and scrambles up on the roof beside Filmer, dropping the raincoat. Jeeves picks up the raincoat and bundles up the swan. Then Bertie, Filmer and Jeeves make their escape.

Filmer suspects that Thomas cast his boat adrift, marooning him. But Jeeves convinces Filmer that it was Bertie who had untied the boat as a practical joke. Bingo's job is saved. Bertie has also benefited by this subterfuge. Aunt Agatha had invited him to Woollam Chersey with the aim of getting Mr Filmer to employ him as his private secretary.

'Jeeves and the Yuletide Spirit' ('Jeeves and the Yule-Tide Spirit')

Published in the December 1927 issue of the Strand Magazine *with illustrations by Charles Crombie, 'Jeeves and the Yuletide Spirit' appeared in* Liberty *magazine on 24 December 1927 with illustrations by Wallace Morgan. It then appeared as 'Jeeves and the Yule-Tide Spirit' in the collection* Very Good, Jeeves.

Lady Wickham has invited Bertie to Skeldings Hall for Christmas, causing him to cancel his plan to visit Monte Carlo, which upsets Jeeves. Bertie then hears from Aunt Agatha that Sir Roderick Glossop is going to be at Skeldings over the holiday. He is to behave himself as Aunt Agatha has gone to great lengths to convince Sir Roderick that Bertie is not insane.

Despite this, Bertie is determined to go to Skeldings for Christmas because one does not get the 'Yule-tide spirit' in Monte Carlo. He also wants to take revenge on Tuppy Glossop, Sir Roderick's nephew, who played a trick on him that resulted in Bertie being dunked in the swimming pool at the Drones Club in his evening clothes. Bertie is also in love with Lady Wickham's daughter, Roberta. Jeeves does not think Miss Wickham a suitable mate.

Later Bertie counters Jeeves's argument that Miss Wickham is 'too volatile and frivolous'. They had been for a walk and she has come up with a scheme to wreak vengeance on Tuppy. At her girls' school, she says, they used to take a long stick with a darning needle tied to the end of it and puncture other girls' hot-water bottles. Jeeves is to provide a stick and a darning needle.

On Christmas Eve, when everyone has gone to bed, Bertie makes for the Moat Room where Jeeves has told him Tuppy is sleeping. He locates the hot-water bottle and stabs it. Sir Roderick Glossop appears. He had changed rooms with Tuppy: Jeeves had been informed of this.

Sir Roderick then notices water dripping from the punctured hot-water bottle. He takes Bertie's bed for the night, leaving Bertie to spend the night in an armchair. When Jeeves brings him his tea on Christmas morning, Bertie upbraids Jeeves for not telling him of the room switch. Jeeves explains that he had not done so because Aunt Agatha was trying to convince Sir Roderick of Bertie's sanity to advance his marriage to Sir Roderick's daughter, Miss Honoria Glossop.

Jeeves then reveals that, during the night, while Sir Roderick was occupying Bertie's bed, someone crept in and punctured his hot-water bottle. The culprit was young Mr Glossop. The idea had been suggested to him, Jeeves says, by Miss Wickham, confirming his view of her.

'Say no more, Jeeves,' says Bertie. 'Love is dead.'

Sir Roderick wants to see Bertie, but Jeeves suggests that he should escape across the fields and hires a car to take him back to London. But will he be safe there from Aunt Agatha? Jeeves reveals that he has forgotten to cancel their tickets for Monte Carlo.

'Jeeves and the Song of Songs' ('Song of Songs')

Published in the September 1929 issue of the Strand Magazine *with illustrations by Charles Crombie, 'Jeeves and the Song of Songs' appeared as 'Song of Songs' in* Cosmopolitan *in the same month with illustrations by James Montgomery Flagg. It then appeared as 'Jeeves and the Song of Songs' in the collection* Very Good, Jeeves.

Bertie is singing 'Sonny Boy' in the bath when Tuppy Glossop arrives. In the sitting room, Tuppy plays 'Sonny Boy' on the piano with one finger and says he is about to get engaged. His intended fiancée, opera singer Cora Bellinger, is a serious-minded woman. She has heard about Tuppy dunking Bertie in the swimming pool at the Drones Club and disapproves. To smooth things over, he is bringing her to have lunch at Bertie's flat that day.

Tuppy has also arranged for Cora to sing at an East End lads' club run by their chum from Oxford, the Reverend 'Beefy' Bingham. To prove to her that he is serious-minded, Tuppy is going to sing there, too. And to show that he has great depth, he is going to sing 'Sonny Boy'.

Tuppy flees when he hears that Mrs Travers is on her way. When Aunt Dahlia arrives, she complains that Tuppy has broken her daughter Angela's heart by dumping her for Cora Bellinger. Bertie says that Angela is better off without him and then relates the story of his soaking at the Drones. But Aunt Dahlia is delighted to hear of Tuppy's exploits.

'You restore my faith in the young hound,' she says.

Jeeves comes up with a plan to break off Mr Glossop's engagement. At the concert, he gets Bertie to sing 'Sonny Boy' before Tuppy. Tuppy then gets pelted with fruit. However, Cora has been delayed and does not witness his humiliation.

Tuppy later turns up at Bertie's flat with a black eye. He says he has changed his mind about Cora, and makes up with Angela.

Jeeves explains that Miss Bellinger hit Mr Glossop in the eye because she had been booed off stage. Jeeves had suggested that she too sing 'Sonny Boy'. When she discovered that both Bertie and Tuppy had sung it before her, she assumed that she had been the victim of another of Mr Glossop's practical jokes.

'Jeeves and the Dog McIntosh' ('The Borrowed Dog'/'Episode of the Dog McIntosh')

Published in the October 1929 issue of the Strand Magazine *with illustrations by Charles Crombie, 'Jeeves and the Dog McIntosh' appeared as 'The Borrowed Dog' in* Cosmopolitan *in the same month with illustrations by James Montgomery Flagg. It then appeared as 'Episode of the Dog McIntosh' in the collection* Very Good, Jeeves.

Aunt Agatha has left her Aberdeen terrier McIntosh with Bertie. However, Miss Roberta Wickham has invited the theatrical manager Blumenfeld and his son – last met in New York in 'Jeeves and the Chump Cyril' – to lunch at Bertie's flat. She is trying to sell Blumenfeld a play her mother, Lady Wickham, has written.

Bertie discovers who Miss Wickham's guests are, he absents himself and lunches at the Drones Club. He returns to find that Miss Wickham has given Master Blumenfeld Aunt

Agatha's dog McIntosh, which is now in their suite in the Savoy.

Bertie goes there to pinch the dog. To make sure McIntosh will come with him, Jeeves sprinkles some aniseed on Wooster's trousers.

Bertie returns with McIntosh and gives Jeeves a fiver. When Mr Blumenfeld arrives, Jeeves advises Bertie to hide behind the settee.

Blumenfeld says that Wooster has stolen his son's dog. He then notices a strange smell. Jeeves explains that Mr Wooster is somewhat eccentric and sprinkles aniseed on his trousers. Blumenfeld concludes that Bertie is 'loony'. Jeeves cautions that Mr Wooster is not dangerous unless roused by the sight of a fat man. Blumenfeld, a gentleman of 'full habit', flees.

Bertie wants to know why Blumenfeld suspected that he had stolen the dog. Jeeves says that he had recommended that Miss Wickham tell Blumenfeld that she had seen Bertie steal the dog, so Blumenfeld would not suspect her of complicity.

But Jeeves now has another fiver – Blumenfeld had given it to him when he handed over the dog. Bertie is aghast, but Jeeves reassures him that McIntosh is safe in his bedroom. He had gone out and bought another Aberdeen terrier, figuring that young Blumenfeld would not be able to tell the difference.

'Jeeves and the Love that Purifies' ('The Love that Purifies')

Published in the November 1929 issue of the Strand Magazine *with illustrations by Charles Crombie, 'Jeeves and the Love that Purifies' appeared in* Cosmopolitan *in the same month with illustrations by James Montgomery Flagg. It then appeared as 'The Love that Purifies' in the collection* Very Good, Jeeves.

Jeeves is taking his annual holiday. Bertie has avoided going to Sippy's because he knows that he will be left to look after

Gwendolen Moon's younger brother, Sebastian. Instead, an invitation from Aunt Dahlia turns up.

At the Travers's he meets a 'moth-eaten septuagenarian' named Mr Anstruther, an old friend of Aunt Dahlia's late father. Lord and Lady Snettisham are also there, along with Aunt Dahlia's son, Bonzo, and Aunt Agatha's loathsome son, Thomas. However, Anstruther has offered the boys a prize of a fiver to whoever behaves best during his stay.

The problem is that Jane, Lady Snettisham, has insisted on having a side bet with Aunt Dahlia – the stake: Anatole. But dirty work is afoot. Jack Snettisham had urged Bonzo to climb on the roof and shout boo down Mr Anstruther's chimney. Bonzo did not succumb because he was distracted by his love for Lilian Gish after seeing one of her films at the local cinema.

Now Aunt Dahlia plans to do a bit of nobbling and she is furious with Bertie because he has not brought Jeeves.

Bertie seeks out Thomas and starts taunting him, but he does not rise to the bait. Thomas offers to bring him cigarettes, matches, drink; Bertie taunts Thomas's school and its uniform. Nothing works. There is only one thing to be done – send for Jeeves.

Jeeves suggests that Mrs Travers should invite Sebastian Moon to stay. He feels that the boy's golden curls and personality, 'which is not uniformly pleasing', will break down Thomas's iron self-control. However, when Sebastian gets a nail in his shoe, Thomas gives him a piggy-back home.

Jeeves has now discerned that the reason for Thomas's good behaviour is that he has fallen for Greta Garbo.

Anstruther is dozing in a deckchair when Sebastian comes into sight pursued by Thomas who has a bucket full of water. Sebastian ducks behind Anstruther just as Thomas lets fly. Anstruther is drenched and Thomas is out of the running.

Jeeves is behind this, of course. He suggested to Sebastian

that he should speak disparagingly of Greta Garbo – it seems he preferred Clara Bow.

'Jeeves and the Spot of Art' ('The Spot of Art')

Published in the December 1929 issue of the Strand Mag-*azine with illustrations by Charles Crombie, 'Jeeves and the Spot of Art' appeared in* Cosmopolitan *in the same month with illustrations by James Montgomery Flagg. It then appeared as 'The Spot of Art' in the collection* Very Good, Jeeves.

Bertie tells Aunt Dahlia that he will not be coming on the Mediterranean cruise she was planning. He has to stay in London to see Gwladys Pendlebury, an artist who he has met at a party in Chelsea. She has painted his portrait, but he feels that Jeeves does not like it, saying it makes him took hungry. Anyway, Bertie dare not go away because he has a rival, another artist named Lucius Pim.

'I shouldn't worry,' said Aunt Dahlia. 'You don't suppose for a moment that Jeeves will sanction the match?'

Bertie objects, but Aunt Dahlia bets him that Jeeves will get rid of the girl and the portrait, and deliver him to her yacht for the cruise.

Back at his flat, Bertie discovers that Miss Pendlebury has visited. She was upset because he had run over a gentleman and broken his leg. The victim is now lodged in Bertie's spare bedroom. The doctor has advised that he should remain there for the time being. The man concerned is Lucius Pim, who had been on the way to the flat to view the portrait of Bertie that Gwladys painted.

Lucius's sister is on her way from Paris. She is married to the wealthy Mr Slingsby, owner of Slingsby's Superb Soups. But he is a mean man and might prosecute Gwladys if he knew she was responsible. So Jeeves tells Mrs Slingsby that Bertie ran over her brother. Pim suggests that Wooster sends her roses to sweeten her, otherwise she may sue.

The following morning Bertie is practising his putting on the sitting-room carpet when Mr Slingsby arrives. He has just returned from America. While he has been away, he says, a man has been importuning his wife and he accuses Bertie because he sent her flowers.

Mrs Slingsby then emerges from the spare room. Mr Slingsby's worst suspicions appear to have been confirmed. He makes for Wooster, but treads on a golf ball and crashes to the floor. Bertie grabs his hat and flees, telling Jeeves to spare no effort to mollify the Slingsbys. Meanwhile, Bertie hides out in Paris.

When he returns to England three weeks later, he finds London plastered with advertisements for Slingsby's Superb Soups featuring his portrait. Jeeves explains that he was instructed to spare no effort to mollify Mr Slingsby, who had threatened to sue. So Jeeves suggested that his portrait might be useful in an advertising campaign. Slingsby dropped any legal action and began negotiating with Miss Pendlebury for the copyright. Mr Pim acted as her agent as he is now her fiancé.

Bertie is broken-hearted. The lads at the Drones will rib him about the soup advert ceaselessly. The only way to get away from the posters is to take a cruise on Aunt Dahlia's yacht. Jeeves has already taken the liberty of calling Mrs Travers to inform her.

'Jeeves and the Kid Clementina'
Published in the January 1930 issue of the Strand Magazine *with illustrations by Charles Crombie, 'Jeeves and the Kid Clementina' appeared in* Cosmopolitan *in the same month with illustrations by James Montgomery Flagg. It then appeared in the collection* Very Good, Jeeves.

Bertie is to take part in the Drones Club annual golf tournament, being held that year at Bingley-on-Sea. However, he is concerned that Aunt Agatha's old friend, Miss Mapleton, runs a girls' school nearby. Bertie does not have fond memories of girls' schools, while Jeeves does not approve of the vivid colour of Bertie's new plus fours. Worse, Bertie has accepted an invitation to join a party of Miss Roberta 'Bobbie' Wickham's in Antibes that summer.

Bertie is knocked out of the tournament in the first round. Then Miss Wickham turns up. She is visiting her cousin Clementina who is at a nearby school. She wants Bertie to take them out as it is Clementina's birthday. Bobbie has a party to go to in London, so Bertie will have to take Clementina back to school afterwards. However, Clementina is at St Monica's, the school where Miss Mapleton is headmistress, so he is going to have to sneak her back in.

Bobbie had been to St Monica's. What girls used to do in her day was take a long piece of string, tie it around a flowerpot from the conservatory, then balance the pot on the tree branch above the conservatory roof. With Clementina stationed near the front door, he should tug the string. The flowerpot will fall on the conservatory, breaking the glass. When someone comes out of the front door to investigate, Clementina can sneak in.

A policeman catches Bertie up the tree balancing the flowerpot on the branch. Then Jeeves arrives.

'Have you got them, officer?' he asks. 'No, I see. It is Mr Wooster.'

Jeeves explains that he was in conference with Miss Mapleton inside the house and stepped outside to see if Mr Wooster had successfully apprehended the intruders. Miss Mapleton was a close friend of Mr Wooster's family. He was paying a visit when he noticed suspicious characters crossing the lawn. Dispatching Jeeves to warn Miss Mapleton, he went to investigate.

The policeman does not believe a word of this and takes them to Miss Mapleton.

'So did you find them, Mr Wooster?' asks Miss Mapleton. She then tells Bertie that she had just finished writing a letter to his Aunt Agatha, but would now have to add a postscript about his gallantry that night, tracking men unarmed through the dark garden.

Afterwards Jeeves explains that, while Bertie was climbing the trees, he went to the back door and asked for an interview with Miss Mapleton. When the maid had gone to convey the request, he returned Clementina unobserved. When he saw Miss Mapleton, he told her that Mr Wooster had been on his way to see her, when he had spotted the burglars and was now giving chase. In gratitude, Bertie cancels the trip to Antibes and sacrifices his new plus fours.

'Jeeves and the Old School Chum'

Published in the February 1930 issue of the Strand Magazine *with illustrations by Charles Crombie, 'Jeeves and the Old School Chum' appeared in* Cosmopolitan *in the same month with illustrations by James Montgomery Flagg. It then appeared in the collection* Very Good, Jeeves.

All is well with Bingo Little. His Uncle Wilberforce has died, leaving him a large income and a country house about thirty miles from Norwich. Then Laura Pyke, his wife's best friend from school, comes to stay.

Bertie visits Bingo to find him complaining that his wife hangs on every word Laura Pyke says. Worse, Miss Pyke is a food crank and they are subsisting on nothing but parsnips and similar muck. And there are to be no cocktails.

Dinner is sparse. Laura Pyke talks incessantly about food reform, holding up Bingo as an example of all that was bad. Jeeves's task is to get rid of Miss Pyke.

That Thursday they go to Lakenham races. Mr and Mrs Little travel in one car. Laura Pyke goes with Bertie, with Jeeves sitting behind in the dickey or rumble seat. When they arrive, they discover the luncheon basket has been left behind. Miss Pyke says that is good; luncheon is best omitted.

Jeeves reveals to Bertie that he removed the luncheon basket. He thinks that a day without food might make Mrs Little less sympathetic to Miss Pyke's views on diet.

At teatime, Mrs Little asks Bertie to drive her and Laura home in Bingo's car. Bingo and Jeeves will follow in Bertie's two-seater after the last race. In the middle of nowhere, the little car Bertie is driving conks out. Laura Pyke gets out to see what is wrong with the car and finds there is no petrol in the tank. Miss Pyke says that Bingo is the type of man who would forget to fill the tank. Mrs Little tells her to stop criticizing her husband.

When Bingo and Jeeves approach, the women are rowing, dredging up old quarrels from school. Mrs Little is delighted to see Bingo, and in high dudgeon Miss Pyke heads back into town.

Bingo then produces a can of petrol and fills the tank. He had filled the tank that morning, but Jeeves had emptied it at the race course, the nub of his scheme being that the two women deprived of their tea would be likely to fall out.

'Indian Summer of an Uncle'

Published in the March 1930 issue of the Strand Magazine *with illustrations by Charles Crombie, 'Indian Summer of an Uncle' appeared in* Cosmopolitan *in the same month, illustrated by James Montgomery Flagg. It then appeared in the collection* Very Good, Jeeves.

Uncle George has decided to marry a young woman named Miss Rhoda Platt, a waitress in his club. Jeeves knows her aunt.

Aunt Agatha arrives. She has heard about the marriage and is against it. She wants Bertie to pay off the girl. The family has done this once previously, before George had been elevated to peerage, when he fell in love with a barmaid at the Criterion named Maudie.

When Bertie arrives at Miss Platt's house, Miss Platt has not made up her mind about the proposal. Uncle George, Lord Yaxley, is rather old. On the other hand, a title is a title. Jeeves then suggests they confront his lordship with Miss Platt's aunt. So Bertie invites them to lunch the following day.

When Miss Platt's aunt, Mrs Wilberforce, arrives, Bertie hands her a cocktail and she reveals that she had once been a barmaid at the Criterion. Bertie ask whether she ever knew a George Wooster. She had. The family had offered her money to give him up.

Uncle George arrives and he and Mrs Wilberforce instantly recognize each other. Bertie leaves them to have lunch alone and goes to the Drones. Aunt Agatha phones, telling Bertie that Uncle George is going to marry a woman of a sensible age named Mrs Wilberforce, but she cannot figure out whether she is from the Essex Wilberforces or the Cumberland Wilberforces.

'Tuppy Changes His Mind' ('The Ordeal of Young Tuppy')
Published in the April 1930 issue of the Strand Magazine *with illustrations by Charles Crombie, 'Tuppy Changes His Mind' appeared in* Cosmopolitan *in the same month, illustrated by James Montgomery Flagg. It appeared as 'The Ordeal of Young Tuppy' in the British (Herbert Jenkins) collection* Very Good Jeeves *but retained its original magazine title in the American (Doubleday, Doran and Company) edition of the book.*

Jeeves is packing. They are going to the home of Sir Reginald Witherspoon in Upper Bleaching, Hampshire, for Christmas.

He is married to Aunt Dahlia's husband's younger sister, Katherine. Tuppy Glossop will be present and Bertie still seeks vengeance for being dunked in the swimming pool in his evening suit.

A telegram arrives from Tuppy asking Bertie to bring his football boots and, if possible, an Irish water spaniel.

Aunt Dahlia has learnt from her sister Katherine that Tuppy, who is more or less engaged to her daughter Angela, is infatuated with Colonel Dalgleish's daughter who lives in Bleaching. She is a 'dog-girl'. This explains the need for an Irish water spaniel.

It seems that Tuppy and Angela had a row before he went to Bleaching. Apparently, he told her she looked like a Pekinese in her new hat and she said she never wanted to see him again.

Aunt Dahlia wants Jeeves to intervene. Nearing Bleaching Court, they see a sea of dogs, along with Tuppy and a large girl wearing tweeds. Bertie apologizes for not bringing the Irish water spaniel. But he has brought the football boots. Miss Dalgleish wants Tuppy to play for Upper Bleaching's team against Hockley-cum-Meston the following Thursday.

According to Jeeves's sources in the servants' hall, the game is a grudge match first played in Henry VIII's time when it resulted in seven deaths, not counting spectators. Recently casualties have been confined to broken bones and other minor injuries. Bertie recommends that Tuppy feign a sprained ankle, but he refuses to let Miss Dalgleish down.

Bertie decides he must save Tuppy. He sends Jeeves to London to send a telegram purporting to come from Mrs Travers. It says that Angela is seriously ill. The telegram is timed to arrive just after the game has started.

The field is muddy and Tuppy is picked out for special treatment because of the orange-and-blue shirt he is wearing. At the first break in play, Bertie goes on to the field to deliver the telegram, but finds he has forgotten to bring it. Tuppy plays on and becomes the star of the match.

After the game, Tuppy discovers that Miss Dalgleish was not there to witness his triumph. She had received a call from someone in London who said they had found an Irish water spaniel but it turned out to be an ordinary English water spaniel. The call, of course, came from Jeeves. Bertie finally produces the telegram. Tuppy borrows Bertie's car and heads for town.

'Jeeves Makes an Omelette' ('Doing Clarence a Bit of Good'/'Jeeves and the Stolen Venus')

First published, with illustrations by James Simpkins, in the 2 August 1958 issue of The Star Weekly, *the nationally distributed weekend magazine supplement of the* Toronto Star *newspaper in Canada. 'Jeeves Makes an Omelette' also appeared in the February 1959 issue of* Lilliput *magazine in the UK with illustrations by John Cooper, the story also appeared in the July 1972 issue of* Argosy *magazine in the UK. It was first anthologized in* A Few Quick Ones *published by Simon & Schuster in the US on 13 April 1959 and by Herbert Jenkins in the UK on 26 June 1959. The first version of this story appeared as 'Doing Clarence a Bit of Good', featuring Reggie Pepper, in the May 1913 issue of the* Strand Magazine, *and as 'Rallying Round Clarence' in the April 1914 issue of* Pictorial Review *in the US. Another version appeared in the August 1959 issue of* Ellery Queen's Mystery Magazine *as 'Jeeves and the Stolen Venus'. These last two short stories come after Jeeves and Wooster have been inhabiting novels for over twenty years. The characters do not seem to have got any older though. Nor have their circumstances changed.*

Bertie Wooster is considering the foundation of a society for the suppression of aunts. He bases his case on the episode of his Aunt Dahlia and the *Fothergill Venus*.

Aunt Dahlia had phoned from Marsham Manor, the Hampshire home of Cornelia Fothergill whose latest novel she wants to serialize in *Milady's Boudoir*. The problem was that Mrs Fothergill wants £800, but Uncle Tom will only stump up £500.

Arriving at Marsham Manor, Bertie is introduced to Cornelia Fothergill, her artist husband, Everard, and his father, Edward, who is also an artist. After tea, Aunt Dahlia collars Bertie. She shows him a stout Venus that Edward Fothergill painted and gave to Everard as a wedding present. A picture painted by Everard, called the *Jocund Spring* in some versions of the story, hangs alongside it.

Cornelia Fothergill has agreed to let *Milady's Boudoir* have her latest novel if her father-in-law's painting, the *Fothergill Venus*, is destroyed. Bertie's job is to pinch it. There is a gang of art thieves working in the area and if the *Venus* goes missing it will be assumed they took it.

At one in the morning, Bertie removes the picture from its frame with four quick cuts with a sharp knife. Before burning the painting, they cut it up. Then Jeeves notices that the signature on the last fragment is that of Everard Fothergill. They have destroyed the wrong picture.

Downstairs Bertie finds Edward Fothergill cutting his own painting from the frame. He mistakenly gave it to his son as a wedding present, so he is using the spate of art thefts in the area as an excuse to steal it back.

Aunt Dahlia fears that Cornelia Fothergill will not let her have the serial when she discovers that they have destroyed one of her husband's valuable pictures. Jeeves suggests that if Mr Wooster was to be found stunned in the vicinity, Mrs Fothergill might conclude that the picture had indeed been taken by art thieves.

Bertie refuses to oblige, then feels a blow on the back of his head. When he comes round, Aunt Dahlia says: 'You can't make an omelette without breaking eggs,' though she admits she is quoting Jeeves.

'Jeeves and the Greasy Bird'

Published in the December 1965 issue of Playboy *magazine with illustrations by Bill Charmatz, 'Jeeves and the Greasy Bird' appeared in the January 1967 issue of* Argosy *magazine with illustrations by Belinda Lyon. It was first anthologized in* Plum Pie, *published in the UK by Herbert Jenkins on 22 September 1966 and in the US by Simon & Schuster on 1 December 1967. It had taken another six years and two novels before Jeeves and Wooster returned to the short story one last time.*

Bertie has just returned from visiting Aunt Dahlia's cousin Percy who has been committed to Sir Roderick Glossop's clinic in Chuffnell Regis. Bertie and Sir Roderick have had a reconciliation since the events outlined in *Thank You, Jeeves*, where they both stalked the streets of Chuffnell Regis with blackened faces. But 'Roddy' is despondent. Bertie puts this down to the presence of Blair Eggleston, an angry young novelist.

However, Jeeves ascribes Sir Roderick's mood to fact that his fiancée, Lady Chuffnell, won't marry him while his daughter Honoria is still single. Jeeves has gleaned this via the Junior Ganymede, a club for gentlemen's personal gentlemen in Curzon Street, Mayfair. Members are required to enter information about their employers in a book. Bertie was surprised to find that there were eleven pages on him.

Aunt Dahlia says that Sir Roderick will soon buck up when he comes to Brinkley Manor for Christmas.

Eggleston is writing a series on the 'Modern Girl' for *Milady's Boudoir*. According to Aunt Dahlia, he is in love with Honoria Glossop, but is too timid to tell her. Aunt

Dahlia then tries to talk Bertie into playing Santa Claus at the children's Christmas party. He refuses.

Bertie has a plan to restore Sir Roderick's happiness. If Eggleston marries Honoria, Lady Chuffnell will marry Sir Roderick. So Bertie is going to make a play for Honoria assuming jealousy will push Eggleston into proposing.

Bertie sets about dining and dancing with Honoria. Soon Eggleston's temperature is rising. When Bertie espies Honoria in Hyde Park, Eggleston turns up, too. So Bertie kisses her and then pushes off. But the plan has backfired. Eggleston had proposed to Honoria the night before. When he sees Bertie kissing Honoria, he instantly breaks it off. Now Honoria says that she is going to marry Bertie.

Bertie explains the situation to Jeeves but, rather than bandy a young lady's name about, he refers to the dramatis personae by letters of the alphabet. Jeeves has it figured out in a moment. If A – Bertie – were betrothed to someone else, the matrimonial plans of B – Honoria – would be rendered null and void.

Bertie meets Catsmeat Potter-Pirbright, an actor, who suggests that he employs an actress to play the part of his fiancée. The following morning, he visits a greasy theatrical agent named Jas Waterbury who says his niece Trixie will play the part.

Aunt Dahlia rings to tell Bertie that Honoria is coming to his flat at four o'clock. Meanwhile Bertie lunches at the Drones where Catsmeat tells him Jas Waterbury once chiselled £2,000 out of Oofy Prosser, as described in the story 'Oofy, Freddie, and the Beef Trust', collected in *A Few Quick Ones*.

Bertie answers the door to Jas and Trixie Waterbury. Honoria is due, so Jas gets his buxom niece to sit on Bertie's lap. The doorbell rings. Trixie goes into a passionate embrace. Waterbury flings open the door and in walks Eggleston.

Bertie introduces Trixie as his fiancée. Eggleston says that Honoria will be relieved. He had come round to tell Bertie that Honoria could never be his as they were going to marry.

Waterbury calls to tell Bertie of the wedding arrangements. When Bertie says that he would not touch Trixie with a ten-foot pole, Waterbury says that is a remarkable coincidence – those were exactly the words Mr Prosser had used. Bertie has announced their betrothal before witnesses and Waterbury threatens a breach-of-promise case. Trixie is heartbroken, but £2,000 will make her feel better. If Wooster does not feel like writing a cheque he will send round an all-in wrestler he used to manage.

Aunt Dahlia is aghast that Bertie can be so stupid, but together with Jeeves she cooks up a plan. When the doorbell rings on the following morning, Jeeves tells Mr Waterbury that Mr Wooster is out. He has gone to pawn his watch to raise a few pounds. Waterbury is shocked. Wooster has a Park Lane flat and a valet. Jeeves explains that he is no longer a valet but, due to Bertie's unpaid wine-merchant's bill, 'the man in possession'. What's more, Mr Wooster's aunt intends to cut his allowance and send him to Canada.

When Aunt Dahlia turns up, Waterbury again threatens a breach of promise suit. Aunt Dahlia says that his niece will have to go to Canada to sue. Bertie is on the next boat and when he gets there he won't have the money to fritter away on a breach-of-promise case. Waterbury gives up and leaves.

Now Aunt Dahlia insists that he plays Santa Claus at the Christmas party. Then Bertie recalls that Jeeves wants to go fishing in Florida even though it will mean missing the Drones Club Darts Tournament.

4

THE NOVELS

By 1933, Jeeves and Wooster stories had been appearing in periodicals for sixteen years and had a well-established readership. Now Wodehouse was ready to let them loose in a full-length novel that, like novels he had written before, would appear first as a serial. What's more, he would add a twist. Throughout the stories that make up *Very Good, Jeeves*, Bertie had been asserting his independence. Now, at the beginning of the first novel, Bertie would sack Jeeves in a narrative coup.

Thank You, Jeeves
First published as a serial in the Strand Magazine *from August 1933 to February 1934 with illustrations by Gilbert Wilkinson,* Thank You, Jeeves *then ran in* Cosmopolitan *from January to June 1934, illustrated by James Montgomery Flagg. It was then published in volume form by Herbert Jenkins in the UK on 16 March 1934 and Little, Brown, and Company in the US on 23*

April 1934. The novel is marred by the casual racism of the day, with Wodehouse's mention of 'nigger minstrels' and blackface. Sympathetic to the black characters in his books, it would not be fair to accuse Wodehouse of racism; sadly, these were the acceptable terms of the day. A 1966 American paperback edition changed the term to 'colored minstrels', though unfortunately by this time, 'colored' was considered by many as almost as offensive as the original.

Wodehouse announces the fact that he is going to let Bertie loose in the world alone by calling first chapter 'Jeeves Gives Notice', though in the serial the chapters are not given headings. In London, Bertie is toying with his banjolele while talking to Jeeves. He says he has seen J. Washburn Stoker and his daughter Pauline, to whom Bertie had been briefly engaged in New York. They were accompanied by Sir Roderick Glossop, who had ended Bertie's engagement to Pauline by telling her father that he was mad. The fourth member of the party was Myrtle, the aunt of Bertie's schoolfriend, Lord Marmaduke 'Chuffy' Chuffnell. Bertie fled.

In the morning, Sir Roderick comes round to complain that one of his patients who occupies the flat below is being disturbed by his banjolele playing. The other neighbours complain, too. But Bertie is wedded to his banjolele and decides to take a cottage in the country to continue playing.

'In that case,' says Jeeves, 'I fear I must give my notice.'

There is a battle of wills. Bertie will not back down. Jeeves is a domestic Mussolini, though a mere valet, while his own ancestors 'did dashed well at the Battle of Crécy'. So he puts his foot down and tells Jeeves to leave.

Bertie then bumps into Chuffy who invites him down to Chuffnell Regis where he will rent him a cottage. There is a troupe of 'nigger minstrels' down there this year, so he can study their technique. But he is not to play his banjolele at Chuffnell Hall.

Hearing that Bertie has sacked Jeeves, Lord Chuffnell immediately takes Jeeves on as his valet.

In Chuffnell Regis, Wooster is billeted with his new valet, Brinkley, in Seaview Cottage, next door to the police cottage of Sergeant Voules. There is a large yacht in the bay. It belongs to J. Washburn Stoker. At the Hall, Chuffy tells Bertie that his aunt is going to marry Sir Roderick Glossop, so he will be rid of the Dowager Lady Chuffnell and her young son, Seabury.

Though landed, Chuffy is hard up. He intends to sell Chuffnell Hall to J. Washburn Stoker who is then going to rent it to Sir Roderick to use as a clinic. Sir Roderick is coming to lunch, along with Stoker, Pauline and her young brother Dwight. Bertie decides to duck out of lunch.

It is clear to Bertie that Chuffy is in love with Pauline. Pauline confides that she loves Marmaduke, too. However, Jeeves says that Lord Chuffnell does not feel in a position to marry someone as wealthy as Miss Stoker if he has no money. Her father had just inherited $50 million from his cousin George, a mental patient that Sir Roderick certifies was sane when he signed the will. So unless Stoker buys Chuffnell Hall, Lord Chuffnell will not feel in a position to propose. He fears that he will be ridiculed as another impoverished English aristocrat marrying a wealthy American heiress for her money.

Lord Chuffnell confided this to Jeeves because Stoker wants Jeeves to go and work for him. However, Lord Chuffnell wants to hold on to Jeeves but has told him not to break off negotiations with Stoker until the sale of Chuffnell Hall has gone through.

Bertie decides to take a hand. After lunch he intends to kiss Miss Stoker and make sure that Chuffy can see him, in the hope that jealousy will force his hand. When Pauline joins

Bertie in the garden, he spots what he thinks is Chuffy's head above a shrub and he kisses her – only to discover that the man approaching is Pop Stoker.

When Chuffy turns up, he wants to know why Bertie had not told him that he had once been engaged to Pauline Stoker. Bertie assures him that it was all over in forty-eight hours and meant nothing. Besides, Pauline had told him that she loves Chuffy. Mollified, Chuffy now announces that Stoker has agreed to buy the Hall and he is engaged to Pauline.

Later Bertie meets Jeeves who tells him there has been a hitch. Inspired by a gangster movie, Seabury had asked Stoker's son Dwight for protection money. There has been a fight, leaving relations between Mr Stoker and the Chuffnells somewhat strained. Sir Roderick sided with Lady Chuffnell and Mr Stoker changed his mind about buying the Hall. Consequently, Lord Chuffnell has had vigorous words with Mr Stoker, who went back to his yacht with Miss Stoker and Master Dwight. Sir Roderick moved into the local inn. All this had happened, before Lord Chuffnell got round to telling Mr Stoker that he was going to marry his daughter. However, Mr Stoker is determined to keep Pauline aboard the yacht to avoid her meeting Wooster, imagining that she still has feelings for him after witnessing the kiss.

Chuffy has now also heard about the kiss and threatens violence. When Bertie returns to his cottage, Chuffy is waiting for him, but Bertie manages to convince him that the kiss was purely fraternal. Even though Chuffy now has no money, Bertie convinces him to write Pauline a letter. Jeeves can take it out to the yacht as Stoker wants to hire him.

Bertie tells Brinkley that he intends to dine out. He drives to Bristol, dines and takes in a show. When he returns it is dark and he finds Pauline Stoker in his bed wearing his pyjamas. She has swum ashore from her father's yacht and shed her wet swimsuit.

Pauline has received Chuffy's letter and she had swum ashore to be with him. But she could not go to the Hall in her swimsuit, so she smashed a window of Bertie's cottage and let herself in. Then comes a knock on the front door. She assumes it is her father and wants to pour water on him. She warns Bertie that he may have a gun.

In fact, Sergeant Voules is at the door with his nephew, Constable Dobson, who has spotted the broken window and saw a 'marauder' climbing through. They want to search the house. Bertie forbids this.

When they are gone, Bertie decides he had better sleep in his car. As he leaves the house, he is grabbed by Constable Dobson who thinks he is a marauder. When Bertie beds down in the car, he is disturbed by Sergeant Voules. In the hope of getting a good night's sleep, Bertie heads for the potting shed in the grounds of the Hall. He is caught there by both Sergeant Voules and Constable Dobson. They conclude he has a touch of the sun and Sergeant Voules fetches Lord Chuffnell, who is at the harbourside.

Chuffy wants to know why Bertie is not sleeping in his bedroom. There is a spider in there, Bertie says. Chuffy concludes Bertie is 'as tight as an owl' and decides they must put him to bed in the cottage. They carry him up to his bedroom.

Fortunately, there is no sign of Pauline Stoker. But when the sergeant leaves, Pauline emerges from a cupboard in Bertie's pyjamas. Chuffy thinks the worst.

Pauline tells Bertie to go, too. She wants to put her swimsuit back on and swim back to the yacht. Later she returns. It is cold so she pinches Bertie's overcoat and leaves a note saying she is going to row back to the yacht in a boat she has found by the landing stage.

Bertie is just calming himself with a whisky and soda when there is another knock at the door. This time it is Stoker. His daughter's stateroom is empty and he has assumed that she has come to see Wooster. He searches the cottage and finds nothing.

In the morning Jeeves arrives, bringing a note from Mr Stoker inviting Bertie to dinner on the yacht. Bertie accepts, thinking that, once he is on board the yacht, he can plead Chuffy's cause. Dinner will be early, at seven, due to Dwight's birthday party. The minstrels will be present and Bertie is particularly keen to speak to the banjo player.

When Bertie arrives on the yacht for dinner, Stoker gives Bertie a tour of the boat and then locks him in one of the cabins. If he were a young man, he says, he would have broken Wooster's neck. On leaving Bertie's cottage he had met Sergeant Voules who took him to the police station to bail Pauline. Constable Dobson had recognized Pauline as the figure he had seen climbing through the cottage window. And when they had arrested her, she was wearing Wooster's coat.

Stoker now intends to keep Bertie prisoner until he marries Pauline and leaves him locked in the cabin to return to his son's birthday party. However, Jeeves has arranged his escape. Bertie is to blacken his face and go ashore as one of the minstrels, then take the next train to London. Jeeves himself is to return to Lord Chuffnell's employ.

Back at the cottage, Bertie finds that soap and water will not remove the burnt cork and boot polish he has used to blacken his face. Downstairs he hears a rumpus. Brinkley has returned drunk. He grabs a carving knife and comes bounding up the stairs. Sergeant Voules intervenes, but Brinkley tells him that the Devil is in the bedroom murdering Mr Wooster. In his drunken state, he knocks over a lamp setting the cottage on fire.

Bertie escapes through the bedroom window, but he has left his banjolele in the sitting-room. He heads for the Hall where he is sure Jeeves will give him butter, which, he believes, will removed his blackface. However, when the back door is opened by a scullery-maid, she screams and faints.

Due to his fight with Dwight, Seabury has missed the birthday party. So Lady Chuffnell persuades Sir Roderick to lay on some entertainment for the child. But Seabury wants to see the minstrels, so Sir Roderick has had to black up.

However, Sir Roderick has refused Seabury's request for protection money, so the child has taken his revenge by making a butter slide. This had provoked Sir Roderick to attack Seabury, causing a rift between Lady Chuffnell and Sir Roderick.

The butter slide has also exhausted the Hall's supply of butter, so Jeeves suggests Bertie should seek shelter in the Dower House. Sir Roderick is also seeking shelter there, as is Brinkley, who flings him out.

Finding themselves in a similar predicament, Bertie and Sir Roderick forget their past grievances and become allies.

Sir Roderick goes to Bertie's garage, which is set away from the cottage, to find petrol. This, he says, is as good as butter for removing blackface. Bertie won't accompany him in case he runs into Sergeant Voules and seeks shelter in the summer house.

In the morning, Bertie sees a maid carrying a breakfast tray into Chuffy's office and sneaks in through the French windows. He is about to seize the tray when he hears footsteps and hides. Jeeves comes in. He tries to phone Sir Roderick at his hotel on Lady Chuffnell's behalf to extend an olive branch. However, their conversation is cut short by the arrival of Mr Stoker, who is hoping that Lord Chuffnell might be able to tell him where Bertie is. Jeeves reveals that it was Mr Wooster's intention to spend the night in the Dower House. When Stoker leaves for the Dower House, Pauline turns up. She has changed her mind about marrying Bertie. As Pauline tucks into Chuffy's breakfast, Bertie is driven by hunger to reveal himself. Pauline screams, bringing Chuffy running to her and they embrace, reconciled.

Mr Stoker returns with a black eye provided by Brinkley. He is still against his daughter marrying Chuffnell, whom he describes as a fortune-hunting English lord. Jeeves returns with a telegram saying that some of Stoker's relatives are contesting cousin George's will, on the grounds that he was insane. Chuffy is delighted. Now Pauline has no money, they can marry.

Stoker is not about to take the news lying down. He needs Sir Roderick to testify that his cousin George was in good mental health. Stoker says he will apologize to Sir Roderick, but first they have to find him. Jeeves reveals that Sir Roderick is in the potting shed where he is being held prisoner by Constable Dobson who caught him trying to break into Bertie's garage. He is being held there because the police cottage, which was next door to Bertie's, also burned down.

Lady Chuffnell appears. She blames herself for Sir Roderick's arrest. When Stoker hears that Sir Roderick has been wandering around the village in blackface, he fears that his testimony in a lunacy case is going to be of little use.

Jeeves points out that, as Sir Roderick is in blackface, all they have to do is to remove him from the potting shed and replace him with Bertie. But first, Bertie makes Stoker promise to buy Chuffnell Hall so Pauline can marry Lord Chuffnell.

Constable Dobson is distracted by the parlourmaid Mary, with whom he is in love. Then Sir Roderick is replaced by Bertie, who can hardly be prosecuted for breaking into his own garage. Besides, Lord Chuffnell is the Justice of the Peace (JP).

After Bertie has eaten a well-earned breakfast, Jeeves reveals that he contacted a friend in New York and got him to send the telegram. No one was contesting the will. By then Stoker had already signed the papers buying Chuffnell Hall.

Now that Bertie's banjolele has been destroyed in the cottage fire and he intends to sack Brinkley, Jeeves offers his services – he can no long work for Lord Chuffnell as he has a policy of never working in the household of a married gentleman. Bertie, of course, accepts.

Right Ho, Jeeves (Brinkley Manor)

First published as a serial in the Saturday Evening Post *from 23 December 1933 to 27 January 1934 with illustrations by Henry Raleigh*, Right Ho, Jeeves *also ran as a serial in* Grand Magazine *in the UK from April to September 1934. It was then published in volume form by Herbert Jenkins in the UK on 5 October 1934 and as* Brinkley Manor *by Little, Brown, and Company in the US on 15 October 1934. Wodehouse was already planning this sequel while working on* Thank You, Jeeves.

Bertie has been in Cannes with Aunt Dahlia and her daughter, Angela. Aunt Dahlia has lost a lot of money at baccarat, while Angela has had an encounter with a shark while aquaplaning. While Bertie has been away, his old friend Gussie Fink-Nottle, who usually spends his time in the country with his newts, has been calling. He has fallen in love with Madeline Bassett but is too timid to propose. She has also been in Cannes and has become friends with Angela. Bertie approves of the match and puts Jeeves on the case. However, Bertie has returned from Cannes with a white mess jacket with brass buttons: Jeeves does not approve.

Jeeves has advised Gussie to go to a fancy-dress ball, where Madeline will be present, dressed as Mephistopheles to embolden him. But Gussie left the invitation and his money behind. Arriving at the wrong address, he cannot pay the cab. He makes a run for it. The cabbie chases after him, grabs his coat which comes off and finds himself confronted with the Devil himself.

Bertie receives a telegram from Aunt Dahlia at Brinkley Court, her country seat in Market Snodsbury, telling him to come at once. He is to give out the prizes at the local grammar school where she is a governor. After his experience giving a speech at a girls' school, as described in 'Bertie Changes his Mind', he is eager to wheedle his way out of this and demurs.

Madeline Bassett has been invited to stay at Brinkley Court, so Bertie arranges an invitation for Gussie. Once he has gone, Bertie has a brainwave and tells Jeeves to send a telegram saying: 'Lay off the sausages.' Gussie should look like he is pining away for love. Misunderstanding, Gussie thinks this is some sort of code.

Jeeves is also to send a wire to Mrs Travers saying that Mr Fink-Nottle will take over the role of giving out the prizes. Aunt Dahlia is furious that Bertie has foisted Gussie on her and insists he come at once. Again Bertie demurs.

Then a telegram arrives saying that Angela and Tuppy Glossop have broken off their engagement, so Bertie decides to go down to Brinkley Court after all. Jeeves tries to leave the mess jacket, but Bertie spots what he is up to and brings it anyway.

Angela has broken off her engagement because, when she told Tuppy about her encounter with the shark, he said it was probably a harmless flatfish. Aunt Dahlia is also worried about telling Uncle Tom about her gambling losses as she needs a cheque for £500 out of him for *Milady's Boudoir*.

Aunt Dahlia wants Jeeves to handle the problem of Angela's engagement, but Bertie insists Jeeves has lost his grip after watching Jeeves's scheme to put Gussie in a Mephistopheles costume go awry.

Bertie bumps into a listless Tuppy. He says that he only poured scorn on Angela's shark because she said he was always thinking of food and was getting fat. Bertie suggests that, at dinner, he should shun food. Later, when everyone has gone to bed, he can sneak down to the larder and eat a steak-and-kidney pie.

Jeeves has an idea of his own. He suggests setting off the fire alarm so that Mr Glossop can endeavour to assist Miss Angela to safety. Bertie dismisses this as too elaborate.

Bertie also suggests that Aunt Dahlia forgo food at dinner to elicit Uncle Tom's sympathy. With Gussie, Tuppy and Aunt Dahlia all refusing food, Anatole is offended, gives his notice and retires to his bed. This upsets Uncle Tom who depends on Anatole because of his sensitive stomach.

That night, when Tuppy sneaks down to the larder for the steak-and-kidney pie, he meets Aunt Dahlia who is also famished. Then comes Uncle Tom, who is worried about burglars, carrying a pistol. He is accompanied by Angela, who finds Tuppy with the pie, and makes a few cutting remarks about Tuppy's enormous appetite.

Tuppy is convinced that there is dirty work afoot. He thinks that Angela has fallen for someone else at Cannes. Bertie says that is impossible because he was with her the whole time. Meanwhile, Bertie's attempts to soften Madeline up for Gussie have resulted in her believing that Bertie is love with her. Thinking he is proposing, she turns him down. She is love with someone else. Gussie. But when Gussie attempts to propose, all he can talk about is newts.

The problem, Bertie decides, is that Gussie does not drink. A gentleman cannot be expected to propose without a few 'stiffeners' inside him. Jeeves counsels against this.

Bertie's next plan is to draw Angela aside and defame Tuppy, expecting Angela to leap to his defence. She does not. Tuppy overhears this and threatens to kick Bertie's spine through the top of his head. He thinks that Bertie is in love with Angela and has stolen her from him.

To counter this, Bertie says that he had fallen for Madeline Bassett. She had turned down his proposal not twenty-four hours earlier.

The following day, Bertie decides to lace Gussie's orange

juice with gin. Carrying out his master's wishes, Jeeves has already done so, giving Gussie a double dose. Meanwhile Gussie has taken Bertie's advice and been drinking whisky. Well fortified, he proposes to Madeline, who accepts him. Then he has to make his speech at the Market Snodsbury Grammar School prize giving. Drunk, he makes such an ass of himself that Madeline breaks off the engagement. On the rebound, Gussie proposes to Angela and, to scorn Tuppy, she accepts. Now it is Gussie, rather than Bertie, whom Tuppy is after to wreak revenge.

Aunt Dahlia tells Bertie that Anatole has withdrawn his notice. Then word comes that Mr Fink-Nottle is making faces at Anatole through the skylight of his bedroom. Tuppy had chased Gussie up on to the roof and Gussie is trying to get through the skylight as Uncle Tom has barred all the other windows for fear of burglars. Seppings, the butler, gets a pole to open the skylight.

Thanks to Gussie, Anatole is leaving the next day. Aunt Dahlia is also less than pleased to hear that Angela and Fink-Nottle are engaged. Then a note comes from Madeline Bassett, accepting Bertie's proposal.

While she says her affection for Bertie will never match the flame-like passion she felt for Augustus she would endeavour to make him happy as his wife. All Bertie can think of saying is: 'Right ho, thanks awfully.'

Jeeves recommends returning to his earlier plan of setting off the fire alarm. He believes that Mr Glossop will hasten to save Miss Angela, while Mr Fink-Nottle performs the same office for Miss Bassett. There is no danger of frightening the housemaids as there is a servants' ball at nearby Kingham Manor that night. The entire staff, with the exception of Monsieur Anatole, are attending.

At 12.30 the fire bell rings and everyone rushes outside. There is no fire, but the door has slammed shut and the only key is thought to be with Seppings who is at the servants' ball.

When it becomes clear that Bertie is responsible for ringing the fire bell he is sent the nine miles to Kingham Manor to get the key. But when he gets there, Seppings says that he left the key with Mr Jeeves.

When Bertie arrives back at Brinkley Court, Madeline Bassett tells him that after he left, Jeeves found the key on the window sill. Then she asks Bertie to release her from their engagement because she wants to marry Gussie. Tuppy has also made it up with Angela.

After Bertie has had a bath to soothe his aching limbs, Jeeves explains his plan had been to unite the quarrelling individuals by providing them with a strong mutual dislike for some third party – in this case Bertie. Tuppy and Angela, Gussie and Madeline, and Aunt Dahlia and Anatole were all quickly reunited. With Anatole consenting to stay on, Uncle Tom had agreed to give Aunt Dahlia the money for *Milady's Boudoir*.

Then Jeeves breaks the bad news. While ironing Bertie's mess jacket, he has accidentally burnt it.

The Code of the Woosters
First published as a serial in the Saturday Evening Post *from 16 July to 3 September 1938 with illustrations by Wallace Morgan,* The Code of the Woosters *was also serialized from 8 September to 21 October 1938 in the London* Daily Mail, *which billed Wodehouse as 'the world's highest paid author'. It was then published in volume form by Doubleday, Doran & Company in the US on 7 October 1938 and by Herbert Jenkins in London on the same day.*

Jeeves wants to go on a round-the-world cruise, but Bertie is not keen. Bertie is summoned by Mrs Travers and heads for her townhouse. She has a job for him. She wants him to go and sneer at an eighteenth-century cow-creamer – a silver cream jug shaped like a cow – that Uncle Tom is going to buy. She hopes that this will make the vendor reduce the price.

Bertie proceeds to the shop in Brompton Road where two gentlemen are examining the cow-creamer. One of them is Sir Watkyn Bassett, Gussie's prospective father-in-law, whom Bertie recognizes from Bosher Street Police Court where he ended up after pinching a policeman's helmet on Boat Race night. Sir Watkyn was on the bench and fined him five quid.

His companion Roderick Spode – who looks like one of those dictators whose pictures were in the papers – accuses Bertie of stealing Sir Watkyn's umbrella, which he has inadvertently picked up.

Thinking he is also trying to steal the cow-creamer, Sir Watkin and Spode call the police. Bertie makes a run for it.

When he gets home there is a telegram from Gussie Fink-Nottle who is at Totleigh-in-the-Wold, Gloucestershire, the country seat of the Bassetts. It says: 'Come immediately. Serious rift Madeline and self.'

Aunt Dahlia also instructs Bertie to proceed to Totleigh Towers. Sir Watkyn had treated the gastrically sensitive Uncle Tom to cold lobster and cucumber. While Tom was indisposed, Sir Watkyn had bought the cow-creamer. Bertie is to steal it back.

Wandering around the house, Bertie happens on the room where Sir Watkyn keeps his collection of silverware. He is examining the cow-creamer when Spode appears at the window with a shotgun and tells Bertie to put his hands up.

Bertie is marched to the library where Sir Watkin is issuing a warrant of arrest. Then Madeline turns up. She explains that Bertie is an old friend. Bertie's previous appearance before Sir Watkyn was for pinching a policeman's helmet, a crime Spode admits that he too was guilty of at Oxford.

Madeline is convinced that Bertie has come to Totleigh Towers to take one last glimpse of her. The rift between her and Gussie was a silly misunderstanding after she caught him taking a fly out of her cousin Stephanie 'Stiffy' Byng's eye. But she has never loved Gussie more. He is no longer the timid creature she first met and has even told Roderick Spode to go and boil his head.

Walking into the drawing room, Bertie hears Gussie tell Spode not to talk rot. The formerly timid Gussie, explains that Sir Watkyn wanted Madeline to marry Spode, who sees himself as a Man of Destiny and would-be dictator. He is the leader of the Saviours of Britain, a fascist organization commonly known as the Black Shorts – there were no shirts left.

In the face of opposition from Sir Watkyn and Spode, Gussie is determined to go through with the marriage. Having to make a speech at the wedding breakfast, he consulted Jeeves who suggested that he should concentrate on the faults of the members of the audience.

In preparation, Gussie has begun writing down all the things he hates about Spode and Sir Watkyn Bassett in a notebook. But he dropped it somewhere. It's all right, though, says Gussie, he has memorized its entire contents. Bertie points out that someone may find the notebook. Gussie panics. If Sir Watkyn reads it, the wedding will be off.

Gussie realizes that he must have dropped the notebook when he pulled the handkerchief out of his pocket to get the fly out of Stiffy's eye. So Stiffy must have the book. Bertie finds her berating a policeman who has nearly run over her Aberdeen terrier, Bartholomew. Stiffy admits she has the notebook, but is much more concerned about Constable Oates who claims that Bartholomew has attacked him. To get her own back, she is going to get her fiancé, the local curate, Bertie's friend Harold 'Stinker' Pinker from Oxford, to pinch his helmet.

Sir Watkyn will not be pleased with the news that his niece intends to marry an impoverished curate. So Stiffy says she will return the notebook if Bertie steals the cow-creamer, then allows himself to be caught by Harold who will be waiting outside. That way Sir Watkyn will be so grateful that he will allow their marriage and give Harold a parish that is in his gift. If Bertie refuses, she will give the notebook to Sir Watkyn.

Spode says he knows Bertie is there to steal the cow-creamer for his Uncle Tom. If it goes missing, Sir Watkyn will send him to prison, but not before Spode has beaten him to jelly.

Bertie outlines the situation to Gussie, who urges him to go through with the scheme to steal the cow-creamer. But Bertie suggests that they try and recover the notebook directly. As it is important to her, Gussie concludes that Stiffy will keep it about her person, probably in her stocking.

Aunt Dahlia arrives with the news that Sir Watkyn has suggested swapping the cow-creamer for Anatole – and Uncle Tom is seriously considering the offer.

Looking for a chink in Spode's armour, Aunt Dahlia asks Jeeves whether Spode has a dark secret. Jeeves agrees to instigate enquiries at the Junior Ganymede. He goes to phone the secretary, but not before revealing that the engagement between Gussie and Madeline is off.

After dinner, Gussie disappears. Bertie goes to his room where he is bearded by Roderick Spode. He is looking for Fink-Nottle. The self-styled guardian of Madeline, he intends to break Gussie's neck.

When Spode is gone, Gussie emerges from under Bertie's bed. Madeline has broken off the engagement after catching Gussie trying to ascertain whether his notebook was in Stiffy's stocking.

Bertie concludes that if the notebook was not on Stiffy's person, it is probably in her room. Stiffy has gone to the village where the curate is giving a talk on the Holy Land with coloured slides.

When Jeeves returns, he confides that Spode does have a secret. But he cannot tell Bertie as he is sworn to secrecy by the rules of the Junior Ganymede. However, to stop Spode in his tracks, Bertie is to say that he knows all about Eulalie. Returning to his room, Bertie finds Gussie knotting his sheets.

Spode approaches. Bertie calls him a fat slob ridicules the Black Shorts: 'I know your secret,' he says. But then can't remember what it is.

Gussie seizes an oil painting and brings it down on Spode's head. Bertie flings a sheet over him, then make a dash for the door, only to run into Aunt Dahlia.

Spode threatens to thrash Bertie to within an inch of his life. Then Bertie remembers what Jeeves said and tells Spode that he knows all about Eulalie. This has an immediate effect. He apologizes.

With Spode neutralized, Aunt Dahlia says that Bertie can walk in and pinch the cow-creamer, but Bertie says they must find the notebook first.

Bertie takes Jeeves to search Stiffy's room. However, Stiffy has left Bartholomew in the bedroom. He has taken a dislike to Bertie and attacks him. Bertie takes refuge on top of the chest of drawers.

Stiffy returns earlier than expected. Harold had dropped the slides when she broke off their engagement because he refused to steal Constable Oates's helmet. She begins to sob. There comes a tapping at the window. It is Harold. He has brought Constable Oates's helmet. To allow Harold in, she locks Bartholomew in the cupboard.

Along with the helmet, Harold has brought her gloves, at least one of them. He had lost the other one. Stinker then reveals that he had not seized the helmet from Constable Oates's head, but crept up behind him when he had taken it off.

They rehearse the plan to steal the cow-creamer. Stinker is to hit Bertie on the nose so there will be lots of blood.

As the scheme to steal the cow-creamer is bound to end in disaster, Jeeves comes up with a better plan. Wooster is to tell Sir Watkyn Bassett that he is engaged to Stiffy. Then when she tells him that she is going to marry the curate instead he will be greatly relieved and give his consent. Stiffy thinks this is a marvellous plan. But she still will not hand over the notebook until Bertie has gone through with it.

When Bertie arrives at the library, Sir Watkyn is briefing Constable Oates. Plainly Wooster is a suspect in the helmet theft. Sir Watkyn says he intends to send the culprit to jail.

Bertie then asks for his niece's hand in marriage. Sir Watkyn is thunderstruck and sends for Miss Stephanie. When she arrives, she tells Bertie that she cannot be his because she wants to marry the curate. Sir Watkyn quibbles, but quickly gives in.

Constable Oates thinks Stiffy stole his helmet because one of her gloves was found at the scene. The helmet is in her room and she must find a safe place to hide it. Then she reveals that she has hidden the notebook in the cow-creamer.

Now that Madeline's engagement to Augustus is at an end, she says she is willing to marry Bertie who insists he can explain what was happening between Gussie and Stiffy.

All will be made clear when she sees the notebook. She goes and looks for it in the cow-creamer, but it is not there.

Then Bertie comes across Spode beating on Gussie's bedroom door. He has found the notebook in the cow-creamer. Bertie demands the book and the cowed Spode hands it over. Bertie gives it to Gussie and tells him to go and show it to Madeline.

Bertie tells Jeeves to pack. Jeeves is stuffing clothes into one of the suitcases when Gussie returns, saying the wedding is off. Gussie had put some newts in the bath. Sir Watkyn had flushed them down the plughole so Gussie told him what he thought of him.

Bertie comes up with a plan: Gussie is to steal the cow-creamer to blackmail Sir Watkyn into permitting the marriage. But Constable Oates is on guard in the collection room. Jeeves suggests that Gussie should tell Constable Oates that Bertie has his helmet. When he comes to recover it, Gussie can sneak into the collection room and pinch the cow-creamer.

As Gussie readies himself to steal the cow-creamer, he says that he has only one regret – that he gave Sir Watkyn the notebook as there were some names in it that he had forgotten to call. So Gussie goes to Sir Watkyn's room to recover it from his dressing-gown pocket.

Constable Oates has been hit on the nose while trying to catch the thief who was stealing the cow-creamer. He saw a dim figure coming out of the French windows, chased it across the garden, only to be assailed by Stinker Pinker. The thief made off, but Constable Oates suspects Bertie and is coming with Sir Watkyn to search his room.

Aunt Dahlia rushes in. She thrusts the cow-creamer into Bertie's hands at tells him to hide it. Jeeves puts the cow-creamer in the suitcase, though they are bound to look in there. Gussie returns. Sir Watkyn has now read the notebook and is after him, so he resumes his earlier plan to tie Bertie's bedsheets together and escape through the window, then borrow Bertie's car and drive back to London. Jeeves suggests that he takes the suitcase with him. Once again disaster is averted. Jeeves then brings out a second suitcase to finish packing, only to find a policeman's helmet in it.

There is only one thing that can be done – throw it out of the window. Sir Watkyn and Constable Oates arrive and accuse Bertie of stealing the cow-creamer. Aunt Dahlia insists that it is the work of an international gang. Bertie protests he was in his room at the time. Jeeves is his witness. Sir Watkyn will not take the word of a manservant. But Spode was there, too. Jeeves is sent to fetch him. As the matter of the helmet is still outstanding, they search his room but find nothing. Then the butler, who had been walking Stiffy's dog outside, arrives with the helmet on a silver salver. He saw Bertie dropping it out of the window.

Bertie is arrested. However, the rules of hospitality prevail and Bertie is allowed to stay at the house, locked in his room with Constable Oates posted outside the window.

Jeeves returns to say that Sir Watkyn has prohibited Stiffy's marriage to the Reverend Pinker after he allows the thief who stole the cow-creamer to escape. He is also prepared to release Bertie in exchange for Anatole. Bertie protests that this is too great a sacrifice. Miffed, Sir Watkyn says that Bertie will have to go to a police cell after all.

But Spode confirms that Wooster had nothing to do with the theft of the cow-creamer, then admits that it was he who stole Constable Oates's helmet. He had done it once before in Oxford. Jeeves's knowledge of Eulalie had persuaded him to take the rap.

Jeeves then points out that Bertie can sue Sir Watkyn for wrongful arrest – unless he consents to Stiffy and Madeline's marriages. As to the cow-creamer, the international gang who stole it might sell it to Uncle Tom, knowing that he is in the market. Nothing more is to be said.

Afterwards Bertie consents to Jeeves's world cruise provided he gives him the lowdown on Spode's secret. Spode, it turns out, is a designer of ladies' undergarments and runs a shop in Bond Street called Eulalie Soeurs – hardly an appropriate profession for a would-be dictator.

Joy in the Morning (*Jeeves in the Morning*)

Joy in the Morning *was first published in volume form by Doubleday and Company in the US on 22 August 1946, illustrated throughout by Paul Galdone, and by Herbert*

Jenkins in London on 2 June 1947. A 1983 Harper & Row edition was retitled Jeeves in the Morning.

The action takes place in Steeple Bumpleigh in Hampshire where Aunt Agatha lives in Bumpleigh Hall with her second husband, shipping magnate Percival, Lord Worplesdon. Also on hand are his daughter, Bertie's former fiancée Florence Craye, and his young son, the Boy Scout Edwin. Jeeves wants Bertie to take a summer cottage in Steeple Bumpleigh so that he can go fishing, but Bertie is determined to avoid Aunt Agatha, Edwin and the other residents.

Miss Zenobia 'Nobby' Hopwood, Lord Worplesdon's ward, arrives at Bertie's London flat. Nobby was in town with Aunt Agatha, but she has gone to minister to her son Thomas, who has contracted mumps at school. Accompanying Nobby was Bertie's old school chum G. D'Arcy 'Stilton' Cheesewright who also now lives in Steeple Bumpleigh.

A call comes from Lord Worplesdon. It is not for Bertie, but for Jeeves. He wants Jeeves to meet him in his office. As Bertie is refusing to take Jeeves fishing, he asks him if he would like a gift. Jeeves asks for an authoritatively annotated edition of the work of the philosopher Spinoza.

When the bookseller goes to see if he can find the Spinoza he leaves Bertie with a book called *Spindrift*, which Bertie thinks 'looked pretty foul'. Florence Craye turns up in the bookshop. She is the author of *Spindrift*, which she signs for him, and is impressed that Bertie reads Spinoza. She sees him in a new light and concludes that he must have hidden depths. He should come to Bumpleigh Hall where she will show him the reviews of *Spindrift* that Edwin has been pasting in an album for her.

Bertie then spots Stilton Cheesewright who is buying an engagement ring. Bertie suspects it is for Nobby, but Stilton reveals she is engaged to fellow member of the Drones,

George 'Boko' Fittleworth. The ring is for Florence Craye. Having escaped the clutches of Florence himself, Bertie wishes to save his friend Stilton and writes to Nobby pointing out all Florence's defects.

Lord Worplesdon wants to see Jeeves as he is planning the merger of his Pink Funnel Line with an American shipping firm headed by J. Chichester Clam. Worplesdon and Clam need to get together secretly to discuss the deal. Jeeves suggests that they meet at a country cottage in Steeple Bumpleigh, which Bertie is to rent, also allowing Jeeves to go fishing after all. The place is called Wee Nooke and it is next door to the home of Boko Fittleworth. Bertie's one consolation is that there is a fancy-dress ball in nearby East Wibley and he buys a Sinbad the Sailor costume with ginger whiskers.

Aunt Agatha wants Bertie to pick up a diamond brooch from Aspinall's in Bond Street. It is a birthday present for her stepdaughter Florence.

Bertie drives to Steeple Bumpleigh with Nobby while Jeeves takes the train. On the way, Nobby reveals that Uncle Percy opposes her match to Boko. Although Boko is making a lot of money as an author and is leaving for Hollywood the following month, Lord Worplesdon does not trust writers. As Nobby is Uncle Percy's ward, she can't marry without his consent and she wants Bertie to put in a good word for her engagement to Boko with Uncle Percy.

After dropping Nobby at the Hall, Bertie goes to visit Boko. He is met with a china ornament that Boko has thrown thinking that Edwin is approaching. Boko wants to know where Jeeves is. He needs his advice. Boko also reveals that he has just had lunch with Uncle Percy to ingratiate himself. To break the ice, he had bought tricks from a joke shop, which did not go down well at all.

Heading for Wee Nooke, Bertie meets Stilton Cheesewright, who is now the local bobby. Having discovered that

Bertie was once engaged to Florence, Stilton accuses Bertie of coming to Steeple Bumpleigh to win Florence back – the last thing on Bertie's mind. But as the meeting between Worplesdon and Clam has to be kept secret, he cannot reveal his true purpose.

Bertie finds Edwin at Wee Nooke. The Boy Scout is tidying up as his daily 'act of kindness'. Then he volunteers to clean the chimney, which he does with gunpowder, and then tries to dowse the flames with paraffin, setting the whole cottage alight. Uncle Percy blames Bertie for the fire. Rushing to rescue his Sinbad the Sailor costume from the conflagration, Bertie loses the brooch.

With Wee Nooke now reduced to a heap of cinders, Jeeves takes up residence in the Hall, while Bertie moves in with Boko. To save Bertie from the wrath of Aunt Agatha, Jeeves returns to London to buy another brooch. Deprived of Jeeves's advice, Boko comes up with another plan to put himself in Lord Worplesdon's good books. Bertie is to pretend to be a marauder and break into the Hall, and Boko is to foil the burglary. But the would-be burglar is spotted by Edwin. As the cottage has been burned down, the meeting between Lord Worplesdon and Clam has been moved to the potting shed. Boko comes bounding up saying that he has caught a burglar in the potting shed. Uncle Percy, furious that Boko has ruined his plan to have a discreet chat with Clam, manages to prevent Stilton from arresting the 'burglar' by insisting that it is merely some harmless wayfarer who has taken shelter in the potting shed.

Jeeves has returned and given the replacement brooch to Florence. Then he comes up with a new scheme to promote the marriage of Nobby and Boko. Bertie is to upbraid Uncle Percy, then Boko is to step in to defend Lord Worplesdon. The plan is set for ten o'clock the following morning.

Edwin hits Bertie over the head with his Scout's stick,

claiming that he mistook him for a burglar. The last chap he mistook for a burglar was his father who got the same treatment. He has also found the missing brooch and has taken it to Florence, saying it was from Bertie.

Stilton has fallen out with Lord Worplesdon after he refused to allow him to arrest the inmate of the potting shed, so Florence has broken off their engagement and consents to be Bertie's wife. Boko had formerly been engaged to Florence and Bertie asks him how he broke it off. But Boko will only reveal 'The Fittleworth System' if Bertie goes through with the plan to upbraid Uncle Percy.

Jeeves discovers that the engagement between Boko and Florence was broken off when Boko kicked Edwin up the backside. But when Bertie boots Edwin, Florence congratulates him. She had wanted to do the same because Edwin pasted the reviews of *Spindrift* into the album the wrong side up.

Now that the Fittleworth System has failed, Bertie has no incentive to upbraid Uncle Percy. However, Nobby says that if he goes ahead she will show Florence the letter he sent outlining her defects, which is then certain to break off his renewed engagement.

The plan was for Bertie to upbraid Uncle Percy in the garden, then Boko was to emerge from his hiding place in the grass. But Uncle Percy treads on Boko while out for a walk and had him escorted from the grounds by a gardener. Bertie is now back in Uncle Percy's good books for kicking Edwin, as he too had been hit with the Scout's stick.

Jeeves has a new plan for the secret meeting between Clam and Worplesdon but he wants Lord Worplesdon to think that Bertie devised the plan so he would be in a strong position to plead with Uncle Percy on Boko's behalf. The plan is for the two shipping magnates to meet, heavily disguised, at that night's East Wibley fancy-dress ball. Uncle Percy is pleased with the idea. When he was young, he used be the toast of fancy-dress balls. Once, he was thrown out of one and arrested with a girl called Tottie. This made the papers the following day, leading to the then young Agatha Wooster breaking off their engagement, so word of that night's foray must not reach Aunt Agatha's ears.

Uncle Percy is to wear Bertie's Sinbad the Sailor costume, leaving Bertie without an outfit. Jeeves provides a policeman's uniform which he 'found' on the riverbank while Stilton was enjoying a swim.

By the time Bertie and Boko reach the ball, Uncle Percy's business has been concluded successfully and he is getting drunk. He wants to take his shoes off, so Bertie takes him out to lie down in the back of Boko's car. He puts in a good word for Boko with Uncle Percy, telling him that Boko also kicked Edwin. Uncle Percy consents to the marriage. Bertie hastens to fetch Boko and then makes his way home.

In the morning, Boko says that everything went swimmingly. Uncle Percy celebrated their engagement with champagne. Stilton arrives and accuses Bertie of stealing his uniform. He was seen wearing it at the fancy-dress ball and Edwin saw it beside Bertie's bed when he was trying to insert a hedgehog.

Stilton is about to arrest Bertie when Boko points out that he needs a warrant. When he goes to get one, Boko advises Bertie to leg it. He dashes to the garage. Opening the door he finds Uncle Percy who has been locked in all night. He had still been in the back of Boko's car when he drove home.

Uncle Percy intends to thrash Boko and sends Jeeves to the Hall for a horsewhip. Then Jeeves breaks the news that her ladyship had returned unexpectedly last night. She has been told that his bed has not been slept in. Worse, Lord Worplesdon is still in his fancy-dress costume.

Jeeves suggests that Uncle Percy change into one of Mr Fittleworth's suits. As he had consented to the union of Miss

Zenobia and Mr Fittleworth, it was only natural that he had gone to talk over the arrangements with the groom. The hour was late and he stayed there the night.

Stilton returns with a warrant. But it must be signed by the local Justice of the Peace – Lord Worplesdon, who is immediately on his guard against any mention of the fancy-dress ball. Jeeves points out that the ball in East Wibley was such a minor affair that a gentleman of Mr Wooster's position would scarcely condescend to participate. Besides, as Lord Worplesdon passed the night in Boko's house, he was in a position to testify that Mr Wooster had never left the premises.

Stilton is so disgusted that he quits. As he is no longer a policeman, Florence agrees to marry him, letting Bertie off the hook.

The car is ready for Bertie to make his escape when he remembers that he had promised to go to the Hall with Uncle Percy to help explain things to Aunt Agatha. Jeeves then admits that Aunt Agatha had not returned to the Hall. It was a subterfuge.

The Mating Season

The Mating Season appeared, condensed, in a single issue of Canada's Star Weekly *magazine on 12 November 1949. It was published in volume form by Herbert Jenkins in the UK on 9 September 1949 and by Didier & Co. in the US on 29 November 1949 with illustrations by Hal McIntosh.*

Aunt Agatha sends Bertie to Deverill Hall, King's Deverill, Hampshire, to lend his services to the village concert being put on by the vicar's niece. His host is Mr Esmond Haddock who has five aunts in residence, along with his cousin Gertrude Winkworth. The butler there is Jeeves's uncle, Charlie Silversmith. Gussie Fink-Nottle will also be there. Madeline

Bassett was supposed to have accompanied him, but at the last moment has had to visit an old schoolfriend in Wimbledon who has suffered a disappointment in love.

Catsmeat Potter-Pirbright calls on Bertie's flat with his actress sister, Cora 'Corky' Pirbright, who is a Hollywood star under the name Cora Starr. It turns out that Corky is the vicar's niece who is arranging the concert. Bertie is booked to be part of a Pat-and-Mike crosstalk act. Catsmeat cannot attend because he is engaged to Gertrude Winkworth, who dare not elope with him because her mother is the fiercest of the aunts, Dame Daphne Winkworth. The problem is that Esmond Haddock is very good looking and is now making a rush on Gertrude. Catsmeat asks Bertie to foil him by being always at her side.

Bertie agrees to this, provided Catsmeat take Gussie Fink-Nottle out that night to cheer him up. Bertie can't do it because he has to take Aunt Agatha's son Thomas to the Old Vic, before putting him on the train to school the next morning.

Corky appears with a dog she calls Sam Goldwyn, which she has obtained from Battersea Dogs Home. She tells Bertie that his partner in the Pat-and-Mike crosstalk act is to be the local rozzer, Constable Dobbs, an atheist who annoys her Uncle Sidney with cracks about Jonah and the whale.

Esmond Haddock is to sing a song. He has turned his attention to Gertrude Winkworth after Cora threw him aside because he would not stand up to his aunts.

Catsmeat turns up that morning to announce that during the drunken revels of the previous evening, Gussie was arrested and sentenced to fourteen days.

If Madeline hears about this, she will break off the engagement and start pursuing Bertie again. So Jeeves suggests that Bertie goes to Deverill Hall pretending to be Gussie. Corky persuades Bertie to take Sam Goldwyn with him and they head off in the two-seater.

At Deverill Hall, the [...] too late to dress for dinn[...] upon by the assembled au[...] a well-known teetotaller, B[...] He tries to explain about the [...] dismiss as 'vulgar'. They go on t[...] was supposed to have arrived that [...] telegram.

When the ladies withdraw, Bertie is [...], who asks him whether he would like to t[...]ort. Bertie readily accedes. Esmond then reveals that [...] is in love with Corky and hopes to win her around with his song at the concert. It is a dreadful hunting song written by two of his aunts. As they rapidly get drunk on port, Bertie suggests new words. They end up giving it a run-through, with Bertie standing on the chair waving the decanter like a baton. Dame Daphne then storms in to tell Esmond that Gertrude is waiting to play backgammon in the drawing room. He follows meekly.

Sam Goldwyn has escaped, finds his way into the drawing room and bites Silversmith. They send the dog to the vicarage to stay with Miss Pirbright, of whom the aunts thoroughly disapprove. Shown to his room, Bertie is told that his valet has arrived. It turns out to be not Jeeves but Catsmeat who wants keep an eye on Gertrude. He masquerades as Meadowes, the name of the valet Bertie sacked before he had Jeeves. As he is a servant, he cannot be seen talking to Gertrude, but they communicate by passing notes.

Gussie has been let off with a fine, and the following morning, he turns up pretending to be Bertie with Jeeves as his valet. Jeeves gauges that, if Mr Haddock's performance at the concert is a success, he will be emboldened to defy the aunts and win Corky, so he sets about organizing a claque.

Gussie is shocked when he hears about the port-and-

...ent. If it comes to Madeline's ears, he is ...ue a stout denial. And if she were to hear that ...was in a crosstalk act, wearing a checked suit and a ...en beard, the engagement would be off. So Gussie, masquerading as Wooster, must play the role. But his qualms vanish when Corky turns up and turns on the charm. Gussie is captivated and starts following her around. This suits Corky as she is trying to make Esmond jealous.

Constable Dobbs is also out of the Pat-and-Mike act after being bitten by Sam Goldwyn, who he arrests. Catsmeat takes over the part. Meanwhile, at Madeline's behest, Bertie, masquerading as Gussie, is to give a recital of Christopher Robin poems while Jeeves takes off to London for a lecture he wants to attend.

Bertie is upbraided by Dame Daphne for not writing to Madeline. Catsmeat has been exchanging notes with Gertrude, eventually persuading her to elope with him. A dab hand with romantic prose, he cooks up a letter for Bertie to send to Madeline. This says that Gussie has sprained his wrist stopping a runaway horse to save a child. That done, Catsmeat goes to play gin rummy with Queenie, the housemaid, to cheer her up. She had just broken off her engagement to Constable Dobbs because of his atheism.

Bertie tells Corky that Esmond still loves her, despite his overtures to Gertrude. He convinces her that, when Esmond's song is a smash, he will defy the aunts. Jeeves has said so. But she must release her hooks from Gussie.

News comes that Aunt Agatha is on her way. Catsmeat is sent to confer with Jeeves. He feels that Aunt Agatha can be diverted if her son Thomas disappears from his school at Bramley-on-Sea. The boy is smitten with film stars, so Corky invites him to stay at the vicarage.

Meanwhile Madeline has received the letter. Hearing that he had been heroically injured, she is coming to Deverill Hall.

Catsmeat decides to drive to Wimbledon and speak to Madeline. After he has gone, Gussie tells Bertie that he has written a letter to Madeline to break off their engagement. He is in love with Corky.

With Madeline unattached, Bertie is in ever-present danger. He travels up to London on the milk train. He arrives in Wimbledon before the mail arrives. After the postman makes his delivery, he slips in through the French windows and grabs Gussie's note before Madeline can read it. However, he finds his retreat cut off. Instead, he flees across the hall into a den, but a gardener outside the window blocks his escape. He looks around and sees a photograph of Madeline. If Gussie saw it, he thinks, it might remind him of how he felt about her.

Madeline and her schoolfriend approach. Bertie hides behind the sofa, but is spotted. Madeline thinks that Bertie is still in love with her and has come to pinch the photograph for himself. Catsmeat then turns up to speak to Madeline, while Bertie makes off back to King's Deverill. Thomas has arrived and brought with him a small rubber cosh. Bertie finds that Corky has not yet released her hooks from Gussie as she has 'a little job' for him to do first. He is to retrieve Sam Goldwyn from captivity in Constable Dobbs's police cottage.

Then comes the announcement that the housemaid Queenie is engaged to Gussie's valet. Catsmeat had found Queenie in tears and tried to comfort her with a kiss when Silversmith walked in. He turns out to be her father. Queenie told him they were engaged. Consequently Gertrude has sent a note saying that the elopement is off.

At the concert that night, the crosstalk act falls flat. However, there is a rousing cheer for Esmond's song.

During the intermission, Bertie realizes that he has forgotten the words to the Christopher Robin poems. He goes into the pub where he meets Jeeves who, on Bertie's instructions, has taken Thomas's cosh away from him. Jeeves suggests that

Esmond might like to read the poems instead. With the claque in place, he can do no wrong.

While Jeeves is away arranging that, Gussie comes in asking for brandy. He is fortifying himself before breaking into the police cottage to release Sam Goldwyn while Constable Dobbs is watching the concert.

When Gussie has gone, Jeeves returns with the news that Constable Dobbs hated the show and that he is going home. So Jeeves and Wooster set off to the police station after Gussie.

On the way Sam Goldwyn comes bounding down the road. Soon after, they see Gussie, still in full Pat-and-Mike costume, being chased down the street by Constable Dobbs. Gussie hastily climbs a tree. Dobbs stands guard below until Jeeves strikes him on the head with Thomas's cosh.

Esmond and Corky are now engaged. She turns up for the after-show drink and sandwiches at Deverill Hall with her father, Reverend Pirbright. Gertrude and the aunts are there, with Jeeves and Queenie serving. Then Silversmith announces the arrival of Constable Dobbs.

Dobbs tells the Reverend Pirbright that he has seen the light after he had been struck by a thunderbolt while standing under a tree. Queenie flings herself on his chest and he smothers her with kisses. Then he addresses Esmond, who is the local JP, saying he is looking for Mr Wooster who has stolen a dog from the police station. But Jeeves insists that he has been with Mr Wooster continuously since they left the concert hall.

If it wasn't Wooster who stole the dog, it must have been the other chap with a green beard and checked suit in the crosstalk act. When Catsmeat appears, Esmond sentences him to thirty days. Gertrude is overcome. She flings herself on his chest and he smothers her with kisses.

Corky steps forward to announce that Gussie's valet is, in fact, her brother Catsmeat. Esmond revokes the sentence, saying that Constable Dobbs must be mistaken.

The aunts are outraged. When challenged by Dame Daphne, Esmond says he will brook no argument. Then he announces that he and Corky are to be married and he will accompany her to Hollywood.

But Aunt Agatha is on her way. Having seen Esmond take on five aunts, Bertie decides to stay and face her. If worst comes to the worst, he can always borrow Thomas's cosh.

Ring for Jeeves (*The Return of Jeeves*)

Adapted from Guy Bolton's script for Come On, Jeeves, Ring for Jeeves *was then published in volume form by Herbert Jenkins in the UK on 22 April 1953 and as* The Return of Jeeves *in the US by Simon & Schuster on 15 April 1954. It also appeared in the 5 September 1953 issue of the* Star Weekly *with illustrations by Jack Hagen and the April 1954 issue of* Ladies' Home Journal. *It is the only Jeeves novel without Bertie in it. Although the plot and dialogue of the American and British books are almost identical, the construction of the plot, especially in the early chapters, is different. The British book (*Ring for Jeeves*) opens with a scene in a country public house before shifting in Chapter Two to a nearby country house, whereas the American book (*The Return of Jeeves*) opens in the country house, with the scene in the pub delayed until Chapter Five.*

Ring for Jeeves is set in the early 1950s when the aristocracy in England is impoverished. Bertie, though retaining his money, has gone to school to prepare for life after the Social Revolution.

In the meantime, he has hired Jeeves out to Lord William 'Bill' Rowcester (Towcester in some American editions) who is strikingly similar to Wooster. He claims ancestors at Agincourt and the Battle of Joppa, says 'what ho!' and other Woosterisms, and frequently checks his quotations with

Jeeves. However, he also claims to have been with the Commandos during the Second World War, something it is hard to imagine Bertie having done, even if he had been young enough. And fitting the more egalitarian era that followed the war, Jeeves speaks up for himself a lot more.

The story in the UK book begins in the coffee room of the Goose and Gherkin where a wealthy American lady sits drinking a gin and tonic. The corresponding scene in the US book is in Chapter Five. Born Rosalinda Banks in Ohio, she married pulp magnate Clifton Bessemer, who was killed in a collision with a truck, followed by millionaire sportsman A. B. Spottsworth, who was eaten by a lion on safari.

Into the pub comes Captain Biggar, the white hunter with that safari. They have not met since the death of her husband. She is on the way to Rowcester (or Towcester) Abbey, having met Lord Rowcester's sister Monica who has suggested that she might like to buy it.

Captain Biggar is on the trail of a bookie called Honest Patch Perkins, who has a patch over one eye and a walrus moustache. He has made off from Epsom Downs race course after the Oaks without paying him his winnings of over £3,000.

Mrs Spottsworth wants to get married again – this time, not for money, but to someone strong and masterful like Captain Biggar. Biggar, for his part, cannot marry a wealthy heiress unless he has money himself. Fortune-hunting is against his code.

Monica, Lady Carmoyle, arrives at Rowcester Abbey with her husband Sir Roderick 'Rory', the tenth baronet, who is now a floorwalker in a department store. He makes jokes about how damp and rundown the place is: Lord Rowcester had once made a big mistake. He had met a rich American widow in Cannes named Mrs Bessemer, but had let her get away.

Jill Wyvern, Lord Rowcester's fiancée, turns up. She is the

daughter of the Chief Constable, who lives nearby, and reveals that Lord Rowcester's fortunes have recently improved. He now has a cook, a housemaid and a butler called Jeeves. He has even paid the phone bill.

The Carmoyles want to know where the money is coming from. Jill is not sure, but Bill goes out in the car most days with Jeeves.

The phone rings. An anonymous caller wants to know the number of Bill's car. They don't know. Then the phone rings again. This time it is the police.

They are not in the drawing room when Honest Patch Perkins enters and pulls off his eyepatch and moustache. Then Jeeves appears, saying that he has put the car in the garage. Patch Perkins is now revealed as Lord Rowcester. He changes quickly and puts the disguise in an old oak chest.

Lord Rowcester is concerned that they cannot go back to Epsom the following day for the Derby and is distraught that he has run out on a bet. But the news that Mrs Spottsworth might buy the house is a godsend.

Monica and Rory then tell Bill about the mysterious phone calls. It is plain that he is concerned.

When Mrs Spottsworth arrives she recognizes Lord Rowcester from the Riviera. Back then, he was plain William Belfry, though she calls him Billiken. She was Mrs Bessemer at that time and he calls her Rosie.

She is interested in spiritualism, so Monica tells her that the ghost of Lady Agatha inhabits the ruined chapel.

While Lord Rowcester is dressing for dinner, Captain Biggar arrives. Mrs Spottsworth immediately asks Monica to invite him to stay.

After dinner, when the ladies have withdrawn, Rory invites Captain Biggar to watch the Derby Dinner on the television in the library. The conversation comes round to Biggar's win on the Oaks. Rory is shocked that the bookmaker did a bolt.

Biggar explains to Lord Rowcester what happens to a welsher in the Far East. He has also discovered the the number of the car Honest Patch Perkins was driving is registered to Lord Rowcester.

Mrs Spottsworth goes out to the ruined chapel to see if she can see the ghost of Lady Agatha. Then she wanders out into the garden where she sits on a rustic bench. Captain Biggar turns up and sits beside her. She drops her $10,000 diamond pendant, which he retrieves.

Mrs Spottsworth then tells Captain Biggar that rich women like her are lonely. He resists her play because of the code vouchsafed to him by Major 'Tubby' Frobisher in the Long Bar in Shanghai.

Lord Rowcester comes out and tries to woo Mrs Spottsworth in the hope of selling the house and honouring his debt to Captain Biggar. Biggar jealously assumes that Rowcester is trying to make love to her – and tells Jill.

Intent on helping her brother sell the house, Monica draws Mrs Spottsworth's attention to the old oak chest. They used to keep costumes in there she says and opens it to reveal her brother's PatchPerkins outfit.

Rory calls everyone through to the library, leaving only Biggar and Rowcester, with Jeeves hovering in attendance. Biggar insists that Rowcester write him a cheque for his winnings. Jeeves points out that, if he does, it won't be honoured. Lord Rowcester has no money. Biggar wants the money as a stake to put on a horse tipped to win the Derby. Then he will have enough money of his own to propose to Mrs Spottsworth without being deemed a fortune-hunter.

He suggests that Lord Rowcester steals – or rather borrows – Mrs Spottsworth's pendant. He will pawn it and put the money on the horse. When it wins, he will redeem the pendant and return it, saying he has found it.

When Lord Rowcester demurs, Biggar tells a long tale of

how he had come by the pendant in the Far East and had given it to Mrs Spottsworth after her husband died. So it really belongs to him.

Lord Rowcester is persuaded and Jeeves comes up with a plan. They must get Mrs Spottsworth back on the rustic bench. Then Lord Rowcester is to pretend there is a spider in the hair and knock open the clasp so the pendant falls to the ground. But when he tries this, the pendant drops down inside her clothing.

Jill discovers that Bill is in the garden again with Mrs Spottsworth and stiffens. Then Rowcester does the Charleston with Mrs Spottsworth in the hope that the pendant will fall off – to no effect other than upsetting Jill further.

After Mrs Spottsworth goes to bed, Jeeves comes up with one more plan. He will go to Mrs Spottsworth's bedroom and tell her that he has just seen the ghost of Lady Agatha. While he escorts her down to the ruined chapel, Lord Rowcester is to sneak into her bedroom and steal the pendant. But when he does so, Mrs Spottsworth's Pekinese alerts Jill, who sees Bill creeping out of Mrs Spottsworth's bedroom. She gives Jeeves her engagement ring to return to his lordship.

The following day, Jill tells her father Colonel Wyvern, Chief Constable of Southmoltonshire (Northamptonshire in some American editions), that she is not going to marry Lord Rowcester because of Mrs Spottsworth. The colonel threatens to horsewhip Rowcester.

Over lunch, Rowcester discovers that Captain Biggar's story about how he acquired the pendant is not true. However, Jeeves points out that, as Biggar has disappeared with the pendant, he will be blamed for stealing it. Then, if Lord Rowcester can sell the house to Mrs Spottsworth, he can then send Captain Biggar his winnings and redeem the pendant – and with it his honour.

Jill gives Jeeves a message for Bill – her father is coming to horsewhip him. Jeeves then reveals that Mrs Spottsworth was not in her bedroom when Jill saw Lord Rowcester leaving it. He has gone there to steal her pendant. His Lordship had been masquerading as Honest Patch Perkins to make enough money to marry her. Everything was going well until Captain Biggar won a double at Epsom. Now he has purloined the pendant so Captain Biggar could put money on Ballymore in the Derby. She runs to Bill and flings her arms around him.

Mrs Spottsworth comes in, saying that she will buy the house – unless it is damp. Rory comes in saying that it has started raining and they had better put out buckets under the holes in the roof.

Then the housemaid comes in to say that a pendant has been stolen. Captain Biggar is suspected. Lord Rowcester sends Jeeves to get Mrs Spottsworth's jewel case, ostensibly so that no one can wipe off the fingerprints. Colonel Wyvern arrives and is thrust, unexpectedly, into an investigation. But the Derby is running. There is a photo-finish. Ballymore loses.

Captain Biggar returns with the pendant. He could not go through with his plan to pawn it. He explains to Mrs Spottsworth that he only wanted to make enough money so that he could ask her to marry him because of the code. Mrs Spottsworth then reveals that Major Frobisher has just married an American widow who is much richer than she is.

Jeeves asks whether they intend to live in the abbey. When Mrs Spottsworth says that it is much too damp, Jeeves suggests that she has it moved stone by stone to California. Bill and Jill now have the money to marry, too. Lord Rowcester asks Jeeves to stay on. But Jeeves regrets he must give notice. Mr Wooster needs him.

Jeeves and the Feudal Spirit (Bertie Wooster Sees it Through)
Jeeves and the Feudal Spirit *was published by Herbert Jenkins in the UK on 15 October 1954 and as* Bertie Wooster Sees it

Through *by Simon & Schuster in the US on 23 February 1955.
It also appeared, illustrated by Alex Redmond and entitled*
Double Jeopardy, *in the 4 December 1954 issue of the* Star
Weekly *in Canada.*

Aunt Dahlia has asked Bertie to take the teetotallers Mr and
Mrs Trotter out for dinner. While he is getting ready a letter
arrives from a Percy Gorringe, the stepson of Mr L. G.
Trotter, asking him for a thousand pounds to back a
dramatization of Lady Florence Craye's novel *Spindrift*. On
Jeeves's advice, Bertie declines. Jeeves then notices that Bertie
is growing a moustache and disapproves.

Bertie is drinking one of Jeeves's special cocktails when G.
D'Arcy 'Stilton' Cheesewright arrives. He wants Bertie to
curb such indulgences as he has drawn Bertie's name in the
Drones Club annual darts sweep and wants him on peak form.

Cheesewright is awaiting Florence Craye. They are dining
with Stilton's uncle. When she arrives, she says she loves
Bertie's moustache. This piques Stilton. He is also jealous
about Percy Gorringe who has been working closely with
Florence.

Dinner with the Trotters does little to raise Bertie's spirits.
Mrs Trotter talks principally about her bitter social rivalry in
Liverpool with Mrs Alderman Blenkinsop.

When Bertie arrives home, Florence turns up. She wants
Bertie to take her to a garish nightclub as research for her next
book. Stilton was to have taken her but they had fallen out
because he refused to grow a moustache like Bertie's. Florence
also says she is going to Brinkley Court the following day
where she is to meet a highly paid fellow authoress, Daphne
Dolores Morehead, who is writing a serial for *Milady's
Boudoir*.

Florence and Bertie go to the Mottled Oyster. It is raided
by the police. Florence makes a run for it. Bertie trips up the

policeman chasing her and gets himself arrested. He appears at Vinton Street Police Court where he is fined £10 by the magistrate, who turns out to be Stilton's Uncle Joseph.

Florence phones to tell Bertie that she has made it up with D'Arcy as he has consented to grow a moustache. While Bertie is on the phone to Florence, Stilton arrives. He suspects that Bertie was with Florence in the Mottled Oyster. Jeeves confirms Bertie's story that he was at home in bed with an improving book. Somewhat mollified by one of Jeeves's special cocktails, Stilton still accuses Bertie of being in love with Florence.

Bertie receives a telegram from Aunt Dahlia, telling him to come to Brinkley to 'buck up a blighter with whiskers' – Gorringe – who is in love with Florence. And he is to bring her pearl necklace from Aspinall's. Bertie is reluctant to go as Stilton has threatened to break his spine if he catches Bertie sniffing around Florence. Then Aunt Dahlia phones and insists that Bertie shows up at Brinkley. The Trotters are there. Mr Trotter owes newspapers in Liverpool and is interested in buying *Milady's Boudoir*, or *Madame's Nightshirt* as Uncle Tom calls it. He wants Aunt Dahlia to sell it because he is tired of funding it.

When Bertie arrives at Brinkley Court, Aunt Dahlia explains that she has invited the Trotters so that Anatole's cooking can sweeten the deal, but it does not seem to be. So the esteemed lady novelist Daphne Dolores Morehead has been brought in to help convince him doing the trick that *Milady's Boudoir* is a going concern.

Florence receives a telegram from Cheesewright, breaking off their engagement. Gorringe is delighted. So is Florence who has discovered that Stilton is so suspicious that he went to the Mottled Oyster and found Bertie's name in the reservations' book. Then Stilton arrives at Brinkley.

When the ladies leave the dinner table, Bertie sneaks off,

too, to avoid Cheesewright. Aunt Dahlia finds Bertie in his room. She is in a nervous state. To pay for Daphne Dolores Morehead's serial, she has pawned the pearl necklace that Uncle Tom had given her. The necklace Bertie collected from Aspinall's is a cheap copy using cultured pearls. However, the following evening, Lord Sidcup is coming to view Uncle Tom's collection. He is an expert on jewellery and is bound spot that the necklace is a fake.

Jeeves suggests that the problem would be solved if a burglar, in the person of Bertie, should steal the necklace that night. After they were all locked out in *Right Ho, Jeeves* (*Brinkley Manor*), Uncle Tom has had the bars removed from the windows. However, when Bertie scales a ladder to break into the house, he mistakenly climbs into Florence's bedroom. She draws the obvious conclusion.

Cheesewright knocks on the bedroom door. He has come to return her letters. Bertie hides in a cupboard. To spite Stilton, Florence says she is going to marry Bertie. Wooster is startled. Hearing a noise, Stilton opens the cupboard and drags Bertie out by the ear.

As Old Etonians do not fight in front of a lady, Stilton awaits Bertie in the corridor outside. Bertie intends to escape through the window but finds the ladder gone. Knowing that he has to go out through the bedroom door and confront Cheesewright, Bertie has the nous to remind him of the Drones Club darts sweep – where Stilton stands to lose fifty-six pounds and ten shillings (£56.50).

Bertie is explaining his failure to steal the necklace to Aunt Dahlia when Uncle Tom turns up, saying he removed the ladder because the place was teeming with burglars. He has now locked the necklace in the safe in the hall.

Nevertheless, Jeeves reports that all is well. Lord Sidcup is the recently elevated Roderick Spode. All Mrs Travers has to do is mention Eulalie Soeurs.

The following day Jeeves has to go to London to chair a luncheon at the Junior Ganymede club. Percy Gorringe is downcast again at the news that Florence is engaged to Bertie. Then he becomes concerned that Bertie is not wearing a hat while out in the sunshine. Cheesewright has sold him a ticket in the Drones Club darts sweep – and Stilton is now looking for Bertie, who catches Jeeves before he leaves for London and tells him to bring back the cosh he took from Thomas in *The Mating Season*.

Bertie meets Aunt Dahlia, who has not had a chance to mention Eulalie Soeurs to Spode as Uncle Tom has him closeted in his collection room. Gorringe arrives to tell Aunt Dahlia that his mother wants to see her.

When Cheesewright finally catches up with him in the hall, Bertie pulls the cosh. Undeterred, Stilton pounces on him. The cosh flies from Bertie's hand and lands near Uncle Tom's safe. Aunt Dahlia's butler, Seppings, interrupts. Again, Cheesewright's code prohibits brawling in front of the staff. Seppings has come to answer the door to Daphne Dolores Morehead. Stilton is immediately dumbstruck. She recognizes D'Arcy Cheesewright as an Oxford rowing Blue and she whisks him off to explore the grounds.

When Bertie returns to collect the cosh, he finds the safe door open, swiftly pockets a pearl necklace and makes off. When he finds Aunt Dahlia, she says that Uncle Tom was called away to the phone when he was showing Spode the necklace. She stepped in and mentioned Eulalie Soeurs, only to have Spode riposte that he had sold the company some time before. She looked down and saw a cosh, grabbed it, knocked Spode out and took the necklace. So whose pearl necklace does he have? Bertie enquires. It belongs to Mrs Trotter.

On his way to put the necklace back, Bertie meets Mr Trotter, who says he is taking to his bed due to a dyspeptic attack. As he goes, he slams the safe door shut, leaving Bertie no chance to return the necklace.

He heads to Aunt Dahlia's room to discover that Mrs Trotter has told her that she will not let her husband buy *Milady's Boudoir* unless Anatole comes to work for them. Aunt Dahlia must sell the magazine to get her necklace out of hock, but Mr Trotter is not going to buy *Milady's Boudoir* if he discovers that her nephew has stolen his wife's pearls.

Mrs Trotter then discovers her pearls are missing. Aunt Dahlia calls for Jeeves. He agrees to return the necklace.

Jeeves has learned from Seppings that Mrs Trotter, being socially ambitious, is eager to see her husband knighted as this would be one in the eye for Mrs Alderman Blenkinsop. However, Mr Trotter, being of a retiring disposition, is not eager to wear satin knee-breeches at the palace. If Mr Trotter learned that the alternative to buying *Milady's Boudoir* was for Mrs Trotter to discover that he had turned down a knight-hood, he might be more easily influenced.

At breakfast the following morning, Stilton is delighted that Bertie has taken Florence off his hands so he can be with Daphne. Mrs Trotter lets out a screech. In *The Times*, she has seen that Alderman Blenkinsop has been knighted. Then Seppings arrives with her pearl necklace on a silver salver. He has found it in Jeeves's room.

Jeeves is summoned. Bertie readies himself to admit that he has stolen the necklace to save Jeeves. But Jeeves brazens it out. He says that he was going to enquire that morning who owned the necklace; he assumed that the trinket belonged to a housemaid. The pearls were cultured. Lord Sidcup confirms Jeeves's assessment.

It transpires that Mrs Trotter had entrusted the necklace to her son Percy. Gorringe had pawned it and replaced with it an imitation. He needed £1,000 to stage *Spindrift*. Florence is overawed that he did this for her.

Mr Trotter is outraged. He says he is going back to Liverpool that morning; he can take no more of Anatole's rich food. Jeeves suggests Mr Trotter might try one of his 'morning mixtures'. It works.

Bertie agrees to release Florence so that she can get engaged to Gorringe. Now that Mr Trotter has revived, he wants to meet Aunt Dahlia in the library, presumably to conclude the sale of *Milady's Boudoir*. In gratitude, Bertie agrees to shave off his moustache.

How Right You Are, Jeeves (*Jeeves in the Offing*)

First published in Playboy *in February 1960 with illustrations by Bill Charmatz, then in the* Star Weekly *on 23 April 1960 with illustrations by Gerry Sevier,* How Right You Are, Jeeves *was serialized in* John Bull *magazine from 29 August to 19 September 1959, illustrated by Richard O. Rose.* How Right You Are, Jeeves *was published by Simon & Schuster in the US on 4 April 1960 and as* Jeeves in the Offing *by Herbert Jenkins in the UK on 12 August 1960.*

Reginald 'Kipper' Herring, an old prep school friend of Bertie's, has come to stay. A former boxer, he now works for the *Thursday Review*. They are having breakfast when Aunt Dahlia phones. She is lunching with Sir Roderick Glossop. Seppings is on holiday so she is hiring a replacement butler. Jeeves is about to go on holiday, shrimping in Herne Bay. So she invites Bertie to stay at Brinkley Court.

Uncle Tom is in Harrogate with Homer Cream, an American tycoon with whom he is trying to conclude a business deal. His wife, Adela Cream, an author of mystery stories, is at Brinkley Court along with her son, Wilbert Cream. Roberta 'Bobbie' Wickham is also there, along with Bertie and Kipper's former headmaster, Aubrey 'Gawd-help-us' Upjohn, who intends to stand as a Conservative candidate for Market Snodsbury, and his stepdaughter Phyllis Mills. Her mother, Jane Mills, was a friend of Aunt Dahlia's and Upjohn is going to give the prizes at Market Snodsbury Grammar School this year.

Kipper has met Phyllis in Switzerland, but did not know that she was related to Upjohn. Recently Upjohn had written a book about prep schools and Kipper has given it an excoriating review. Before he leaves, Jeeves warns Bertie that in New York the playboy 'Broadway Willie' Cream is notorious for letting off stink bombs in night clubs and other pranks.

Bertie then gets a phone call from Bobbie's mother, Lady Wickham. She wants to know if the awful thing she has read in *The Times* is true, then faints. Bertie finds in Jeeves's copy of *The Times*, to his horror, the announcement of his forthcoming marriage to Roberta Wickham.

Arriving at Brinkley Court, Bertie searches the grounds for Bobbie. He bumps into Willie Cream and Phyllis Mills. Wilbert is reading poetry to Phyllis and clearly has designs on her.

Bertie finds Bobbie by the lake. She says she put the notice in *The Times* to soften her mother up. When Lady Wickham realizes that Bobbie is not going to marry Bertie, she will be so relieved that she won't mind her marrying Reggie Herring.

At tea Bertie discovers that Aunt Dahlia's new butler is Sir Roderick Glossop, whom Bobbie has mischievously dubbed Swordfish. Bertie is so shocked he spills a cup of tea over Aubrey Upjohn's trousers. It appears that Upjohn is urging Phyllis to marry Wilbert Cream. Aunt Dahlia is against the match, thinking playboy Willie Cream an unsuitable match for the daughter of her old friend, and she has called in Glossop to observe him discreetly to see if he can be written off as a loony. Mrs Cream must not know, of course, or it would jeopardize Uncle Tom's deal with her husband. Aunt Dahlia also wants Bertie to follow Wilbert and Phyllis around so that he does not get a chance to propose.

Bertie goes to tell Phyllis to come in for tea, while Wilbert takes her dachshund Poppet for a walk. Phyllis asks Bobbie where her stepfather is, to be told that he has gone to London. He is 'all of a doodah' about the piece in the *Thursday Review*.

Mrs Cream is suspicious of Swordfish, thinking that he is not a real butler. Wilbert then shows an interest in Uncle Tom's cow-creamer, which Bertie finds odd for a playboy. After lunch, Phyllis goes to her room to finish typing her stepfather's speech for the prize-giving. Aunt Dahlia has been called away to tend her son Bonzo who has German measles. When she phones, Bertie tells her of Mrs Cream's suspicions, but she is more worried about what is going on between Phyllis and Wilbert.

Bertie's attentions are causing aggravation in that quarter. Fearing that there may be a fight, Aunt Dahlia says that, if anyone hits Wilbert, they must have no connection to the Travers family. She suggests that Bertie invite Kipper to come to Brinkley Court to assist him.

Bertie receives a letter from Jeeves warning him that Willie Cream is a kleptomaniac. Concerned for Mr Travers's silverware, Bertie and Bobbie go to the collection room where they find the cow-creamer is missing. Bertie goes to search Wilbert Cream's room for it. Looking on top of a cupboard, he falls and becomes entangled in a chair. The noise attracts Mrs Cream who wants to know what Bertie is doing in her son's room. He claims he is looking for a mouse. When she catches him a second time, she recommends that he consult Sir Roderick Glossop.

Bobbie takes off to see her mother at Skeldings Hall, while Kipper turns up at Brinkley Court. He has seen the notice in *The Times*, too, and is stunned. Only a couple of days earlier, he says, Bobbie was engaged to him. So after dinner, he intends to propose to Phyllis Mills.

Sir Roderick Glossop volunteers to search Wilbert Cream's

room. He tells Bertie he finds the idea rather exciting as, when he was at prep school, he would sneak into the headmaster's study to steal biscuits – as did Bertie. Recognizing that they are brothers at heart, Bertie starts calling Sir Roderick 'Roddy'.

Kipper now reveals that, after reading the notice in *The Times*, he had written a stinker of a letter to the red-headed Bobbie, calling her a carrot-topped Jezebel. But now he has learned that the notice was just a ruse and she still loves him. He phones Skeldings Hall and tells her not to open the letter. She does and explodes, saying that she is now free to marry Bertie.

Bertie decides there is only one thing to do: drive to Herne Bay to see Jeeves, who agrees to return with Bertie to Brinkley Court. On the way, Bertie spots Bobbie's roadster outside a wayside inn and stops to talk to her. She says that she did not mean what she had said to Kipper. She was just blowing off steam. So her engagement to Bertie is off.

When they reach Brinkley Court, Aunt Dahlia has returned. She reveals that Wilbert Cream did not steal the cow-creamer. He had phoned Uncle Tom in Harrogate who agreed to sell it to sweeten the deal with his father. Bobbie is now upset because Kipper, thinking it was all over, has got engaged to Phyllis Mills.

News comes that Upjohn is returning from London where he has started a libel action against the *Thursday Review*. Kipper is likely to lose his job. His review contained caustic but mostly legitimate criticism. However, it concluded by saying Upjohn's school served sausages made from pigs that had died of 'glanders, the botts and tuberculosis' – which was libellous. But Kipper had not written this. Bobbie had added it when Kipper showed her the proofs. As the author of his misfortune, Bobbie gets engaged to Kipper again.

Sir Roderick comes up with a plan for Kipper to ingratiate

himself with Upjohn. Bobbie is to point out a large fish in the lake. As Upjohn bends over to look at it, Bertie is to push him in, then Kipper is to dive in and rescue him. When they repair to the garden, Wilbert Cream comes up with Poppet and asks Bertie about the mouse in his room. While he was looking for it, Wilbert enquires, did he come across a cow-creamer that has now gone missing?

As Bobbie and Bertie prepare to push him in the lake, Upjohn is called away to speak to his lawyer on the phone. Phyllis arrives with a cat. Poppet shoots between Bertie's legs and topples him into the water. Kipper jumps in to rescue Bertie, thinking that he is Upjohn, and Wilbert dives into to rescue Poppet. As he has saved her doggie, Phyllis gets engaged to Cream.

When Aunt Dahlia hears of this, she upbraids Upjohn for allowing the daughter of her friend Jane Mills to marry a playboy who lets stink bombs off in nightclubs – the infamous Broadway Willie. Upjohn points out that it is Wilbert's younger brother Wilfred who is the notorious playboy, Broadway Willie.

Hearing from his lawyers that the author of the piece in the *Thursday Review* is his fellow guest, Reginald Herring, and says 'either he goes, or I go'. Aunt Dahlia takes offence so Upjohn is packed off to the pub in Market Snodsbury. Jeeves packs for him, but fails to include the speech that Phyllis was typing for him. He gives it to Bobbie who presents Upjohn with an ultimatum. Either he drops his libel suit or he doesn't get his speech back. As Upjohn cannot make a speech without the typescript – and if he does not make the speech at the prize-giving he will not be selected as the Conservative candidate – he has no choice but to withdraw his action.

Stiff Upper Lip, Jeeves

First appearing in the February and March issues of Playboy *magazine with illustrations by Bill Charmatz,* Stiff Upper Lip,

Jeeves *was published in volume form by Simon & Schuster in the US on 22 March 1963 and by Herbert Jenkins in the UK on 16 August 1963.*

Aunt Dahlia's butler went sick and she borrowed Jeeves for a house party. Sir Watkyn Bassett had been present and was impressed by Jeeves's bultering skills. Aunt Dahlia tells Bertie that her husband, Bertie's Uncle Tom, suffered agonies through Sir Watkyn's gloating about a black amber statuette he had just added to his collection, an *objet d'art* Uncle Tom himself coveted.

Meanwhile Bertie goes for lunch at the Ritz wearing his new blue Alpine hat with a pink feather, of which Jeeves disapproves. His guest is Emerald Stoker, Pauline's younger sister. She is on her way to Totleigh Towers and wants Bertie to tell her about the people she is likely to meet there. One of them is Gussie Fink-Nottle, who Emerald has already met at a studio party.

After a drink in the Drones, Bertie returns home. Reverend Harold 'Stinker' Pinker turns up, complaining that Sir Watkyn still has not given him the vicarage Stinker needs so he can marry Stephanie 'Stiffy' Byng. Then Stinker says that Stiffy wants Bertie to come to Totleigh Towers to do something for her, but she won't say what. Fearing trouble, Bertie refuses to go.

After Stinker has gone, Gussie Fink-Nottle turns up. He has fallen out with Madeline; nevertheless he on his way back to Totleigh Towers on the same train as Emerald. Jeeves recommends that Bertie should head for Totleigh Towers to make peace between Gussie and Madeline – otherwise he may find himself engaged to her again.

When Bertie arrives, Madeline assumes that he is lovesick and cannot stay away from her. She sheds a tear. Roderick Spode, Lord Sidcup, threatens to break his neck. He has been in love with Madeline for years, but has kept his feelings to himself. Bertie should do the same now she is engaged to Fink-Nottle.

Over dinner, Bertie tries to make conversation about the black amber statuette, which is the centrepiece of the table. Madeline says that Sir Watkyn bought it from a man named Plank who lives nearby in Hockley-cum-Meston. Stiffy says that it is worth £1,000.

While Madeline is still sweet on Gussie, Gussie is not happy with her because she has put him on a vegetarian diet. However, the cook had promised him a cold steak-and-kidney pie if he comes to the kitchen after everyone has gone to bed. It turns out that the cook is Emerald Stoker. She had lost her allowance on a horse and had taken the job as cook to support herself.

When Bertie awakes to find himself hungry she sneaks down to the kitchen and help himself to some of the steak-and-kidney pie. In the dark, he bumps into Gussie then knocks over a grandfather clock. This awakes Pop Bassett. They are attacked by Stiffy's Aberdeen terrier Bartholomew and take refuge on top of a chest. Stiffy comes to their rescue.

Once Sir Watkyn Bassett has returned to bed, Stiffy tells Bertie that she wants him to steal the amber statuette and return it to Plank as Bassett cheated him by giving him just £5 for it. If he doesn't, she will tell Madeline that she saw Gussie sneaking down to the kitchen to eat steak-and-kidney pie. Madeline will then break off her engagement and come after Bertie again.

Jeeves advises against trying to steal the statuette as it is now locked in Sir Watkyn's collection room. Jeeves had overheard Sir Watkyn and Spode talking. Having caught Bertie sneaking around in the dark at night, they believe he intends to steal the statuette for Mr Travers. However, Stiffy has a key to the collection room, steals the statuette and gives it to Bertie to return it to Plank.

Bertie drives over to Hockley-cum-Meston. Rather than being a humble labourer, as Bertie imagined, Major Plank is the lord of the manor, an African explorer and Empire builder. He is also a rugby player who is looking for a prop forward for the local team. Nevertheless, Bertie tries to sell the statuette back to him for the original £5. Plank assumes that he has stolen it from Sir Watkyn and threatens to call the police.

At that moment, Jeeves enters through the French windows, claiming to be Chief Inspector Witherspoon of Scotland Yard. He says he is there to arrest 'Alpine Joe', a criminal mastermind who goes about stealing statuettes, known for his distinctive headwear. Jeeves then marches 'Alpine Joe' out of the house. While Bertie has been away, Stiffy upbraided Sir Watkyn for cheating Plank by buying the statuette for just £5. Sir Watkyn admitted that he had actually paid £1,000 for it, but had only told Mr Travers that he had paid £5 to annoy him. Learning this, Jeeves set off after Bertie in Stiffy's car.

Jeeves then offers to return the statuette to Totleigh Towers, which is just as well because Spode searches Bertie and his car when he returns.

That afternoon there is to be the local school treat in the grounds of Totleigh Towers. A boiled egg is thrown at Sir Watkyn, who blames the Reverend Pinker for not keeping order, ruling him out as a candidate for the vicarage. Meanwhile Gussie goes for a walk with Emerald Stoker.

Seeing him kissing the cook, Spode declares Gussie a libertine and threatens to break his neck. Bertie heads off to warn Gussie. Meanwhile Bartholomew has bitten Gussie. While Madeline has sided with the dog, Emerald has tended the wound, so he kissed her. She also made him a round of ham sandwiches.

Spode arrives. Stinker steps forward to protect Gussie. Spode hits him on the nose and Stinker, a Boxing Blue, knocks him out. When Spode regains consciousness, Emerald brains him with a basin. Viewing the fallen Spode, Madeline tells Gussie that he is a brute and she hates him. Standing his ground, he takes a bite out of a ham sandwich and Madeline breaks off their engagement.

At cocktail hour, Bertie finds Sir Watkyn in the drawing-room. Stiffy arrives to announce that there will be no dinner. The cook has eloped with Gussie. Pop Bassett is so happy that Gussie is not going to be his son-in-law that he plies Bertie with drink and offers Stinker the vicarage.

Aunt Dahlia phones. Gussie has lodged Emerald at Brinkley Court while he goes off to get a special licence. She has taken over as cook as Anatole has come down with *mal au foie*. She wants Bertie to buy the statuette for Uncle Tom – but Spode assumes she is instructing Bertie to steal the statuette.

When Sir Watkyn learns that Spode's black eye was inflicted by Pinker, he withdraws the offer of the vicarage. Free of Gussie, Madeline now intends to marry Bertie.

Plank turns up, looking for the Reverend Pinker. He has heard of Stinker's prowess as a prop forward and offers him the vicarage at Hockley-cum-Meston.

When Bertie breaks the good news to Stiffy, she produces the statuette, which she had stolen again, intending to blackmail Sir Watkyn into giving Stinker the vicarage. Jeeves takes it from her to return it to the collection.

Spode offers to marry Madeline to save her from marrying Wooster. She says that she must marry Bertie because he loves her so. But Spode says that Bertie did not come to Totleigh Towers to be near her, but to steal the statuette. Jeeves then tells Madeline that Bertie is a kleptomaniac and gives her the statuette, which he says he found hidden in Bertie's room. Madeline consents to marry Spode and become Lady Sidcup. Pop Bassett is delighted. He calls Constable Oates and Bertie is arrested.

This time Bertie is locked in a cell. In the morning, news comes that Sir Watkyn is not pressing charges, provided that Jeeves comes to work for him. Jeeves has agreed but says that, after perhaps a week, differences will arise and he will be compelled to resign and return to Bertie's employ – on condition that the young master gets rid of his Alpine hat.

Much Obliged, Jeeves (*Jeeves and the Tie that Binds*)
Much Obliged, Jeeves *was published by Barrie & Jenkins in London on 15 October 1971 – Wooster's 90th birthday – and as* Jeeves and the Tie that Binds *in New York by Simon and Schuster on the same day.*

Aunt Dahlia summons Bertie to Brinkley Court to canvass for his old friend Harold 'Ginger' Winship who is standing as the Conservative candidate in the by-election in Market Snodsbury. Ginger is in London that day. When Bertie meets him for lunch, Ginger refuses a cocktail. He is under the thumb of his new fiancée Florence Craye; Percy Gorringe has been given the push after the stage version of *Spindrift* flopped.

Ginger is only standing for Parliament because Florence wants him so to do. She has arranged his candidacy through her friend, Cabinet minister A. B. Filmer. Ginger is in town to hire a secretary, an American named Magnolia Glendennon who had worked for Boko Fittleworth when he and Ginger shared a flat.

Walking home after lunch, Bertie trips up and is snatched from the path of an oncoming taxi by an unseen hand. It is Jeeves, who takes Bertie to recover over a whisky and soda at the Junior Ganymede. Jeeves reveals that Mr Winship has seven pages in the club book which, if the contents were known, would turn the voters of Market Snodsbury against him. It is vital that this information does not get out; Florence will hand him his hat if he does not win.

Bingley – formerly Brinkley, Bertie's relief valet in *Thank You, Jeeves* – arrives at the Junior Ganymede. He addresses Jeeves as 'Reggie' and acknowledges his former employer. Bingley has come into some money and is no longer in service, but remains a country member of the Junior Ganymede and lives in Market Snodsbury.

Bertie and Jeeves drive down to Brinkley Court with Ginger and Magnolia. Bertie takes a stroll in the garden and sees a camera. Fearing rain, he picks it up to take it into the house. At that moment, a stout individual wearing a Panama hat with a pink ribbon emerges from the bushes and asks what Bertie is doing with his camera. Later, through the French windows, Bertie hears the camera chap talking to Roderick Spode, Lord Sidcup, who says that Wooster was trying to steal the camera.

Aunt Dahlia has invited Spode to Brinkley Court so that he can make speeches supporting Winship in the election. Spode is a renowned orator; Ginger is not. Madeline Bassett is there to be near Spode and Florence is present to help her fiancé's campaign. Understandably, Uncle Tom has sought refuge in the South of France.

The camera chap is L. P. Runkle, owner of Runkle's Enterprises. He had employed Tuppy Glossop's late father, a research chemist who invented the headache pills Runkle's Magic Midgets. A popular hangover cure, they have made millions, but Tuppy received none of the money as an inheritance. Instead, it stayed with the company. Aunt Dahlia has invited Runkle to Brinkley Court, hoping that, after a few days of Anatole's cooking, he might hand over some of the proceeds to Tuppy so he can finally marry her daughter, Angela.

Madeline is happy with her betrothal to Spode and tells Bertie that he must be brave. A gnat flies into Madeline's eye. Bertie is fishing it out with his handkerchief when Spode comes in. He accuses Bertie of trying to win Madeline from him.

Early the next morning, Bertie goes out canvassing. The first house he visits belongs to Mrs McCorkadale, the opposing candidate. On his way out, Bertie meets Bingley entering. He says that Winship hasn't a chance and Bertie should bet on McCorkadale.

Mrs McCorkadale turns up at Brinkley Court. Bingley has tried to sell her the Junior Ganymede's book, which he has stolen, so she can use the information on Winship to wreck his campaign. She prides herself on fighting fair and sent Bingley away with a flea in his ear.

Aunt Dahlia is afraid that Bingley might sell the book to the *Market Snodsbury Argus-Reminder*, a local newspaper that opposes the Conservative Party. The damaging secret in the Junior Ganymede's book is that Ginger has done time – overnight in the cells for stealing policemen's helmets on Boat Race night.

When both Bertie and Aunt Dahlia fail to retrieve the Junior Ganymede's book, Jeeves goes to see Bingley and gets the book by the simple expedient of slipping him a Mickey Finn.

Aunt Dahlia decides that Runkle has been softened up enough by Anatole's cooking and goes to talk to him about Tuppy's inheritance. But Jeeves does not think she will be able to persuade him. Bingley, he knows, once worked for Runkle and found him to be a 'twenty-minute egg'.

Sent by Florence to get Harold, Bertie finds Ginger in the summer house in a passionate embrace with Magnolia. Ginger explains that he is in love with Magnolia and, to get Florence to break off their engagement, proposes to lose the election.

But thanks to a speech by Spode, the odds have now turned in Winship's favour. Madeline is now in tears. After the success of his speech, Spode plans to renounce his title and stand for the House of Commons. That means, if she marries him, Madeline will not be Lady Sidcup, but plain Mrs Spode. She has broken off her engagement, deciding once more to marry Bertie.

As her appeal to Runkle has fallen on deaf ears, Aunt Dahlia has pinched the porringer, an ornate silver ladle, he was trying to sell to Uncle Tom. She intends to return it to him in exchange for Tuppy's inheritance. Jeeves does not think this will work. The porringer sold at auction for just £9,000, while Aunt Dahlia was looking to get between £50,000 and £100,000 out of Runkle.

Bertie is delegated to return the porringer. But when he enters Runkle's room he finds him there and retreats still in possession of the stolen porringer. His suspicions aroused, Runkle finds the porringer gone, accuses Bertie of stealing it and calls the police.

Jeeves informs Bertie that the police will not be able to search his room without a warrant, so Bertie borrows Ginger's car and takes off for the day. As a result he misses the election debate. When he returns, he finds Ginger waiting in the drive. He wants his car back to drive Magnolia to London where they intend to marry. Ginger has egg in his hair.

Back at the house, Jeeves is tending to a housemaid who has been struck by a turnip. The debate had ended in uproar because Ginger announced he was going to vote for Mrs McCorkadale and advised the audience to do the same. The proceedings broke up in a shower of eggs and vegetables, and Florence broke off the engagement. The stratagem, of course, had been created by Jeeves.

Spode was hit in the eye by a potato. This convinced him not to renounce his peerage and stand for Parliament, so his engagement to Madeline is back on.

Florence appears covered in egg. She tells Bertie that she will now consent to be his wife. But Runkle intervenes, telling her that Bertie is going to spend a longish stretch in prison, and she changes her mind.

Bingley turns up to see Runkle. They are in cahoots. Bertie's bedroom is found open. Bingley has plainly broken into it and found the porringer. Aunt Dahlia offers to admit stealing the porringer to clear Bertie, but Bertie begs her not to. He would rather go to jail than be engaged to Florence again.

Runkle offers to drop the whole thing if he can have Anatole. Aunt Dahlia complains that this is blackmail. Jeeves disagrees and gives an example of blackmail: suppose you tried to obtain money by threatening to reveal that someone had served a long prison sentence in America for bribing a juror. The person in question is Runkle and the details were recorded in the Junior Ganymede club book by Bingley, along with details of Runkle's real estate fraud and the fact that he had jumped bail.

Tuppy gets his inheritance and Jeeves destroys the eighteen pages concerning Bertie in the Junior Ganymede's book. In the British version of the book, to this news, Bertie simply replies: 'Much obliged, Jeeves.'

In the American version, Jeeves explains that he has destroyed the pages concerning Bertie because he intends to stay on in his employ permanently. Bertie then asks why Jeeves would want to stay on with him when his superlative gifts must be in demand. Jeeves replies: 'There is a tie that binds, sir.'

Aunts Aren't Gentlemen (The Cat-nappers)
First published by Barrie & Jenkins in the UK in October 1974, Aunts Aren't Gentlemen appeared as The Cat-nappers published by Simon & Schuster in the US on 14 April 1975.

Bertie discovers that he has spots on his chest and goes to the doctor. On the way to Harley Street, he sees Vanessa Cook, a radiant beauty who once turned down his proposal, leading a demonstration. She is accompanied by Orlo J. Porter who Bertie knew from Oxford. There is a fracas. Orlo jumps into Bertie's car. As they make their getaway, Orlo explains he had socked a cop who was arresting the woman he loved – Vanessa Cook. When Bertie lets slip that he knows her, Orlo is instantly jealous.

Orlo and Vanessa are engaged, but cannot marry. Her father is the trustee of the money Orlo's Uncle Joe has left him and he will not hand it over to a communist. Deprived of funds, Orlo is making a living as an insurance salesman and, learning of Bertie's spots, sells him life cover.

In the waiting room in Harley Street, Bertie bumps into Major Plank (from *Stiff Upper Lip, Jeeves*). Malaria has left him absent-minded. All he can remember is that Bertie is called Al something.

The doctor says the spots are nothing to worry about, but recommends that Bertie go out to the countryside for fresh air and plenty of exercise.

Aunt Dahlia is going to stay with the Briscoes at Eggesford Hall in Maiden Eggesford, not far from the popular seaside resort of Bridmouth-on-Sea in Somerset. She says she will arrange a country cottage for Bertie there. Colonel James 'Jimmy' Briscoe has dozens. Bertie then has to break the news to Jeeves who had his heart set on going to New York. His consolation is that he has an aunt who lives in Maiden Eggesford and he visited frequently as a boy.

Maiden Eggesford is a quiet village, just what the doctor ordered, except Bertie spots Major Plank.

The following day, Bertie is invited to the Briscoes' for lunch at Eggesford Hall. Having been prescribed exercise, he decides to walk. Jeeves gives directions. Nevertheless, Bertie gets lost. When he sees a large house, he heads for it. On the way, he comes across a black-and-white cat and picks it up.

A small, red-faced man brandishing a hunting crop approaches. He accuses Bertie of trying to steal the cat. Then Major Plank appears and Bertie realizes that he is at Eggesford Court, rather than Eggesford Hall, and the man with the crop is the owner, Vanessa's father, Mr Cook. Plank suggests that Bertie stays for lunch as company for Vanessa who has been summoned home from the Slade for her revolutionary activities. When Bertie explains that he is lunching with the Briscoes at Eggesford Hall, Cook goes to call the police – and Bertie legs it.

Jeeves has learnt that there is bad blood between Mr Cook and Colonel Briscoe, who are both racehorse owners. The forthcoming race at Bridmouth-on-Sea is a duel between Cook's Potato Chip and Briscoe's Simla, and the presence of the stray cat is vital to Potato Chip's wellbeing.

Bertie goes on to lunch at Eggesford Hall where he meets the Colonel's niece, Angelica. But Bertie is not his usual outgoing self. After lunch he tells Aunt Dahlia that he is unsettled by the accusation of cat-napping.

Having heavily waded into the port after lunch, Bertie stops for a snooze on the way home. He is awoken by Orlo Porter, who complains that his snoring is disturbing a Clarkson's warbler – Orlo is a keen birdwatcher. Orlo then accuses Bertie of being a slimy serpent who has come to steal Vanessa away from him.

When Bertie gets back to the cottage, Vanessa turns up. She accuses him of following her. But she loves Orlo and no one else. Bertie tells her that he has just bumped into Orlo.

As Orlo must be staying in the Goose and Grasshopper – the only decent inn around – Bertie must go there and tell him to meet her at Bertie's cottage at three. Bertie does as he is told, addressing Orlo as Comrade, 'for there is never anything lost by being civil'.

While Bertie is out, he bumps into Angelica, who asks mysteriously: 'Has he brought it yet?'

Back at the cottage, Jeeves overhears Vanessa insisting that Orlo confront her father over his inheritance. Otherwise, he should steal the cat to use as a bargaining tool. Orlo refuses. She breaks off the engagement, then catches up with Bertie and tells him: 'I will be your wife.'

She dislikes the name Bertie and is going to call him Harold and he is to give up smoking and cocktails.

Then Angelica turns up at the cottage and says: 'Has he brought it yet?' She is followed by Aunt Dahlia, who says: 'Has he brought it yet?

'Brought what?' asks Bertie.

'The cat, of course, you poor dumb-bell.'

Aunt Dahlia has put a large bet on Simla. If she loses, it will upset Uncle Tom's digestion. So Angelica has arranged for local poacher Herbert 'Billy' Graham to steal the cat whose presence is essential to Potato Chip's equilibrium.

Jeeves then appears with the cat, which Billy Graham has just delivered. Then Plank arrives. He is still struggling to remember Bertie's name when he thinks he hears a cat. Bertie explains Jeeves passes the time imitating cats. The cat has disappeared from Cook's, says Plank, and he is thinking of calling Scotland Yard.

Rattled, Bertie insists that the cat must go back. Jeeves suggests that he hires Billy Graham to return it. Aunt Dahlia is outraged that Bertie has sent the cat back.

Orlo Porter phones and, according to Jeeves, makes proposals of a 'crudely surgical nature'. To draw Orlo's fangs, Jeeves reminds Bertie that Orlo has sold him insurance and his employers are hardly going to be pleased if he collects.

Jeeves then comes up with a plan to rid Bertie of Vanessa. To heal the rift between her and Orlo, he must encourage Orlo to confront her father over his inheritance. He should do this after dinner when Mr Cook is liable to be mellower. Meanwhile, Jeeves takes the night off to visit his aunt.

Graham returns, saying that he has taken the cat back, but it has followed him home. Bertie gives him another £10 to take the cat back again.

Vanessa returns, accompanied by a large dog. She brings him a slim volume called *The Prose Ramblings of a Rhymester*. When they are married, she says, he will give up his membership of the Drones.

Her father arrives and Vanessa flees through the kitchen. Plank has regained his memory and has named Bertie as the notorious crook, Alpine Joe. Clearly he is in the pay of Colonel Briscoe to steal the cat. Then Mr Cook sees the book that Vanessa has left and his hunting crop twitches.

Recalling how Gussie Fink-Nottle thwarted Roderick Spode in *The Code of the Woosters*, Bertie crowns Cook with an oil painting and then tangles him up in a tablecloth. After that, he goes to the Goose and Grasshopper to see Orlo. Bertie explains Jeeves's plan and they become bosom pals.

Aunt Dahlia phones. She had told Jimmy Briscoe about the cat ruse and, and being an honorable man, he threatened to scratch Simla if the cat was not returned. Bertie assures her the matter was in hand. But when she rings off, Graham appears from the kitchen and explains that when he came to collect the cat he found Mr Cook in such a temper that he did not dare return to Eggesford Court.

If Bertie does not return the cat Aunt Dahlia threatens to bar him from Anatole's cooking. So Bertie heads off in the dark and slips over in what he thinks is mud. The cat shoots from his arms. Then he bumps into Vanessa's dog, which starts barking. Two men approach. One pokes Bertie in the ribs with a shotgun. They march him up to the house to see Mr Cook, but the butler will not let them in because Bertie smells so bad. Instead, they lock him in the stables.

Bertie escapes, but falls in the swimming pool. He is joined there by Orlo, who has just been to see Mr Cook, with no success.

With Jeeves at his aunt's, Bertie has breakfast the following morning in the Goose and Grasshopper. Orlo is waiting for Vanessa. Impressed that Orlo had the courage to confront her father, she steals daddy's Bentley so they can elope.

Vanessa has left a note for her father. Orlo has also written a letter for Mr Cook which he gives to Bertie to deliver. But when Bertie gets home, he is confronted by Cook and Major Plank. They are there to prevent him eloping with Vanessa.

Cook brandishes his daughter's letter. In it, she says that she is going away with the man she loves. Bertie explains that he is not the man she loves, Orlo is. To prove it, Bertie produces Orlo's letter.

Cook apologizes, but then the cat strolls in. They tie Bertie up so that Cook can take the cat back to the stables while Plank fetches the police. Jeeves returns and, expressing no surprise, unties Bertie.

Plank returns. Unable to find a policeman, he is delighted to see Inspector Witherspoon there. Jeeves denies being Inspector Witherspoon. He says he is Mr Wooster's account-ant and his client has sufficient funds not to go around selling stolen statuettes for £5 or stealing cats. Plank must have a touch of the sun and is hallucinating.

Jeeves's aunt has lost her cat that answers the description of the one from Eggesford Court. Bertie and Jeeves agree to lease the cat to Cook until the race is over, provided he gives Orlo his inheritance.

In New York, Bertie receives a letter from Uncle Tom. Celebrating her winnings, Aunt Dahlia fell over and injured her wrist. An enclosed cutting explains that, nearing the finish, Simla was ahead of Potato Chip by a full length when a cat ran across the course, causing him to shy and unseat the jockey. As the cat belonged to Mr Cook, the race was awarded to Colonel Briscoe.

Both Jeeves and Wooster decide that New York is much more restful than Maiden Eggesford. There are no aunts there.

5

BERTRAM WILBERFORCE WOOSTER

Bertram Wilberforce Wooster is the son of unnamed parents. He comes from an old and noble family. Bertie says that the Woosters 'came over with the Conqueror and were extremely pally with him'. They also did their bit in the Crusades. One Wooster 'would have won the Battle of Joppa single-handed, if he hadn't fallen off his horse'. They 'did dashed well at the Battle of Crécy' in 1346 and Sieur de Wooster was at the Battle of Agincourt in 1415. He makes references to some old Puritan strain in the Wooster blood – though, despite not having a title, one would have thought his forebears would have been Royalists. A Wooster also saw service during the Peninsular War – 'Wellington used to say he was the best spy he had,' according to Aunt Dahlia.

In 'Jeeves and the Kid Clementina', Bertie mentions that his mother thought him intelligent, but that is only in riposte to Jeeves remarking that his own mother thought him intelligent when Bertie asks him if he were brilliant as a boy. When he was about seven, Bertie says his mother used to praise him for his recitation of Tennyson's 'The Charge of the Light Brigade', though he practically always fluffed his lines.

Bertie's father was a good friend of Lord Wickhammersley, according to 'The Great Sermon Handicap'. He is mentioned again in *Much Obliged, Jeeves* (*Jeeves and the Tie that Binds*) where it is revealed that, the day before Bertie's christening, his father won a packet on an outsider in the Grand National and insisted dubbing the child 'Wilberforce' to carry on the name.

Throughout the period covered by the books, though, Bertie is parentless. He does have a sister, a Mrs Scholfield who lives with her three daughters in India. She is supposed to be returning home in 'Bertie Changes His Mind', but must have changed her mind as she makes no appearance. There is, of course, a large extended family consisting of at least four aunts, up to fourteen uncles and some eight cousins. Bertie does not intend to reproduce though. In *Joy in the Morning*, he describes himself as 'the Last of the Woosters'.

Bertie's money comes from his Uncle Willoughby of Easeby Hall in Shropshire on whom, he says in 'Jeeves Takes Charge', he is 'more or less dependent'. There is no further mention of Uncle Willoughby and it is assumed that he has died, leaving Bertram his fortune. However, Uncle Willoughby may simply have been a trustee and, when Bertie took control of his money at the age of twenty-five, he took a back seat. Bertie is certainly free with his money and in *Jeeves and the Feudal Spirit* (*Bertie Wooster Sees it Through*) he says that he was 'stagnant with the stuff'. There is certainly enough for him to travel freely back and forth across the Atlantic, indeed around the world. Hotels bills, renting country cottages and paying for large apartments in both New York and London are not a problem. Number 6A Crichton

Mansions, Berkeley Street, and 3a Berkeley Mansions, Berkeley Square, are two of the London addresses he gives. Both are in upmarket Mayfair. Bertie is so unworldly that he is quite shocked when he discovers that others in his circle are short of cash.

He can also afford to run a car – a Widgeon Seven. They seem to be a popular model. Gwladys Pendlebury has a red one in 'Jeeves and the Spot of Art'. It is a two-seater with a dickey or rumble seat at the back, just large enough to accommodate Jeeves in 'Jeeves and the Old School Chum'. He keeps it in a garage near his flat where other vehicles are available. When Bertie takes Biffy, Sir Roderick and Jeeves to the British Empire Exhibition at Wembley, they need a four-seater and Jeeves says: 'The grey cheviot lounge will, I fancy, be suitable.'

Jeeves and Wooster are not in a two-seater then they give Peggy Mainwaring a lift back to school in 'Bertie Changes His Mind'. She says the car is a Sunbeam and they do not contradict her. Later, after his speech, he leaps into the tonneau – the rear seating compartment of the car – and covers himself with the rug. This is clearly not a dickey.

Bertie knows nothing of what goes on under the hood of a car. In *Much Obliged, Jeeves*, Ginger gives him a lift because his own sports model is 'at the vet's with some nervous ailment'. His talents, he says, are limited to 'twisting the wheel and tooting the tooter'. And he is not so good at that. On their way back from Wembley, when Jeeves drops the bombshell that Mabel, Biffy's intended, is his niece, there is nearly a collision.

'If I might make a suggestion, sir,' says Jeeves. 'I should not jerk the steering-wheel with quite such suddenness. We very nearly collided with that omnibus.'

Bertie has certainly never had a job. In 'The Great Sermon Handicap', he is a little concerned that Lady Cynthia

Wickhammersley, who was pretty and attractive, was the 'sort of girl who would want a fellow to carve out a career and what not'. Of course, he once wrote a piece on 'What the Well-Dressed Man is Wearing' for the 'Husbands and Brothers' page of *Milady's Boudoir* and found this hard work, 'taxing the physique to the utmost'. Although he disparages authors, he is, in fictional terms, the author of all the Jeeves and Wooster stories, except for 'Bertie Changes His Mind', which is supplied by Jeeves (how dare Jeeves be so familiar) and *Ring for Jeeves* (*The Return of Jeeves*), which is in the third person. His literary output is truly remarkable given that, at school, for English composition, his report usually read: 'Has little or no ability, but does his best.' Over the course of the years, of course, he has picked up a vocabulary of sorts from Jeeves. He claims that he is not nearly so hot at drawing a word-picture as his valet. But when comparing their literary output, Bertie's prose is much the more vivid.

Plainly Bertie is not cut out for work. When Jeeves dismisses him as mentally negligible, Pauline Stoker echoes the sentiment. Most see him merely as chump. Aunt Agatha, always his severest critic, says he had a brain the size of a peahen. She describes him as 'barely sentient' and says she often wonders if the best thing would be to put him in a home of some kind. Elsewhere she says he is a vapid and unreflective nitwit who should have been put in a mental home and, most damning off all, a 'guffin' – something Lady Wickham also calls him, along with a 'gaby'. Even the beloved Aunt Dahlia admits calling him 'a brainless poop who ought to be given a scholarship at some good lunatic asylum'. On another occasion, she says: 'It's simply because I am fond of you and have influence with the Lunacy Commissioners that you weren't put in a padded cell years ago.' However, Jeeves also notes that his employer is pleasant and amiable, and it is generally agreed that he has a heart of gold. After all, the code of the Woosters is 'never let a pal down'. Bertie himself admits that, during the day he is pretty much a total loss, 'but plunge the world in darkness, switch on the soft lights, uncork the champagne and shove a dinner into him, and you'd be surprised'.

As a child Bertie had a nurse. At the age of six, he gave her a 'juicy over the top-knot with a porringer'. He stayed with Nurse Hogg in Basingstoke, in a semi-detached villa called Balmoral. She, apparently, suffered from hiccups. At some point he attended dance classes with Corky Pirbright. He had worn a Little Lord Fauntleroy suit and was covered in pimples.

Bertie then went, possibly, to two prep schools where he won a prize for the best collection of wild flowers and the Scripture Knowledge prize, an accolade that he mentions repeatedly. His only other claim to fame is that, at the age of fourteen, he won the Choir Boys' Handicap cycle race after being given a half-lap start. Even then the odds-on favourite was scratched when his elder brother repossessed his bike.

At Malvern House, he spent four years under the Reverend Aubrey Upjohn. One of Wooster's formative experiences was sneaking down to the Reverend Upjohn's study to steal the biscuits he kept in a tin on his desk, only to be confronted by the pedagogue himself. This earned him six of the best. On other occasions, he was sent for after morning prayers. Perhaps some of it was deserved. Looking back on his own childhood when he sees Mr Anstruther dozing in a deckchair in 'Jeeves and the Love that Purifies', Bertie says that he could never resist the spectacle of an old gentleman asleep in a deckchair. He would have done something to him, no matter what the cost – probably with a pea-shooter. At prep school, he admits putting sherbet in the ink. Earlier, at his dance class, admittedly at the bidding of Corky Pirbright, he threw a mildewed orange at the teacher. Then, as a stripling, he was told off by Aunt Agatha for breaking a valuable china vase with a catapult and, at the age of fifteen, Lord Worplesdon caught him smoking one of his special cigars in the stable yard and chased him for a mile across difficult country with a hunting-crop.

According to the Reverend Upjohn, at school Bertie was called 'Bungling Wooster' – if there as a chair in a room, he would fall over it. However, according to Gussie Fink-Nottle, he was called 'Daredevil Bertie' by the boys.

Bertie was not happy at prep school. The food was 'garbage' – boiled mutton with caper sauce and margarine. On Sundays, they got sausages made 'not from contented pigs but from pigs which had expired, regretted by all, of glanders, botts and tuberculosis'. However, Uncle Tom used to send him postal orders sometimes for as much as ten shillings (50p).

Wooster then went on to Eton and Oxford. He says that he went to Magdalen College where, after getting well oiled on bump-supper nights, he would ride a bicycle naked around the quadrangle, singing comic songs. He does not say what he read at Oxford, though there is speculation that it was French as he lards the text with French words and phrases that are spelt and, by and large, used correctly. He does mention the sports he participated in, though. He got a Blue partnering Harold 'Beefy' Anstruther at rackets. He also rowed; Stilton Cheesewright was his coach. There is speculation that he even got into Magdalen's first eight.

His interest in sport did not end when he came down from Oxford. At the Drones, he played squash, darts – a runner up in tournaments in both disciplines – snooker-pool and golf, with a handicap of sixteen. Elsewhere he plays tennis. Though he knows about bridge, he is far happier spending 'a restful afternoon throwing cards into a top-hat with some of the better element'. In his younger days he had been 'pretty hot stuff' at tiddlywinks and is indignant when Aunt Dahlia says that she let him beat her.

There is a swimming pool at the Drones, but Bertie does not seem to use it apart from the occasion when Tuppy Glossop bet him that he could not swing himself across the pool in full evening dress by the ropes and rings, and then looped the last ring back leaving him with no alternative but to drop in the water. He swims in the river in *Joy in the Morning*; he rides, but does not hunt, and he shoots well enough to be invited on a shooting party in Norfolk but, with both Mortimer Little and Rosie M. Banks after him in 'Bingo and the Little Woman', he was so dashed jumpy he couldn't hit a thing. In *How Right You Are, Jeeves (Jeeves in the Offing)*, Bobbie Wickham ways he is in training for the Jerk the Cucumber Sandwich event at the next Olympic Games. His favourite sport, though, is horse racing. But when it comes to betting he is bested by Jeeves.

All this exercise seems to have been effective. Despite the amount he eats and drinks, he remains tall, willowy and sylphlike. In 'Comrade Bingo', Bingo Little describes him as 'the tall, thin one with the face like a motor mascot', while Bertie described himself as a man of slender physique. Percy Gorringe calls him a 'weedy butterfly' in *Jeeves and the Feudal Spirit*. He has ghastly taste in clothes, but he is elegantly turned out, thanks to Jeeves. Twice he grows a moustache – his David Niven found favour with Florence Craye – but on both occasions, Jeeves makes him shave it off. There is also one reference to him wearing a monocle. In 'Jeeves and the Spot of Art', Gwladys Pendlebury paints his portrait, which is then used in an advertising campaign for Slingsby's Superb Soup and Bertie returns from Paris to see a poster showing him slavering through a monocle about six inches in circumference at a plateful of soup.

His taste in reading is confined to mysteries, thrillers and detective novels. There are mentions of Erle Stanley Gardner, Agatha Christie and Poirot. He is clear that he is familiar with the work of Sir Arthur Conan Doyle. Bertie sees himself and Jeeves as a Sherlock Holmes–Dr Watson team though he never clearly states which he thinks is which. He makes several references to the 'Secret Nine', but cannot have been a fan of Enid Blyton whose Secret Seven series did not start until 1949.

Bertie also reads the newspapers – the *Mirror*, *Mail*, *Morning Post*, various evening papers and the *Sporting Times*. He does not read the business pages nor is he much concerned about the news. Occasionally he borrows Jeeves's *Times* to do the crossword and has been known to attempt the crossword in the *Telegraph*. He has a pleasant light baritone voice, which he exercises in the bath and, occasionally, on the public stage. He can also play the piano with one finger and makes a serious attempt to master the banjolele. He also goes out dancing. In 'The Metropolitan Touch', Bertie has been at the Embassy swinging 'a practically non-stop shoe from shortly after dinner until two a.m.' and claims to be able to 'out-Fred the nimblest Astaire'.

The Jeeves and Wooster saga begins when Bertie is twenty-four. In 'Jeeves Takes Charge' he recounts how he first took Jeeves on at the time when he was still dependent on Uncle Willoughby. There he recalls the incident of Lord Worplesdon chasing him with a hunting-crop when he was fifteen which, he says, occurred nine years before. In the stories, Bertie passes four Christmases in England and, according to 'Jeeves and the Unbidden Guest', he spent more than a year in America. So the saga ends when he is about twenty-nine. Other ages and time lapses in the books concur with that. The period covered could certainly not have been much more than five years as Bertie and the other characters, especially the troublesome young boys, do not seem to age significantly. In *How Right You Are, Jeeves* (*Jeeves in the Offing*), one of the later novels, Bertie says that he has not seen the Reverend Upjohn for fifteen years. If he went to Eton at thirteen or fourteen, that would be about right.

However, it is possible to spot all sorts of anachronisms. Mussolini and Stalin, both of whom are mentioned, did not come to power until 1922, seven years after the first Jeeves and Wooster story was written. There are mentions of Al Capone, Ernest Hemingway, Bing Crosby, Betty Grable, Dorothy Lamour, Jennifer Jones, Hedda Hopper, Rodgers and Hammerstein, Ernie Bevin, Stafford Cripps and Billy Graham, all of whom did not come to prominence until much later. The combination 'lend-lease', which appears in *Aunts Aren't Gentlemen*, was not used until 1941. *Lost Week-End*, which is mentioned in *The Mating Season*, did not appear as a novel until 1944 and as a film until the following year. Then there is *Ring for Jeeves* (*The Return of Jeeves*), which is set in the early 1950s. A middle-aged Bertie does not appear but we learn that he is still alive and well. Jeeves, now butler to Lord Rowcester, has changed little, apart from being much more garrulous.

Thanks to Anatole, Bertie is something of a gastronome. He is much more at home lunching at the Ritz or Claridge's than at the tea-and-bun shop Bingo takes him to in 'Jeeves in the Springtime' where the only thing he can face is a roll and butter and a small coffee. Usually, though, he lunches, if not at home, at his club. The usual hour for lunch is one-thirty, but he can hardly have been hungry. After a rousing cup of tea or one of Jeeves's prairie oysters at some time after ten, he tucks into a substantial fried breakfast or kippers. He has luncheon and dinner of at least three courses, and usually there is afternoon tea, if not supper, thrown in. Then there is his drinking.

Aunt Dahlia thinks that Bertie never stops drinking, even when he is asleep. Bertie complains this is unfair.

'Except at times of special revelry, I am exceedingly moderate in my potations,' he says. 'A brace of cocktails, a glass of wine at dinner and possibly a liqueur with the coffee – that is Bertram Wooster.'

On another occasion, he claims that some people call him 'One Martini Wooster'. He underestimates. Every evening, Jeeves can be relied to be on hand with a whisky and soda and, at times of stress, brandy and a splash. There seem to be plenty of special revelries, especially at the Drones. Then there is Boat Race night – 'Then, if ever, you will see Bertram under the influence,' he says in 'Without the Option'.

However, there are only four recorded incidents where Bertie needs one of Jeeves's pick-me-ups and there are always extenuating circumstances. The first occurs when Bertie first encounters Jeeves – indeed, it is the reason he hired him. The night before, he said, he has been present at 'a rather cheery supper'. But he was under pressure. Florence Craye was trying to make him read *Types of Ethical Theory* and his former valet Meadowes has been stealing his socks. When Jeeves arrives and says he is a valet, Bertie says he would have preferred an undertaker.

The second is after the Boat Race night, where he gets fined a fiver and Sippy gets sent down. He certainly needs one after Pongo Twistleton's birthday party and Aunt Dahlia tells him he is supposed to hand out the prizes at Market Snodsbury Grammar School. The night before he had mistaken a standard lamp for a burglar. The fourth is required after celebrating Gussie Fink-Nottle's betrothal to Madeline Bassett at the Drones.

He was drunk on several occasions at Oxford. On one occasion he got so drunk he insisted that he was a mermaid and wanted to dive into the college fountain and play the harp there. This has convinced some scholars that Wooster was at Christ Church as Magdalen does not have a fountain. But he could have been visiting.

In 'Jeeves and the Spot of Art', when he drops into Drones for a refresher, he says he seldom drinks in the morning. However, in *Joy in the Morning*, he goes to the Bollinger Bar in Bond Street after his brush with Florence Craye in the bookstore and, in 'Extricating Young Gussie', when first arriving in New York he has a couple of 'lightning whizzers' first thing. He visits a pub before singing 'Sonny Boy' in 'Jeeves and the Song of Songs'; enters another to suss out the opposition in 'Tuppy Changes His Mind' ('The Ordeal of Young Tuppy') and repairs to the Goose and Cowslip in *The Mating Season* when he has forgotten the words to the Christopher Robin poems he is supposed to recite.

Fortifying himself at lunch before attempting to dowse Sippy's old headmaster with flour, he has a 'nicely balanced meal, preceded by a couple of dry Martinis, washed down with half a bot. of nice light, dry champagne, and followed by a spot of brandy'. Before lunching with Lord Yaxley and former barmaid Maudie, Bertie produces the near lethal cocktail consisting of 'Martini with a spot of absinthe'. It is not recorded whether these are Jeeves's 'specials' that he has instead of Martinis to brace himself before having dinner with the Trotters. Normally, he limits himself to two cocktails.

With his brandy after dinner he would smoke a cigar. At other times he would smoke a thoughtful cigarette. There is also an allusion to a twelve-inch cigarette holder.

There have been attempts to make out that there is a homosexual relationship between Jeeves and Wooster. However, Bertie has been interested in girls from a young age. At fourteen he wrote to Marie Lloyd for her autograph, he admits in 'The Love that Purifies', 'but apart from that my private life could bear the strictest investigation'. This may not be entirely true. In the original version of 'Leave it to Jeeves', which appeared in *My Man Jeeves* in 1919, Bertie says: 'Goodness knows there was fuss enough in our family when I tried to marry into musical comedy a few years ago.' This was excised from the version that appeared as 'The Artistic Career of Corky' in *Carry on, Jeeves!* in 1925.

Bertie considers himself to be a man of chilled steel, though he is wax in the hands of the opposite sex. He appears to have been engaged some twenty times, but he is usually trying to get out of it rather than pushing on towards marriage. Jeeves describes Wooster as 'essentially one of Nature's bachelors'. But then he had a vested interest. He makes it a rule not to serve in the household of married men. As Aunt Dahlia says: 'I won't believe you're married till I see the bishop and assistant clergy mopping their foreheads and saying: "Well, that's that. We've really got the blighter off at last."'

However, Bertie is not inured to the charms of the fairer sex. He finds Lady Cynthia Wickhammersley 'dashed pretty and lively and attractive'. He was in love with her until he surmised that she was the sort of girl that would want a fellow to carve out a career. And in *The Mating Season* he notes that Cora Pirbright is 'gowned in some clinging material which accentuated rather than hid her graceful outlines, if you know what I mean'.

Even Florence Craye is handsome, with a terrific profile and 'might, so far as looks are concerned, be the star unit of the harem of one of the better-class Sultans'. She was also 'well equipped to take to the office as a pin-up girl'. Bertie knows about harems and pin-ups.

True, Bertie is not a Bingo Little who, before he marries Rosie M. Banks, falls in love with practically every young woman he sees and is so warm-hearted that he should have worn an asbestos vest. Nor is he a Freddie Widgeon of whom it was said that, if all the girls he had loved and lost were laid end to end, they would have reached halfway down Piccadilly – or further as some of them were pretty tall.

Nevertheless, Bertie considers Bingo Little's waitress Mabel in 'Jeeves in the Springtime' as 'rather a pretty girl'. The parlourmaid who tries to get him arrested when he attempts to steal the cylinder from Rosie Little's dictating machine in 'Clustering Round Young Bingo' is 'not a bad looking girl'. Mary, the parlourmaid in *Thank You, Jeeves*, is 'full of sex appeal'. Then there is Angelica Briscoe in *Aunts Aren't Gentlemen* who is 'a very personable wench with whom, had I not been preoccupied, I should probably have fallen in love'. Once he told Gussie Fink-Nottle that he had got engaged three times at Brinkley Court alone – though 'no business resulted, but the fact remains'.

Bertie tells the reader repeatedly that he is a *preux chevalier* – a valiant knight. He prides himself on his chivalrous attitude to women. While 'girls never make sense', he is careful not to bandy their names around. He learnt this gallant code from an early age. Although at six, he hit his nurse with a porringer, 'the lapse was merely a temporary one. Since then, though few men have been more sorely tried by the sex, I have never raised a hand against a woman.'

This is not entirely true. At his dance class he once forgot himself to the extent of socking Corky Pirbright on the topknot with a wooden dumb-bell, but 'I had always regretted the unpleasant affair, considering my action a blot on an otherwise stainless record'.

As a child, he nearly let 'a revered aunt have it on the side of the head with a *papier mâché* elephant'. Aunt Dahlia gets rapped on the topknot with a paper knife of oriental design in *Much Obliged, Jeeves* (*Jeeves and the Tie that Binds*). Bertie contemplates taking a cosh to Aunt Agatha in *The Mating Season*. And in *How Right You Are, Jeeves* (*Jeeves in the Offing*) he has to remind himself that 'an English gentleman does not slosh a sitting redhead' – Bobbie Wickham – 'no matter what the provocation'.

He is always ready to ride to the rescue of a damsel in

distress – 'I don't suppose there is a man in the W1 postal district of London more readily moved by a woman's grief than myself,' he says in *The Code of the Woosters*. And in 'Aunt Agatha Takes the Count', he springs to the defence of the chambermaid Aunt Agatha has accused of stealing her pearls, one of the few occasions he is prepared to stand up to the harridan.

Bertie is particularly quick to intervene in the matter of a broken heart. When Stiffy Byng is in tears after breaking off her engagement to Stinker Pinker, Bertie 'ached with sympathy with her distress' even though she was capable of 'doing something which even by female standards was raw'. Whenever his cousin Angela and Tuppy Glossop split up, he rushes to mend the rift – as he does when Gussie Fink-Nottle and Madeline Bassett part, but there is self interest there. If she is not engaged to Gussie, she is certain to turn her matrimonial sights on Bertie.

He even sympathizes with Madeline Bassett's brokenhearted friend Hilda Gudgeon in *The Mating Season*, even though he does not know her. Although he is hiding behind the sofa in her den, he says he 'mourned for her distress, and had circumstances been different, might have reached up and patted her on the head'.

Indeed, he is so gracious to women that, when Madeline Bassett, Florence Craye and Vanessa Cook consent, unbidden, to be his wife, he is too polite to say no. He considers himself to be a reputable bachelor who has never had his licence so much as endorsed and prides himself in his scrupulous delicacy in his relations with the other sex. Pauline Stoker learnt this for herself. When she turns up in his bed in Chuffnell Regis, even though they had once been engaged and, presumably, found each other attractive, Bertie does nothing to take advantage of the situation. He merely remarks: 'The attitude of fellows towards finding girls in their bedroom shortly after midnight varies. Some like it. Some don't. I didn't. I suppose it's some old Puritan strain in the Wooster blood.'

Then in *Jeeves and the Feudal Spirit* (*Bertie Wooster Sees it Through*), he climbs by mistake into the bedroom of Florence Craye, freshly sundered from Stilton Cheesewright, again, and finds her sitting up in bed in a pink boudoir cap (there is no mention of a nightdress; perhaps Bertie didn't notice). When she says she supposed that he had come to kiss her softly while she slept, he leaps six inches in the direction of the ceiling and knocks over a chair. He does not like it thought that he is the type of fellow who deliberately shins up ladders at one in the morning in order to kiss girls while they sleep.

They have a long conversation, which embraces a novel that he is reading, suggestively titled *The Mystery of the Pink Crayfish*. This seems to have an effect, on Florence at least. He notices a shudder run though her slender figure that is more or less hidden beneath the bedclothes. 'Oh, Bertie,' she says. It is only when Stilton Cheesewright knocks on the door that she reaches for a dressing gown. But that's as hot as it gets.

Despite getting engaged numerous times, he seldom even kisses a girl. When he got engaged, briefly, to Pauline Stoker he never reached that consummation because 'a waiter came into the room with a tray of beef sandwiches and the moment passed'. For the remainder of the two days of their engagement he was in bed with a nasty cold. However, he always looks upon Pauline as one of the nicest girls to whom he has been engaged. Indeed, in *Thank You, Jeeves*, Bertie kisses her in the garden, but only to make her boyfriend Lord Chuffnell jealous.

'It wasn't one of my best,' he admits, 'but it was a kiss within the meaning of the act.'

During the bedroom scene with Florence at Brinkley Court, he kisses her, but only because she has asked him to and 'one has to be civil'.

'I didn't like the general trend of affairs,' he remarks, 'the whole thing seeming to me to be becoming far too French.' This is an expression Bertie uses again in *How Right You Are, Jeeves* (*Jeeves in the Offing*) when Kipper Herring reports kissing Phyllis Mills.

Then when Bertie broke out of the clinch with Florence, he finds her regarding him in the way a governess regards a new pupil.

Bertie even kisses, horror of horrors, Honoria Glossop, but only in an attempt to make her boyfriend Blair Eggleston jealous and thus promote the romance between Sir Roderick and Lady Chuffnell. It seems that Bertie is happier playing with toy ducks in the bath, as he does in *Right Ho, Jeeves*.

6

JEEVES

In *Bring on the Girls*, Wodehouse suggests that Jeeves was based on the butler Eugene Robinson, whom Wodehouse once described as a 'walking *Encyclopaedia Britannica*'. However, Robinson worked at the house in Norfolk Street and Wodehouse did not move there until 1927, long after the birth of Jeeves. His fiction had long been peppered with valets and butlers. Indeed, Wodehouse tells of a perfect manservant called Jevons in the story 'Creature of Impulse', which appeared in the October 1914 issue of the *Strand Magazine*.

In a letter written in 1960, Wodehouse explained the origin of the name Jeeves: 'I was watching a county match on the Cheltenham ground before the first war, and one of the Gloucester bowlers was called Jeeves. I suppose the name stuck, and I named Jeeves after him.' This is thought to be the Warwickshire bowler Percy Jeeves who died at the Battle of the Somme in 1916.

Since then Jeeves has achieved the ultimate accolade: his

own entry in the *Oxford English Dictionary*, where he is 'the perfect valet, used allusively'. 'Jeevesian' and 'Jeeves-like' also appear. Wooster also appears in the *OED*, but he is not in *Debrett's*.

Jeeves does not get a first name until *Much Obliged, Jeeves* (*Jeeves and the Tie that Binds*) in 1971 when Bingley – formerly Brinkley, Moscow's finest from *Thank You, Jeeves* – addresses him as 'Reggie'. Bertie is stunned by the revelation, 'It had never occurred to me before that he had a first name,' he says. Then Bertie speculates how embarrassing it would have been if he had also been called 'Bertie'.

In 'Jeeves and the Kid Clementina', Jeeves refers to himself as a 'gentleman's personal gentleman'. This means that he is there to take care of his master's personal needs, not wait on a household. However, in *Stiff Upper Lip, Jeeves*, Bertie says: 'If the call comes, he can buttle with the best of them.' Indeed, Bertie often lends Jeeves out as a butler, if needs be. His motto is 'Resource and tact'. He sees himself as a thane and vassal, and the word 'feudal' is offered as a compliment for his loyalty.

Jeeves's origins are obscure. We learn that his mother thought him intelligent. His parents must have been reasonably well off as he was privately educated. He was obviously at some top-notch establishment as he quotes freely from Lucretius, Pliny the Younger, Whittier, Fitzgerald, Pater, Shelley, Kipling, Keats, Scott, Wordsworth, Emerson, Marcus Aurelius, Shakespeare, Browning, Moore, Virgil, Horace, Dickens, Tennyson, Milton, Henley, the Bible, Stevenson, Gray, Burns, Byron, Longfellow, Rossetti and Rosie M. Banks. For relaxation he reads Spinoza, Dostoevsky and the great Russian novelists. Nietzsche he believes to be 'fundamentally unsound'. And in 'Bertie Changes His Mind', he finds the opinions of Professor Mainwaring, author of a well-known series of philosophical treatises, 'somewhat empirical'. He exhibits a broad knowledge of science and politics, and can type and take shorthand. The one thing he does not know about is rugby football, but soon gets up to speed in *Stiff Upper Lip, Jeeves*.

In *Stiff Upper Lip, Jeeves*, he says he rarely attends cinematographic performances. However, the plot of 'Fixing it for Freddie' depends on Jeeves having seen the mawkish film, *Tiny Hands*.

His education has led him to be punctilious in the use of the English language. As well as offering Bertie suitable literary quotations, he frequently corrects his solecisms. Their different approach to the tongue can be seen in an exchange in 'Leave it to Jeeves' ('The Artistic Career of Corky'):

> 'The scheme I would suggest cannot fail of success, but it has what may seem to you a drawback, sir, in that it requires a certain financial outlay.'
>
> 'He means,' I translated to Corky, 'that he has got a pippin of an idea, but it's going to cost a bit.'

However, Jeeves's remarks are usually confined to 'Yes, sir', 'No, sir', 'Indeed, sir', 'Thank you, sir', 'Very good, sir', 'Perfectly, sir', 'Unsuitable, sir', 'Too ornate, sir', 'I beg your pardon, sir', 'Most disturbing, sir' and 'Will that be all, sir?'

Like Bertie, Jeeves has an extended family – at least three aunts, two uncles, several cousins and a niece. Aunt Annie is the peacemaker of the family who is called in at times of domestic disagreement. Aunt Emily is interested in psychical research and there is a Mrs P. B. Pigott, but all we know of her is that her address is Balmoral, Mafeking Road, Maiden Eggesford, and that she owns a cat. Then there are various other mentions of aunts. One paid five shillings to improve her social standing by having a moving-picture actor over for tea. An aunt obtained considerable relief from applying

Walkinshaw's Supreme Ointment to her swollen lower limbs, sent an unsolicited testimonial and took pride in seeing her photograph in the paper. This may be the same aunt as the one who lives in south-east London. Her swollen lower limbs would explain her passion for taxi-cabs. One has almost a complete set of Rosie M. Banks novels, though she cannot, surely, be the same one who read Oliver Wendell Holmes's poem, 'The Organ Grinders', to Jeeves when he was a child.

Jeeves's Uncle Charlie is Silversmith, the butler at Deverill Hall, so his daughter Queenie is Jeeves's cousin. Uncle Cyril told him the tale of two men on a tandem named Nicholls and Jackson who had an unfortunate accident with a brewer's van. It was impossible to know which bit belonged to Nicholls and which to Jackson, so the parts were collected and buried together as Nixon. Bertie thinks a lot about this cheery little anecdote as he cycles through the night in *Right Ho, Jeeves* (*Brinkley Manor*). He is glad to learn that Cyril is dead. One or other of these uncles – or a third, possibly – appears to have been wild as a youth.

Jeeves has always been fond of this cousin Egbert, who is the local bobby in Beckley-on-the-Moor, and he once spent some months studying jewellery under the auspices of another cousin. A cousin George appears in *Right Ho, Jeeves*, but – as so often – we get to learn little about him because Bertie cuts Jeeves off. Then there is his niece Mabel whom Biffy gets engaged to in 'The Rummy Affair of Old Biffy'.

Though unmarried, Jeeves has an eye for the ladies. In 'Jeeves in the Springtime', Jeeves has an 'understanding' with Mortimer Little's cook, Jane Watson. He contrives to get her married off so that he can move in on Bingo's Mabel, though as she had bought Bingo Little a crimson satin tie decorated with horseshoes it is hard to see what he saw in her. He also has enough of an eye for the ladies to judge a bathing-belles contest. The young ladies that attract his attention are from Brixton, Tulse Hill and Penge, all of which are in south-east

London, an area for which Jeeves seems to have a particular affinity. Indeed, in his nineties, Wodehouse wrote the lyrics for a Jeeves and Wooster musical comedy called *Betting on Bertie* and gave Jeeves a solo in which we learn that he hails from Brixton and longs to return there.

Jeeves both drinks and smokes. In *The Mating Season*, he shares a drink with Bertie in the Goose and Cowslip, and in *Thank You, Jeeves*, when Bertie asks him for a cigarette, he says: 'Turkish or Virginia, sir?' His only other vice is playing bridge at the Junior Ganymede club. He is prepared to bend, if not break, the rules there. According to rule eleven, all members are to enter into the club book information regarding their employer – an archive amassed over eighty years – but they are not allowed to pass that information on to non-members. Jeeves tells both Bertie and Aunt Dahlia about Roderick Spode's involvement in the lingerie business. Further, the eleven pages in the book in *Jeeves and the Feudal Spirit* that have swelled to eighteen pages by *Much Obliged, Jeeves*, presumably by Jeeves own hand, are destroyed by Jeeves by the end of the tale. This, we can only assume, ends his membership of the club. However, throughout the saga Jeeves has his own intelligence network: the staff of various members of the aristocracy who can be relied on to relate their masters' secrets.

After leaving his private school, Jeeves was plunged straight into service as a pageboy in a school for young ladies. He then 'dabbled to a certain extent' in the First World War. Before he fetched up on Bertie's doorstep, he had a rich and varied career. He worked for Lord Worplesdon, but left when he did not see eye-to-eye with his lordship who dined in dress trousers, a flannel shirt and a shooting coat. He was also in the service of the financier Mr Montague-Todd, who was in the second year of his sentence in 'Bertie Changes His Mind'. Then there was Lord Brancaster who, to overcome the lethargy suffered by his pet parrot, fed the bird seed cake steeped in '84 port. The parrot then bit his thumb, sang a sea shanty and lay on its back on the bottom of its cage for some time. Jeeves worked for Lord Bridgeworth, who marketed his patented depilatory as Hair-o and was elevated to the peerage for his services to the Party. Shortly before he entered Bertie's service, Jeeves also worked for Lord Frederick Ranelagh who was ripped off by Soapy Sid and Aline Hemmingway.

When he quits Bertie's service over the banjolele, Jeeves is quickly snapped up by Lord Chuffnell and then takes employment with J. Washburn Stoker to advance his employer's affair with Pauline. Quite how loyal he is to his new employer, it is hard to tell. He sends Pauline Stoker to her ex-lover Bertie in a swimsuit at night and she ends up in his bed. She was supposed to be lying low there to pick up some clothes, but what clothes is Bertie supposed to provide her with? Perhaps Jeeves is trying to rekindle their affair so that he can continue in service with an unmarried Lord Chuffnell.

While working for Bertie, Jeeves also serves as valet to Bicky Bickersteth to impress his uncle in 'Jeeves and the Hard-Boiled Egg' and Rocky Todd in 'The Aunt and the Sluggard'. He is co-opted back into service for Lord Worplesdon in *Joy in the Morning*. In *The Mating Season*, he is valet to Gussie Fink-Nottle while he is pretending to be Bertie. In *Ring for Jeeves (The Return of Jeeves)*, he is working for Lord Rowcester (or Towcester) while Bertie is in training to survive after the forthcoming Social Revolution. In that role, Jeeves also dons a false moustache and works as clerk to bookmaker Honest Patch Perkins. And in *Stiff Upper Lip, Jeeves*, he is lent out to Aunt Dahlia and Sir Watkyn Bassett.

However, Bertie considers him not so much a valet as a Mayfair consultant. 'The highest in the land bring their problems to him' – that is, Bertie's friends and family – 'I shouldn't wonder they didn't give him jewelled snuff-boxes.'

This is a reference to the jewelled snuff box that the King of Bohemia gives to Sherlock Holmes after 'A Scandal in Bohemia'.

Jeeves is a tallish man, with a dark, shrewd face and eyes that gleam with the light of pure intelligence. Bertie puts this down to eating fish and the phosphorous it contains. He wears a size eight bowler hat; Bertie thought it should be a number eleven or twelve. Bertie and others sometimes remark on the bulge at the back of his head.

As well as being phenomenally intelligent and well read, he has an encyclopaedic knowledge of horse-racing and a mastery of all forms of betting. When he is not reading 'improving books', he likes to spend his time fishing, whether it is shrimping in Herne Bay or catching tarpon off Florida. He has the uncanny ability to move around like a noiseless zephyr, oozing from Spot A to Spot B like some form of gas. Bertie compares him to a fakir – 'one of those birds in India who bung their astral bodies about . . . who having gone into thin air in Bombay, reassemble the parts and appear two minutes later in Calcutta' – announcing his presence with a gentle cough that sounds like a 'very old sheep clearing its throat on a misty mountain top'. He registers surprise or emotion by a flicker of the eyebrow, raising one a fraction of an inch, or, in *Ring for Jeeves* (*The Return of Jeeves*), by a slight twitch of the small muscle at the corner of his mouth. But, as a rule, his features preserve a uniform imperturbability, like a cigar-store Indian.

In *Aunts Aren't Gentlemen*, when Bertie tells him he is engaged to be married, Jeeves betrays no emotion and continues 'to look as if he had been stuffed by a good taxidermist'.

Jeeves is, surprisingly, a man of violence, decking Sippy Sipperley with a golf club in 'The Inferiority Complex of Old Sippy', coshing Constable Dobbs in *The Mating Season* and slipping Bingley a Mickey Finn in *Much Obliged, Jeeves*. He also takes physical action against Bertie's white mess jacket in *Right Ho, Jeeves*. Elsewhere he imposes his sartorial tyranny more subtly, giving his check suit to the under-gardener in 'Jeeves Takes Charge', stripping Bertie of his bright scarlet cummerbund in 'Aunt Agatha Takes the Count', giving his purple socks to the lift attendant in 'Jeeves and the Chump Cyril', disposing of both his pink tie and Broadway Special in 'Jeeves and the Unbidden Guest', burning his Old Etonian spats in 'The Delayed Exit of Claude and Eustace', sending back his soft silk shirts in 'Clustering Round Young Bingo', giving his new plus-fours to the poor in 'Jeeves and the Kid Clementina' and handing his blue Alpine hat with a pink feather on to Sir Watkyn Bassett's butler Butterfield to assist him in his courtship in *Stiff Upper Lip, Jeeves* rather than burning it. However, in *Ring for Jeeves* (*The Return of Jeeves*), he dons a check suit and a walrus moustache, despite his evident distaste for facial hair.

He also gets his way in taking holidays in Monte Carlo, Florida and New York, and on Aunt Dahlia's yacht in the Mediterranean. He gets a round-the-world cruise after *The Code of the Woosters* and scuppers Bertie's trip to Antibes with Bobbie Wickham in 'Jeeves and the Kid Clementina'.

Bertie tries to stand up against Jeeves predations. He even sacks him in 'Jeeves Takes Charge' but immediately rehires him.

7

AUNTS AND UNCLES

With no parents to protect him, Bertie is constantly at the beck and call of aunts – and not just his own. Uncles are kindlier coves, though, often sharing an interest in drinking.

Aunt Agatha

The dreaded Aunt Agatha, née Wooster, makes her first appearance in 'Extricating Young Gussie' where she has an 'eye like a man-eating fish'. She bosses around her husband Spencer, later Spenser, Gregson, her sister-in-law Aunt Julia and Bertie's cousin Gussie Mannering-Phipps. Bertie curls into a ball when he sees her coming. When Aunt Agatha wants you do to a thing, you do it, he says, making him wonder why people made all that fuss about the Spanish Inquisition.

She also appears as Mrs Spencer and Mrs Spenser. Curiously, her butler's name also appears to be Spenser. She is cold and haughty. Bertie has been afraid of her since he was a child. He calls her the 'Pest of Pont Street', claims that she kills rats with her teeth, devours her young, eats broken bottles and turns into a werewolf – or makes human sacrifices – at full moon.

Five foot nine with a lot of grey hair, she looks like 'a tall, thin vulture in the Gobi Desert'. She has a beaky nose and an eagle eye, though she has a way of drawing her eyebrows together that makes her nose look like an eagle's beak. Her voice is like that of a sergeant major or a herdman who calls the cattle home across the sands of Dee.

Despite this, she marries twice. Her first husband, Spenser Gregson, is a 'battered little chappie on the Stock Exchange'. He cleans up on Sumatra rubber, which allows him to lash out on a country estate at Woollam Chersey in Hertfordshire where there are miles of rolling parkland, rose gardens, stables, outhouses and a lake. Sadly, by *The Code of the Woosters*, he is dead.

They had a son, Bertie's cousin Thomas. In 'The Love that Purifies', this 'scourge of humanity' is a chunky fourteen-year-old with a snub nose, green eyes, a saint-like smile and the general aspect of someone studying to become a gangster. He has already proved himself in 'Jeeves and the Impending Doom', where he strands Cabinet minister A. B. Filmer on an island with a ferocious swan. And he once put a match to a parcel of fireworks to see what would happen.

However, he mends his ways due to a juvenile infatuation with Greta Garbo. By *The Mating Season* Cora Starr has taken over as his screen idol and he is soon getting a shilling a piece for her autograph at his prep school. But he is soon back to his old ways, having bought a cosh in Seven Dials to use on a boy named Stinker. Bertie has the task of taking him to the Old Vic see *King Lear*, *Hamlet* and *Macbeth*, which Thomas slept through. However, Bertie refused to take Thomas to the British Museum, the National Gallery or to see anything by Chekhov.

Aunt Agatha goes on to marry Lord Worplesdon and acquires a loathsome stepson, Edwin.

Aunt Julia

Julia Mannering-Phipps is the widow of the late Cuthbert Mannering-Phipps, father of Gussie and uncle of Bertie. There are some who maintain that Bertie's name in 'Extricating Young Gussie' is Mannering-Phipps as no surname is given. Julia was in pantomime at Drury Lane when Cuthbert, who was the scion of one of the oldest families in England, met her twenty-five years earlier. She had also been knocking them cold at the Tivoli. The family was against the match, but made the best of it.

Aunt Agatha took her in hand until, even with a microscope, you couldn't tell Aunt Julia from a genuine dyed-in-the-wool aristocrat. She kept her looks, too, with very large brown eyes, a mass of soft grey hair and the complexion of a girl of seventeen. Bertie claims she is the most dignified person he knows. He says she is like a stage duchess about to instruct the butler to tell the head footman to serve lunch in the blue room. However, Mannering-Phipps had no title. Uncle Cuthbert was 'wickedly extravagant' and left her with very little money for a woman in her position. Her home, Beechwood, needed a great deal of keeping up. Bertie's Uncle Spenser does what he can to help.

Uncle Alexander

Alexander Worple is the artist Bruce Corcoran's uncle in 'The Artistic Career of Corky'. He is a fifty-one-year-old jute magnate, who believes that Corky should quit art and go into the jute business, starting at the bottom and working his way up. The author of *American Birds* and *More American Birds*, Worple in no time captures Corky's fiancée Muriel Singer, a showgirl and putative author of *The Children's Book of*

American Birds, and marries her so she becomes Aunt Muriel, though she is not a proper aunt in the Wodehousian sense of the word. They quickly produced a young cousin, who launches Corky's career as author of the cartoon strip 'The Adventures of Baby Blobbs'.

Aunt Isabel
Rocky Todd's aunt, Isabel Rockmetteller, sends money so that Rocky can live it up in New York and report back. But the letters, actually written by Jeeves, make New York so enticing that she steams in from Illinois to see for herself. Then Jeeves takes her to a revival meeting. She turns against drink and dancing and urges Todd to do the same.

Uncle Willoughby
Bertie's Uncle Willoughby lives in Easeby Hall and is the source of his income in 'Jeeves Takes Charge'. He was a contemporary of Percy Craye, Lord Worplesdon, at Oxford, and lived on the 'Tabasco side' as a young man, enough to write a spicy memoir. He and Percy were thrown out of a music-hall in 1887. Little more is known about the incident, though Worplesdon's daughter Florence is shocked. Uncle Willoughby does not appear in later stories and it is assumed that he died and left his money to Bertie.

Lady Malvern
A friend of Aunt Agatha, Lady Malvern is the mother of Wilmot, Lord Pershore, who she dumps on Bertie in New York in 'Jeeves and the Unbidden Guest'. She then goes off to write a book about social conditions in the United States, a companion volume to her *India and the Indians*, which took her less than a month on the subcontinent to complete. She has to get back for the season. She is a hearty, happy, healthy, overpowering woman who, like Aunt Agatha, makes Bertie feel about ten years old.

While not tall, she measures about six feet 'from the O.P. to the prompt side' (i.e. from one side to the other on stage) and fits into his biggest armchair as if it had been build around her by someone who knew that they were wearing armchairs tight around the hips that season. She has bright, bulging eyes, a lot of yellow hair and a mouth that shows about fifty-seven front teeth when she speaks.

Her son Motty is a meek-looking twenty-three year-old. He is tall and thin, with the same yellow hair as his mother, parted in the middle and plastered down. His eyes bulge, too, but they are not bright. Instead, they are grey with pink rims. He has no eyelashes to speak of, a chin that gives up the struggle about halfway down and, when he is not chewing on his walking stick, he sits with his mouth open.

Bertie sums him up as a 'furtive, sheepish sort of blighter'. His mother says that he is a 'vegetarian and a teetotaller and is devoted to reading', but as soon as her back is turned he is out on the town. But then, before he came to New York, he was cooped up in the ancestral home in Much Middlefold, Shropshire.

Duke of Chiswick

The uncle of Bertie's friend Francis 'Bicky' Bickersteth, the Duke owns half of London and about five counties in the north, though he is a notoriously prudent spender. He wears a top hat and argues with cab drivers over the fare. While he hates America, Americans are prepared to spend money to shake his hand. He is further outraged when they want proof of his credentials. When he discovers that selling introductions is his nephew's money-making scheme he foams at the mouth and cuts him off without a penny. However, he also hates reporters and, to prevent his nephew going to the newspapers, he is forced to take him on as his secretary at a salary of £500 a year.

Uncle Mortimer

Bingo Little's Uncle Mortimer has made a goodish pile out of Little's Liniment – 'It Limbers Up the Legs'. He suffers from gout and lives at 16 Pounceby Gardens. In 'Jeeves in the Springtime', after Bingo reads Rosie M. Banks's novels about love between the classes, Uncle Mortimer marries the cook Jane Watson, allowing Jeeves to move in on Bingo's fiancée, Mabel.

Uncle Mortimer and his wife go on to become Lord and Lady Bittlesham. He owns Ocean Breeze, favourite for the Cup at Goodwood. After he receives a threatening letter from Comrade Bingo, who is posing as one of the Sons of the Red Dawn, Bertie bumps into him out the Devonshire Club, where he 'quivered from head to foot like a poleaxed blancmange. His eyes were popping and his face had gone sort of greenish.'

Aunt Emily

We know of Aunt Emily largely because she is the mother of the twins Claude and Eustace who stay with Bertie's Uncle Clive after being sent down from Oxford. They are thought to have inherited the late Uncle Henry's eccentricity. He kept eleven pet rabbits in his bedroom.

But Claude and Eustace are bright boys, Aunt Agatha asserts. They were at school with Bertie during his last summer term and he spent his whole time getting them out of frightful rows.

At Oxford they are candidates for the Seekers Club, but are sent down for squirting soda-water over the Senior Tutor. Bertie concedes that they were 'bright', but then they are about as useless at gambling as he is. Their various scams cost him money. They did not impress Marion Wardour either. Thankfully, Aunt Emily has a friend in South Africa named Mr Van Alstyne who will give them a job in Johannesburg.

In 'The Rummy Affair of Old Biffy', Aunt Emily also has a six-year-old son named Harold. Bertie attends his birthday party and attaches his card to a toy aeroplane provided by his Uncle James, pocketing the squirter he had bought for use later.

Aunt Dahlia

Dahlia Travers, née Wooster, married twice, though we know nothing of her first husband. She is a large, jovial soul, built along the lines of Mae West, though elsewhere she is said to be short and solid like a rugby scrum-half. Though she is often rude to Bertie, she is so in an affectionate way. Bertie says she is beloved by all and their relations have always been 'chummy to the last drop'. Although she chides him for his drinking, when they are together she keeps up glass for glass.

In her younger days she spent much of her time on horseback, riding in foxhunts based in the villages of Quorn and Pytchley, leaving her with permanently reddened cheeks. She speaks like she is still in the saddle and summoning a crony a quarter of a mile away.

She is a governor of Market Snodsbury Grammar School and editor of the struggling journal *Milady's Boudoir*, for which Uncle Tom begrudgingly pays until she manages to sell it in *Jeeves and the Feudal Spirit* (*Bertie Wooster Sees it Through*). However, she seems to have it back again by 'Jeeves Makes an Omelette'.

She is a woman prepared to take matters into her own hands, stealing a cow-creamer, coshing Roderick Spode and using blackmail when necessary. She certainly takes no nonsense from actor's agent Jas Waterbury. On the other hand, she is a sociable lady, always laying on a good spread, thanks to Anatole, whom she goes to great lengths to keep hold of, though in *The Code of the Woosters* she volunteers to give him up to keep Bertie out of jail. When Bertie was a child, she saved his life by removing a rubber comforter from his throat and wonders whether she had done the right thing in the long run.

She has two children, Angela and Bonzo. Bertie says Bonzo has been a pest since the cradle, but he is an ordinary plate seller to the classic yearling that is Aunt Agatha's son, Thomas.

Uncle Tom

Aunt Dahlia's second husband, Thomas Portarlington Travers made a pile out East, but ruined his digestion, hence Aunt Dahlia's need to keep Anatole as all costs. Uncle Tom hates income tax and socialistic legislation, and is afraid of fires and burglars. He dislikes the country, though he eventually settles at Brinkley Court. However, he dislikes the house-guests Dahlia invites there, and occasionally seeks sanctuary in the South of France; though in *Right Ho, Jeeves* when Dahlia, Cousin Angela and Bertie holiday in Cannes at the beginning of June, Tom choses to stay at home because he can't stick the south of France at any price. He also maintains a townhouse at 47 Charles Street, Berkeley Square, where Aunt Dahlia edits *Milady's Boudoir*.

Apart from making, and keeping, money, Uncle Tom's major interest in life is ornamental silverware. He buttonholes Bertie and talks of sconces and foliation, scrolls, ribbon wreaths in high relief and gadroon borders. Bertie has a soft spot for Uncle Tom, who would send him postal orders when he was at school.

Aunt Vera

Miss Sipperley of the Paddock, Beckley-on-the-Moor, supports her nephew Oliver 'Sippy' Sipperley in 'Without the Option'. She is organizing a village concert, but Sippy is excused as he has a writing engagement on the colleges of

Cambridge. Consequently, he has to go and stay with her friends, the Pringles.

The Paddock is a medium-sized house with a tidy garden, a gravel drive and shrubbery that looked as if it has just come back from the dry cleaner – the sort of house you would expect an aunt to live in. Aunt Vera is plainly a keen gardener. She is a stout woman with a red face, the sort of woman you would expect to be annoyed if she heard that her nephew was in chokey. Instead, she is delighted.

Uncle George

Sir George Wooster, later Lord Yaxley, has had an eventful love-life. When Aunt Dahlia was a girl, she saw him kiss her governess. Then as a young man he fell for Maudie, the barmaid at the Criterion, and the family was forced to buy her off. In middle-age he settled into routine, making his way from club to club, having a couple of drinks in each. Bertie says that he discovered that alcohol was a food well in advance of modern medical thought. However, after the shock of seeing Eustace, who was thought to be on his way to South Africa, he resorts to drinking barley water.

Then in 'Indian Summer of an Uncle', he tries to recapture his lost youth by proposing to, Rhoda Platt, the young waitress in his club. Deftly Jeeves puts him back in touch with Maudie again. As he grows older, he seems to enjoy his food more. With each year, Bertie says, he grows wider.

Dowager Lady Myrtle Chuffnell

Aunt of Lord Marmaduke 'Chuffy' Chuffnell, she is the relic of the Fourth Baron Chuffnell, supposedly consigned to the Dower House but then returned to the Hall with her twelve-year-old son from a previous marriage, Seabury.

A powerful woman, she looks like a female Master of the Hounds. Nevertheless, Sir Roderick Glossop is attracted to her, though Seabury does everything he can to get in the way of the match. Then Lady Chuffnell refuses to marry Sir Roderick while his daughter is still unwed. When her marriage is accomplished in 'Jeeves and the Greasy Bird', we can only assume that Sir Roderick and the new Lady Glossop live happily ever after.

Uncle Percy

The second husband of Aunt Agatha, Percival Craye, Lord Worplesdon, had been thrown out of the music-hall with Uncle Willoughby in 1887. It appears he drank a quart-and-a-half of champagne before beginning the evening. He was then engaged to the youthful Agatha Wooster. However, he was thrown out of a Covent Garden fancy-dress ball and ended up in Vine Street Police Station with a girl named Tottie. Agatha broke off their engagement within three minutes of the story appearing in the evening papers.

He married and fathered Florence and Edwin Craye. One day, according to Jeeves, he came down for breakfast, lifted the first cover and cried: 'Egg! Eggs! Eggs! Damn all eggs!' Then he legged it for France, never to return to his family – which was lucky for them as he had the worst temper in the country.

By the time he marries Agatha, he is a shipping magnate. They settle in Bumpleigh Hall, Steeple Bumpleigh, Hampshire, where his study is dominated by an intimidating portrait of Lady Agatha. It was Edwin who told his father that Bertie was smoking his special cigars, resulting in Worplesdon pursuing Bertie across country with a hunting crop. Edwin later joins the Boy Scouts.

Worplesdon is also guardian to Zenobia Hopwood, daughter of his old friend, the writer Roderick Hopwood, who was 'too fond of pink gin'.

Dame Daphne Winkworth

Aunt of Esmond Haddock, Dame Daphne is the widow of the historian P. B. Winkworth, mother of Gertrude and Madeline Bassett's godmother. She is a rugged light-heavyweight with a touch of Wallace Beery in her make-up who had once run a girls' school. At Deverill Hall, she is head of a gaggle of aunts and will brook no opposition. As we discover in 1965's *Galahad at Blandings* (U.S. title: *The Brinkmanship of Galahad Threepwood*) she also has a revolting young son named Huxley. In that later Blandings book she comes out of retirement to be a headmistress with a vengeance.

8

FIANCÉES AND SWEETHEARTS

Bertie has a problem with women. Both viragos and soupy sentimental girls pursue him – or, at least, they do so when their first choice has given them the slip. However, he is frequently attracted by other men's fiancées, but he is too much of a gentleman to muscle in. He has had a few conquests of his own, though. As Aunt Dahlia says: the girls he has been engaged to would, if placed end to end, reach from Piccadilly to Hyde Park Corner.

Ray Denison
Ray Denison is Gussie Mannering-Phipps's fiancée in 'Extricating Young Gussie'. Daughter of old trouper, Joe Danby, she is a vaudeville performer with a voice that lifts them out of their seats at Mosenstein's. However, when Bertie first sees her, he decides that she is a 'deucedly pretty girl' and sits down beside her. She is rather small, with great big eyes and a ripping smile. Then he discovers that she is Gussie's girl.

He gives up extricating young Gussie and lets them get on with it.

Muriel Singer

Bruce 'Corky' Corcoran's secret fiancée in 'Leave it to Jeeves' or 'The Artistic Career of Young Corky', Muriel is a chorus girl in the show *Choose Your Exit*. When Bertie meets her, he is attracted to her. He says she is one of those quiet, appealing girls who have a way of looking at you with their big eyes as though you were the greatest thing on earth and wondered why you had not caught on to it yourself.

She makes him feel protective. He wants to stroke her hands and say: 'There, there, little one!' or words to that effect. There is nothing he would not do for her. He compares her to an innocent-tasting American drink that creeps imperceptibly into your system and makes you want to change the world and, if necessary, tell the large man in the corner you are going to knock his head off. She makes him feel like a dashing knight-errant. Even though she is out to marry Corky, he says, 'I felt that I was with her in this thing to the limit.'

However, she marries Corky's uncle, who is wealthy, instead.

Florence Craye

Bertie and Florence get engaged four times – in 'Jeeves Takes Charge', *Joy in the Morning*, *Jeeves and the Feudal Spirit* and *Much Obliged, Jeeves*. She is also engaged to Stilton Cheesewright in *Joy in the Morning* and *Jeeves and the Feudal Spirit*; Boko Fittleworth in *Joy in the Morning*; Percy Gorringe in *Jeeves and the Feudal Spirit*; and an unnamed gentleman jockey and Harold 'Ginger' Winship in *Much Obliged, Jeeves*.

Bertie and Aunt Dahlia decide that Florence's former fiancés form clubs and societies, perhaps calling themselves the Old Florentians, and have annual dinners. However, in *Joy in the Morning*, Nobby Hopwood tells Bertie: 'I've often thought that, of all the multitude Florence has been engaged to, you were the one she wanted.' But in his letter to Nobby, Bertie lists all her defects, not only as a prospective bride, but as a human being.

Lady Florence is the daughter of Lord Worplesdon, so when he marries Bertie's Aunt Agatha she becomes Bertie's cousin by marriage. Tall, willowy and handsome, with luxuriant platinum-blonde hair, she is indubitably comely and has 'as many curves as a scenic railway'.

But there is a problem. She is an intellectual, 'her bean crammed to bursting point with little grey cells', and she is 'steeped to the gills with serious purpose'. When we first meet her in 'Jeeves Takes Charge' she is trying to get Bertie to read *Types of Ethical Theory*. Worse, she has plans to inflict Nietzsche upon him. But then she made Stilton read Karl Marx. She is also known as a perfectionist and has no time for a loser.

She is the author of the novel *Spindrift*, which is 'Book Society Choice of the Month'. It goes into five editions and is soon to be translated into Scandinavian. Bertie can't bring himself to read it, but Jeeves skims through it and says he considers it 'a somewhat immature production lacking in significant form'. However, it is widely reviewed and is 'like ham and eggs with the boys with the bulging foreheads out Bloomsbury way'. Percy Gorringe turns the book into a play, which closes after three nights. At the beginning of *Jeeves and the Feudal Spirit*, Florence is threatening to write another book.

Jeeves disapproves of her because she is imperious with her staff. She is also a threat to Bertie's bachelor life and, consequently, his employment.

Florence has all the makings of an aunt and, with Aunt Agatha as her stepmother, she could hardly want for training.

She promises to 'mould' Bertie, though Bertie makes it very clear that he does not want to be moulded, and on one occasion she tells him off in front of seventeen Girl Guides. Nobby blames Bertie for that fact that Florence is constantly pursuing him.

'It's your fault for being so fascinating,' she says.

Florence has her chance with Bertie, repeatedly, and with other men. But at the end of the saga, she is unmarried.

Honoria Glossop

The only daughter of Sir Roderick and Lady Glossop (née Blatherwick) of 6b Harley Street and Ditteridge Hall, Honoria Glossop was the brainiest women of her year at Girton College, Cambridge, which extended her brain to frightful extent. She read Nietzsche and Ruskin, and expects Bertie to take an intelligent interest in Freud. Not only is she brainy, she has gone in for every kind of sport and is 'the sort of girl who reduces you to pulp with sixteen sets of tennis and a few rounds of gold, and then comes down to dinner as fresh as a daisy'. This has left her with the physique of a middle-weight catch-as-catch-can wrestler. Bertie is not sure that she did not box for the varsity while she was up.

She compares unfavourably with her friend Daphne Braythwayt, who is 'tallish with blue eyes and fair hair'. Bertie takes to Daphne immediately and says, if he had the spare time, he wouldn't have minded talking to her for a bit. But before he gets the chance, Bingo Little moves in.

Honoria has a voice like a lion tamer making some authoritative announcement to one of her troupe and a laugh variously described as sounding like 'the Scotch express going under a bridge', 'a steam-riveting machine', 'waves breaking on a stern and rock-bound coast' and, more famously, 'a squadron of cavalry charging over a tin bridge'. Naturally Aunt Agatha thinks she would make the perfect wife for

Bertie – she will mould him. 'But I don't want to be moulded,' Bertie responds. Aunt Agatha tells him not to be troublesome.

By the end of 'Scoring off Jeeves', Bertie is engaged to her. Fortunately, her father, Sir Roderick, concludes that he is a looney and the engagement is broken off, much to Bertie's relief.

'If I had been engaged to her another week, her old father would have had one more patient on his books,' he says.

In 'The Rummy Affair of Old Biffy', she gets engaged to Biffy Biffen, but Jeeves reunites him with his lost love, Jeeves's own niece Mabel.

Bertie has another brush with Honoria in 'Jeeves and the Greasy Bird', where he gives her the rush in the hope of making young novelist Blair Eggleston angry (though he surely cannot be that angry if he writes for *Milady's Boudoir*). Unfortunately Bertie goes too far. After kissing her, he finds he is engaged to her again, only to be extricated with the help of the buxom actress Trixie. This leaves Honoria free to marry Eggleston. Bertie and Aunt Dahlia agree that they had it coming to them.

Aline Hemmingway

In earlier versions of 'Aunt Agatha Takes the Count', Bertie meets Aline Hemmingway on the train to Roville-sur-Mer where he is going to escape Aunt Agatha, following the severing of his first engagement to Honoria Glossop. After helping Aline with her luggage, he lunches with her in the restaurant car. He finds her sympathetic, unlike modern girls who are all bobbed hair and gaspers. However, Aunt Agatha is in hot pursuit.

In later versions, Aunt Agatha is in Roville-sur-Mer and summons Bertie there to meet Aline, whom she says is a great friend of hers, because she is the sort of girl he should marry. She would be such a good influence in his life.

Aline is a nice, quiet girl, so different from the bold girls one meets in London. Her brother is a curate at Chipley-in-the-Glen in Dorset, though he tells Aunt Agatha that they are connected to the Kent Hemmingways. She is a charming girl. Bertie feels a grim foreboding.

But when he meets her, he is smitten. He doesn't know when he has met anyone so respectable. Her dress and hair are plain and she has a face that is mild and saint-like.

'I don't pretend to be a Sherlock Holmes or anything of that order,' says Bertie, 'but the moment I looked at her I said to myself, "The girl plays the organ in the village church!"' I think we can assume that is not an innuendo.

In the earlier version, while Jeeves warns about the dishonest characters that infest fashionable French watering-places, Bertie protests that Aline is 'the sweetest girl in the world'. He also says: 'If Love hadn't actually awakened in my heart, there's no doubt it was having a good stab at it, and the thing was only a question of days.'

But it is not to be,: she and her brother are unmasked by Jeeves as a couple of international jewel thieves.

Charlotte Corday Rowbotham

Named after the assassin of Jean-Paul Marat during the French Revolution, Charlotte is a member of the Heralds of the Red Dawn, the revolutionary group that Bingo has joined in 'Comrade Bingo'. While Bertie finds her father 'moth-eaten' and Bingo's rival for her hand, Comrade Butt, 'like one of the things that come out of dead trees after the rain', he shows interest in Charlotte herself. Although she takes him 'straight into another and a dreadful world', she is not exactly bad-looking. If she laid off starchy foods and did some Swedish exercises, she might be quite tolerable.

'But there was too much of her,' he says. 'Billowy curves. Well-nourished, perhaps, expresses it best.'

He notes that she has a heart of gold, and also a gold tooth. When Bingo asks that he thinks of her, all Bertie can bring himself to say is: 'I must say I've seen cheerier souls.'

The marriage is off when Bingo is unmasked as the nephew of Lord Bittlesham and his horse Ocean Breeze loses at Goodwood, robbing him of the money he needs to wed. She consoles herself with Comrade Butt.

Lady Cynthia Wickhammersley

The youngest daughter of Lord Wickhammersley of Twing Hall, Gloucestershire, she is a 'dashed pretty and lively and attractive girl'. Bertie had known her since she was seven. It appears that Bertie once screwed up his courage to propose, but she gave him the bird and nearly laughed herself into a permanent state of hiccoughs. However, he still considers her a 'dear sweet thing'.

Bingo Little, of course, falls in love with her. He turns a light green when he discovers that she is engaged to the Reverend James Bates, winner of the Great Sermon Handicap.

Mary Burgess

Bingo describes his latest armour as sweetly grave and beautifully earnest, not one of those flippant, shallow-minded modern girls. She reminds him of – his youthful heart-throb Marie Lloyd, Bertie interjects – no, Saint Cecilia. Bingo believes that she yearns to make him a 'better, nobler, deeper, broader man'. But his production of the local concert turns into a disaster and she gets engaged to the Reverend Hubert Wingham, the curate at Twing.

Marion Wardour

A showgirl from the Apollo, she has been a pal of Bertie's for some time when he foolishly introduces her to his cousins Claude and Eustace at Ciros. The twins then fall in love with her. She expects Bertie to rescue her, but it is, of course, Jeeves who rids her of her unwanted admirers.

Rosie M. Banks

Bingo Little first espies Rosie M. Banks when he is working at the Senior Liberal Club, where he and Bertie dine when the Drones Club is having its annual wash and brush-up. She is working there to collect material for her latest novel *Mervyn Keene, Clubman*. (The storyline is spelt out in *The Mating Season*.)

Bertie is impressed. She is a tall, lissom girl with soft, soulful, brown eyes and a nice figure. She also has rather decent hands. 'I must say she raised the standard of the place quite a lot,' he remarks. To Bingo, she is an angel.

Bingo and Rosie marry in the registrar's office in Holborn. Bingo's Uncle Mortimer comes round because he is a great fan, as is one of Jeeves's aunts, who owns nearly a complete set of her books. Titles include *All for Love*, *A Red, Red Summer Rose*, *Only a Factory Girl*, *Madcap Myrtle*, *'Twas Once in May* and *The Courtship of Lord Strathmorlick* – what Bertie calls 'some of the most pronounced and widely-read tripe ever put on the market'.

She writes 'How I Keep the Love of My Husband-Baby' for *Milady's Boudoir*. The article is not published because she falls out with Mrs Travers, who has, with Jeeves's help, pinched Anatole. Rosie is so successful that, in 'Jeeves and the Impending Doom', she is off on a lecture tour of America. She plainly disapproves of Bingo's gambling. When he blows the six weeks of housekeeping money she has left him on a single race, he has to put her Peke in a kennel and take a job tutoring.

Heloise Pringle

In 'Without the Option', Bertie has to dodge the attentions of Heloise Pringle who thinks he is Sippy Sipperley. They have not met since Sippy was ten. She resembles Honoria Glossop 'in the most ghastly way'. Indeed, she was an even more brilliant scholar. Honoria's cousin, she is the daughter of Professor Pringle, who is 'a thinnish, baldish, dyspeptic-lookingish cove with an eye like a haddock', and his wife, whose 'aspect was that of one who had had bad news round about the year 1900 and never really got over it'.

Over lunch, Heloise's eyes are fixed on Bertie in a rummy manner that reminds him of the way Honoria looked at him immediately before their engagement – 'the look of a tigress that has marked down its prey'.

Although he tries to avoid her by climbing down the drainpipe, she corners him in the summer house. She asks him not to smoke. It is bad for him. And he should not sit outside without an overcoat. Plainly, he needs someone to look after him.

His flesh creeps when she tells him to get rid of Jeeves. Then she notices the name 'Bertie Wooster' in the flyleaf of his detective novel. If he is a friend, he should drop him. Then she recalls that when she and Sippy were children he cried because she would not let him kiss her.

As she gets close to him, her shoulder squashed against his, her black hair tickling his nose, Bertie is seized with the perfectly looney impulse to kiss her, but he is saved at the last moment by Aunt Jane who accuses him of once trying to kill her cat.

Gwendolen Moon

We do not actually get to meet poetess Gwendolen Moon, Sippy Sipperley's intended in 'The Inferiority Complex of Old Sippy', but she has a part to play in the saga. She is the authoress of *Autumn Leaves*, *'Twas on an English June* and the poem 'Solitude', which she submitted to the *Mayfair Gazette*, edited by Oliver Randolph Sipperley. Thanks to

Jeeves's intervention, they are to be married at 11 a.m. sharp on 1 June at St Peter's, Eaton Square.

However, they are still engaged at the beginning of 'The Love that Purifies', written three years later. Miss Moon, her mother and her golden-haired younger brother Sebastian are at Sippy's country residence in Hampshire in August. Curiously, in *Right Ho, Jeeves* (*Brinkley Manor*) she is misremembered as Elizabeth Moon.

Roberta 'Bobbie' Wickham

The daughter of the late Sir Cuthbert and Lady Wickham of Skeldings Hall, Hertfordshire, she appears in three Jeeves and Wooster short stories and one novel, *How Right You Are, Jeeves* (*Jeeves in the Offing*). However, she also appears in three Mulliner stories and two where she takes the central role. Constructed along the lines of film star Clara Bow, she is a slim, boyish-looking girl who 'resembled a particularly good-looking schoolboy who had dressed up in his sister's clothes'. She has bright red hair, which is sometimes shingled.

Aunt Dahlia describes her as a one-girl beauty chorus. Bertie agrees that 'her outer crust was indeed of a nature to cause those beholding it to rock back on their heels with a startled whistle'. She is 'equipped with eyes like twin stars, hair ruddier then a cherry, oomph, *espièglerie* [mischievousness] and all the fixings'.

Although Jeeves grants that Miss Wickham is in possession of desirable qualities, the vivid red hair is a danger signal. Miss Wickham, he says, 'lacks seriousness', which makes her not a matrimonial prospect 'for a gentleman of your description'. Bertie concedes that she has the disposition and general outlook of a ticking bomb. You feel like she might go off pop at any moment. You never know what she is going to do next or into what murky depths of soup she will carelessly plunge you. Bertie realizes that Jeeves is right when she suggests to both Bertie and Tuppy Glossop the trick of busting one another's hot-water bottles with a darning needle tied to a pole.

In *How Right You Are, Jeeves* (*Jeeves in the Offing*), Aunt Dahlia expresses surprise that she is not one of the gaggle of girls to whom he has been engaged. 'That was merely because she wouldn't meet me half way,' Bertie explains. Under the influence of her 'oomph' he has proposed to her several times. When a marriage notice appears in *The Times* he incorrectly assumes that, on one of these occasions, his attention must have wandered when she drooped her eyes and came through with a 'Right ho'. After they finally do get engaged, and break it off, Bertie becomes convinced that she is indeed 'a carrot-topped Jezebel'.

Bobbie is a prankster. She has obviously been like this from her days at St Monica's school in Bingley-on-Sea where girls used an elaborate ruse to get back into school after hours. In the Mulliner story 'Something Squishy', she puts a snake in Sir Claude Lynn's bed after he had asked her to marry him. He leaps out of bed, proving he is human. But Bobbie shares Jeeves's prejudice against mauve pyjamas and decides that there will be no wedding bells. She also drives a fast car, once getting fined for doing forty miles-an-hour down Piccadilly. On another occasion she crashes a car while uninsured.

Having toyed with Bertie, she ends up engaged to Kipper Herring.

Cora Bellinger

Thirty-year-old opera singer Cora Bellinger is Tuppy Glossop's amour in 'Jeeves and the Song of Songs'. She has a wonderful voice and, according to Tuppy, dark flashing eyes and a great soul. However, she has a rather serious outlook on life and balks at anything in the shape of humour. Practical joking, in particular, is out.

According to Bertie, she is pretty massive, built on the lines of the Albert Hall, but Tuppy cannot take his eyes off her chassis. Bertie insists that she is a light-heavyweight with a commanding eye and a square chin. She looks like Cleopatra would have done if she had gone too freely with the starches and cereals. But then women who have anything to do with the opera always appear to run to surplus poundage.

Worse, when Jeeves offers Tuppy a cocktail in front of her, he recoiled from it as if it were a serpent. Bertie acknowledges that she was one from whom he, personally, would have steered clear. Jeeves saves Tuppy from his fate, sparing him for Bertie's cousin Angela.

Gwladys Pendlebury

Bertie describes Gwladys Pendlebury, an artist he met in Chelsea, as 'slightly divine'. But Aunt Dahlia warns that no good can come of associating with 'anything labelled Gwladys or Ysosbel or Ethyl or Kathryn'. Like Bertie, she drives a Widgeon Seven, a red one, and has been seen doing sixty miles-an-hour through the park. Also, like him, she is not the greatest driver and runs over Lucius Pim.

As an artist she 'swings a jolly fine brush', in Bertie's estimation at least. Jeeves does not like the portrait she has done of the young master, though.

In the end, Bertie loses out to Lucius Pim, who is a strong, masterful type who criticizes her hats and says nasty things about her chiaroscuro. Worse, he has wavy hair.

Laura Pyke

Bertie admits that, if he 'had not been informed in advance of the warped nature of her soul', he might have been favourably impressed by Laura Pyke when he first met her. She is rather good-looking – 'a bit strong in the face but nevertheless quite attractive'. However, she would never have clicked with

Bertram Wooster. 'Her conversation was of a kind which would have queered Helen of Troy with any right-thinking man . . . She spoke freely of proteins, carbohydrates, and the physiological requirements of the average individual.' She believes that the carrot is the best of all vegetables and a racy story that she tells about a man who refused to eat prunes makes Bertie a non-starter for the last two courses at dinner.

As well as being a food crank, she opposes cocktails, saying that they corrode the stomach tissue. And she picks on Bingo – 'Twice during dinner tonight the Pyke said things about young Bingo's intestinal canal which I shouldn't have thought possible in mixed company even in this lax post-War era.'

She has little time for Bertie either. The 'Tchah!' she lets out when he explains he knows nothing about cars possesses much of the timbre and brio of Aunt Agatha's exclamations and nearly lifts the top of his head off. Naturally, Miss Pyke does understand about cars and quickly discerns that it is out of petrol. Then she turns on Bertie like a wounded leopardess.

She was, however, Mrs Little's dearest friend at St Adela's. Then, in pique, she recalls how Rosie fawned on the captain to get into the hockey team and won the Scripture prize by cheating. Bertie sums her up as 'unfit for human consumption'. They celebrate her departure with hot Scotch-and-water with a spot of lemon in it.

Rhoda Platt

A waitress at the Buffers Club, Miss Platt is the object of Bertie's Uncle George's matrimonial designs. This has to be stopped. She is, after all, too young for him and not of the right social class. Rhoda herself wonders if Lord Yaxley is too old, but 'a title is a title'. Bertie is dispatched to Wisteria Lodge, Kitchener Road, East Dulwich, to buy her off. But when Uncle George reconnects with his former love, Maudie, the barmaid of the Criterion, Rhoda is free to marry Jeeves's friend, Smethurst.

Angela Travers

Bertie's cousin Angela has an on-again-off-again relationship with Tuppy Glossop, which concerns Bertie. He is extremely fond of Angela. Indeed, he is devoted to her. There is nothing he likes better than a ramble in her company. He has known her since he was 'so high'. She is a 'young prune' and 'soundish sort of egg'.

In 'Jeeves and the Song of Songs', he puts Jeeves on the case to break up Tuppy and Cora Bellinger. Then Jeeves has to ride to the rescue again to free Tuppy from the clutches of the dog-girl, Miss Dalgleish – a largish, corn-fed girl who wears tailor-made tweeds and thick boots – after a row about a hat. Tuppy later concedes that Angela, appropriately, is an angel in human form – 'the sun is once more shining'.

In *Right Ho, Jeeves*, Tuppy is jealous because of the amount of time Angela and Bertie have spent together in Cannes. Bertie admits they were practically inseparable, right down to the mixed bathing and moonlight strolls, but you don't fall in love with close relations. There is something in the book of rules about a man not marrying his cousin, says Bertie, 'Or am I thinking of grandmothers?' She is even briefly engaged to Gussie Fink-Nottle. But Angela and Tuppy make it up in the end. It seems they finally get married at the end of *Much Obliged, Jeeves*.

Pauline Stoker

Daughter of American multi-millionaire J. Washburn Stoker, Pauline was 'of a beauty so radiant that strong men whistled after her in the street'. Not a blonde, rather 'darkish in her general colour scheme'. But the effect she had on Bertie is shattering.

'She got right in among me,' he says. 'Her beauty maddened me like wine.'

Two weeks after meeting her in New York, he proposes, though he cannot fathom why she accepts him. She explains that there is a sort of 'woolly-headed duckiness' about him. They were engaged for forty-eight hours, until Sir Roderick Glossop put an end to it by telling her he was looney.

There is something about her manner that attracts Bertie. When they meet again at Chuffnell Regis, she is 'as cool as an oyster on the half-shell and as chirpy as a spring breeze'. When speaking of Pauline, Lord Chuffnell goes deep crimson and looks like 'a stuffed frog with a touch of the Soul's Awakening about it'.

Despite being one of the most beautiful girls he has ever seen, she has a grave defect. She is 'one of those girls who want you to come and swim a mile before breakfast and rout you out when you are trying to snatch a wink of sleep after lunch for a merry five sets of tennis'. As Chuffy rides, swim, shoots, chivvies foxes and generally bustles about, Bertie thinks they make the perfect pair.

For himself, 'of the ancient fire which had caused me to bung my heart at her feet at the Plaza there remained not a trace'. His broken heart is soon mended. Consequently, he is unmoved when she turns up in his bed – the only girl to do so – in his heliotrope pyjamas with an old gold stripe, though she does 'look fine in that slumber-wear'. She is similarly unmoved when he kisses her in Lord Chuffnell's garden, but then the kiss was not one of Bertie's best. However, she does say that if she was not so crazy about Marmaduke she could easily marry him and there is a hint of nudity when Pauline changes out of Bertie's pyjamas and back into her swimsuit.

Although her father tries to make her marry Bertie by imprisoning him on his yacht, Pauline and Chuffy are reunited and, in *Stiff Upper Lip, Jeeves*, they are married.

Madeline Bassett

Daughter of Sir Watkyn Bassett, JP, Madeline is 'undeniably of attractive exterior – slim, svelte . . . and bountifully equipped with golden hair and all the fixings'. Physically, she is in the pin-up class, Bertie concedes, though elsewhere he rates her only as 'pretty enough in a droopy, blonde, saucer-eyed way, but not the sort of breath-taker that takes the breath'. While any red-blooded Sultan or Pasha, if offered the chance, would take her into his harem without hesitation, he would regret his impulsiveness within a week.

A Roedean girl, she is as mushy a character as ever broke a biscuit, convinced that stars are God's daisy chain and every time a fairy blows its nose a baby is born. She is soupy, droopy, squishy and sentimental with melting eyes and a cooing voice, and cannot even prepare the simplest meal – though that, surely, goes for Bertie too. Her favourite reading is Christopher Robin, Winnie the Pooh and Rosie M. Banks's novels, particularly *Mervyn Keene, Clubman*.

Despite describing her as 'a ghastly girl' and 'England's premier pill', Bertie finds himself engaged to her on four occasions. She also gets engaged to Gussie Fink-Nottle on five occasions. After he runs off with Emerald Stoker, she falls under the thrall of Roderick Spode, now Lord Sidcup, and they marry.

Stephanie 'Stiffy' Byng

The ward of Sir Watkyn Bassett, Stiffy Byng lives at Totleigh Towers with her cousin Madeline Bassett. She is 'petite', a 'smallish girl of about the tonnage of Jesse Matthews' – presumably the sylphlike star of the musical stage of the 1930s rather than the more substantial figure Miss Matthews developed later on. Elsewhere Stiffy is described as 'the little squirt with the large blue eyes'. Jeeves finds her a most charming young lady. She gets Bertie to tell her guardian that they are engaged, then denies it, making her intended, the curate Harold 'Stinker' Pinker, look good by comparison.

In *Stiff Upper Lips, Jeeves*, Bertie compares her to an upas tree – 'It's not safe to come near her. Disaster on every side is what she strews.' The engagement secured in *The Code of the Woosters* survives *Stiff Upper Lip, Jeeves* and in *Much Obliged, Jeeves* she is introduced as the Reverend Mrs Stinker Pinker.

Zenobia 'Nobby' Hopwood

Daughter of penniless writer Roderick Hopwood, Zenobia Hopwood was made the ward of Lord Worplesdon on her father's deathbed. He told Worplesdon to watch her like a hawk 'or she'll go marrying some bally blot on the landscape'. She is a close friend of Florence Craye.

When we meet her in *Joy in the Morning*, she is twenty. She is a blue-eyed little half-portion with an animated dial, who wears her hair in a style that does not require curling pins and is liberally endowed with oomph. She claims that she is devoted to Bertie because, when she was a child, he once gave her threepennyworth of acid drops.

After Jeeves engineers her guardian's consent to her marriage to Boko Fittleworth, they are not heard of again. Presumably they head off to Hollywood and live happily ever after.

Cora 'Corky' Pirbright

Sister of Claude Cattermole 'Catsmeat' Potter-Pirbright, Cora comes from a theatrical family. Her father wrote the music for *The Blue Lady* and other hits. Her mother, Elsie Cattermole, was a star on Broadway. Her uncle is the vicar of King's Deverill where she is organizing the village concert. She also spends her time straightening her uncle's tie and tells him he smokes too much.

She attended dance classes with a youthful Bertie where she persuaded him to throw a mildewed orange at the teacher. He did this without a murmur, knowing full well how bitter the reckoning would be. From the age of sixteen, she has been wowing people with her oomph and *espièglerie* and went on to become a Hollywood star under the screen name Cora Starr.

A lissom girl of medium height, she is constructed along the lines of Gertrude Lawrence, and she has always been worth more than a passing glance. Her hair and eyes are a kind of browny hazel. The general effect is of an angel who has eaten a lot of yeast.

Bertie remarks that if you had to pick someone to be cast away on a desert island with, your first choice would be Hedy Lamarr, but Corky Pirbright would inevitably come high up in the list of honourable mentions. Her outlines are graceful and shown off to good effect in clinging gowns. She can bowl over the strongest man and Catsmeat reminds Bertie that he made a colossal ass over her at one time. In the end she wins Esmond Haddock and whisks him off to Hollywood, though her ambition is to settle down as a farmer's wife.

Hilda Gudgeon

School tennis champion Hilda Gudgeon was with Madeline Bassett at Roedean. She broke off her engagement to Bertie's college chum Harold 'Beefy' Anstruther when he hogged the court during a game of mixed doubles, though they make it up again. As a tennis player, she is fortunate to live in Wimbledon, in a suburban villa called The Larches near Wimbledon Common.

A solid, strapping girl, she plays hockey and squash. She also wields a pistol at Bertie when she finds him hiding behind the sofa in her den. When she makes it up with Anstruther, she gives Bertie a slap on the back; and gives him another when she establishes that Bertie is a friend of Harold. When Bertie braces himself for a third, she changes policy and prods him in the ribs. She claims to have a lot of influence with Madeline and, on Bertie's behalf, she will 'talk to her like a mother'. The very idea makes him forgo her invitation to breakfast – a huge sacrifice for Bertie – and hurry on elsewhere.

Daphne Dolores Morehead

Lady novelist Daphne Dolores Morehead is frightfully expensive, but Aunt Dahlia hires her to write a series for *Milady's Boudoir* in the hope that she can sell the magazine. She has blonde hair, whiffs of Chanel No. 5 and Bertie classifies her, at a single glance, as a pipterino of the first water. And when he describes her as a pipterino, he says, 'you will gather that she was something pretty special'. He had been expecting an elderly lady with a face like a horse and gold-rimmed pince-nez attached to her top button with black string.

Bertie waxes lyrical over her. Her hair is the colour of ripe corn and her eyes cornflower blue. She has a tip-tilted nose and 'a figure as full of curves as a scenic railway', cf. Florence Craye. He says that she could walk into any assembly of international beauty contestants and the committee of judges would lay down the red carpet for her. 'One could imagine fashionable photographers fighting for her custom.'

Stilton Cheesewright soon forgets about Florence when he meets her and is soon goggling her like a bulldog confronted with a pound of steak. The feeling is mutual and Daphne immediately makes a play for Cheesewright, whom she recognizes as an Oxford rowing Blue.

Phyllis Mills

The stepdaughter of Audrey Upjohn, Phyllis is a 'well-stacked young featherweight'. However, Bertie immediately spots goofiness in her. She had a mild 'Soul's Awakening' expression which made it clear that, while not super-goofy like some girls he has met, she is goofy enough to be going on with. Although shaky on the IQ, physically she is a pipterino of the first water, Bertie says. Her eyes are bluer than the skies above and the simple summer dress she wears accentuates rather than hides the graceful outlines of her figure. He does not blame Wilbert Cream for reaching for a book of poetry and making a beeline to the nearest leafy glade with her.

Emerald Stoker

The American younger daughter of J. Washburn Stoker, Emerald is not as attractive as her older sister, Pauline. She is plain, except for a touch of the Pekinese about the nose and eyes, and a plethora of freckles. In England to study art at the Slade, she loses her allowance on Sunny Jim at Kempton Park, which came in sixth out of seven. Rather than risk her father's wrath, she takes a job as a cook at Totleigh Towers, home of Sir Watkyn Bassett.

There, she takes pity on Gussie Fink-Nottle who Madeline Bassett has put on a vegetarian diet. They fall in love over cold steak-and-kidney pie. Her lasting achievement is beaning Roderick Spode with a basin. She then elopes with Gussie and takes over from Anatole at Brinkley Court when he comes down with *mal au foie* and takes to his bed, while Gussie goes to see the Archbishop of Canterbury to get a special licence.

Magnolia Glendennon

A shorthand-typist from South Carolina, Magnolia's face would not launch a thousand ships but, as Ginger Winship is engaged to Florence Craye at the time, he does not dare take on anyone as a secretary who might have done well in the latest Miss America contest. However, she is the 'sweetest, kindest, gentlest girl that ever took down outgoing mail in shorthand'.

Vanessa Cook

An art student at the Slade, Vanessa has rejected Bertie's proposal and gone into radical politics with Orlo Porter. She is a large girl who packs a hefty punch, but her outer aspect 'would have drawn whistles from susceptible members of America's armed forces'. The pin-up to end all pin-ups, she reminds Bertie of his childhood dancing mistress. In another thirty years, Bertie reckons, she will look just like Aunt Agatha, 'before whose glare . . . strong men curl up like rabbits'.

9

DRONES AND OTHER ACQUAINTANCES

When Bertie is in town the Drones Club is the centre of his life. He drops in for a snifter, a smoke, a chat or a game of snooker-pool or darts. Most of his male friends are Drones. They were at school and university together and many are still known by the nicknames they were stuck with at school. Indeed, in *Thank You, Jeeves*, Bertie affects not to know that 'Chuffy' Chuffnell's first name is Marmaduke. Even when a Drone does not have a nickname, a diminutive is used. Augustus is always Gussie.

Augustus 'Gussie' Mannering-Phipps
Bertie's cousin Gussie, son of Aunt Julia and the late Uncle Cuthbert, is a romantic who is always losing his head over 'creatures'. He is not clever, but is good-looking and had excellent letters of introduction to contacts in New York to make good.

In the United States, he falls for vaudeville singer Ray Denison and, as her father Joe Danby will not let her marry outside the profession, takes to the boards himself under the name George Wilson. He appears on stage wearing a purple frock coat and brown top-hat, trips over his feet and blushes. But Ray singing from the stalls helps him overcome his stage fright. Then, following the *rapprochement* of Aunt Julia and Mr Danby, he marries Ray and goes on to do well on the stage.

Bruce 'Corky' Corcoran

As a portrait painter with a studio near Washington Square, Corky is unsuccessful and remains dependent on his uncle, jute magnate Alexander Worple. When Corky finally gets a commission – from his uncle who had married Corky's fiancée – it is to paint the couple's offspring, who is going to deprive Corky of his inheritance. As an artist, he cannot stop his feelings showing through. His uncle is outraged and stops his allowance. However, thanks to Jeeves, he uses the portrait to establish himself in strip cartoons.

Rockmetteller 'Rocky' Todd

Long Island poet, Rocky Todd never gets up before twelve and writes poetry three days a month. On the other 329 days a year, he rests. He hates New York, but is forced to live there by his Aunt Isabel, who pays him an allowance. But when she gets religion, thanks to Jeeves, he happily give up the bright lights and returns to the countryside.

Francis 'Bicky' Bickersteth

Bertie had been at Oxford with Bicky. His father, the late Captain Rollo Bickersteth of the Coldstream Guards, left him no money and his uncle, the Duke of Chiswick, sent him to the United States to become a rancher in Colorado, but he prefers to stay in a boarding house in New York. They meet again at a party in Washington Square. Bertie is feeling homesick and they get together for a quiet snort in a corner, where Bicky endears himself to Bertie by his ability to imitate a bull-terrier chasing a cat up a tree. Once his uncle cuts off his allowance, he develops an ambition to become a chicken farmer, but ends up going into politics as his uncle's secretary.

Cyril Bassington-Bassington

Foisted on Bertie by Aunt Agatha, Cyril Bassington-Bassington, in the United States for the first time, mistakes a policeman for a postman and gets arrested. He is tall and thin, with a lot of light hair and pale-blue goggly eyes that make him look like one of the rarer kinds of fish. Despite this, he wants to go on the stage, but his ambition is thwarted by New York impresario Blumenfeld's son who calls him 'fish-face'. After this setback, he continues on his way to Washington, DC in preparation for a career in the diplomatic service.

Richard P. 'Bingo' Little

Born in the same village as Bertie within a couple of days, they attended the same kindergarten and went on to Malvern House, Eton and Oxford together, where Bingo got some sort of degree. During his bachelor days Bingo is supported by his Uncle Mortimer, but when they fall out he falls back on tutoring. Later he inherits a large income and a country house from his Uncle Wilberforce.

According to Bertie, 'at school Bingo had the finest collection of actresses' photographs of anyone of his time; and at Oxford his romantic nature was a byword'. He repeatedly falls in love. In 'The Pride of the Woosters is Wounded' ('Scoring off Jeeves'), Bertie compares him to 'the hero of a musical comedy who takes the centre of the stage, gathers the boys round him in a circle, and tells them all about his love at the top of his voice'.

The objects of his love included the waitress Mabel in 'Jeeves in the Springtime', Honoria Glossop and Daphne Braythwayt in 'The Pride of the Woosters is Wounded', Charlotte Corday Rowbottom in 'Comrade Bingo', Lady Cynthia Wickhammersley in 'The Great Sermon Handicap' and Mary Burgess in 'The Metropolitan Touch'.

Then comes his marriage to Rosie M. Banks and they set up the marital home in St John's Wood. In her article for *Milady's Boudoir*, she describes Bingo as 'half god, half prattling, mischievous child'. To discourage his gambling, she keeps him on a tight budget, forcing him to return to tutoring in 'Jeeves and the Impending Doom'. They have a baby and, despite his inheritance and his wife's considerable income, Bingo has to take a job as the editor of *Wee Tots*, a journal for the nursery and the home. This is only secured using Rosie's considerable influence. The proprietor, P. P. Purkiss, is parsimonious and, week after week, Bingo attempts to ask him for a pay rise. It is only after his child wins a baby contest in South Kensington that Bingo gets the courage to go into Purkiss's private office and demand an additional 'ten fish' in his pay packet, starting the following Saturday.

Although a married man, he attends Gussie's dinner at the Drones in *The Code of Woosters*. He also has a life in Wodehouse fiction outside the Jeeves and Wooster stories, returning to political activism in 'Bingo Bans the Bomb' in the collection *Plum Pie* (1966).

Charles Edward 'Biffy' Biffen

Biffy is the absent-minded son of Mr and Mrs E. C. Biffen of 11 Penslow Square, Mayfair. His godmother died leaving him a place in Herefordshire, where he retires to become a country gentleman, landowner and to 'prod cows'. After he loses the love of his life, Jeeves's niece Mabel, at the customs house in New York, Bertie says of Biffy: 'I am no master-mind myself;

but compared with Biffy I'm one of the great thinkers of all time.'

Anatole

In *Much Obliged, Jeeves*, Bertie considers going to pay his respects to Aunt Dahlia's chef Anatole, but decides not to as he is 'inclined to the long monologue when he gets you in his power'. He suffers from *mal au foie* and talks rather too much about his liver for Bertie's taste. He rustles up a vast range of gourmet French dishes, though he can turn his hand to steak-and-kidney pie as well, and he is much in demand. After Aunt Dahlia steals him away from Bingo and Rosie Little, she sees off attempts by Jane Snettisham, Sir Watkyn Bassett and Mrs Lemuel Trotter to take him from her. Aunt Dahlia even postpones her Mediterranean cruise for a month because Anatole comes down with influenza.

Anatole has an impulsive Provençal temperament and flies off the handle at the slightest provocation. When people push away his food, he retires to his room. He is a tubby little man with a moustache of the outsize or soup-strainer variety that turns up at the ends like a sergeant major's when all is well and droops when his soul is bruised.

Before working for the Littles, he spent a couple of years with an American family in Nice and learned his fractured English from their chauffeur, a man named Maloney from Brooklyn. It seems he is also something of a ladies' man. In 'Clustering Round Young Bingo', there were 'two young persons, both of whom he had led to assume . . .'

Oliver Randolph 'Sippy' Sipperley

In 'Without the Option', Sippy is a twenty-four year-old author who is supposed to be writing a series of articles on the colleges of Cambridge, rather than singing at his aunt's village concert. However, on Boat Race night, he follows

Bertie's suggestion, steals a policeman's helmet and ends up in jail.

He goes on to become editor of the *Mayfair Gazette*. As a freelance, he had been a cheery cove, full of happy laughter. But as editor, he becomes careworn. He looks haggard, drawn, with circles under his eyes. This all changes when he screws up his courage to reject the work of his old headmaster, Mr Waterbury, and tells poetess Gwendolen Moon how he feels about her.

Once they are engaged, Sippy invites Gwendolen, her mother, her brother and Bertie, who declines, to his Hampshire residence, though he clearly keeps a place in London, to which Gussie Fink-Nottle repairs on the night he finds himself out on the town in a Mephistopheles costume without a penny. They were students together.

Freddie Bullivant

Usually the life and soul of the Drones, Freddie is found in a dark corner of the smoking-room looking like the last rose of summer after Elizabeth Vickers breaks off their engagement. Bertie decides to take him down to Mavis Bay to get over it. He plays the piano, is good at polo and is spoken of as the coming man at snooker-pool.

Hildebrand 'Tuppy' Glossop

Nephew of Sir Roderick Glossop, Tuppy has a long-term relationship with Bertie's cousin Angela, punctuated by infatuations with Cora Bellinger and Miss Dalgleish, and a row over Angela's shark. Although Bertie can never forgive the incident at the Drones when Tuppy dunked him in the swimming pool in full evening dress, he helps him in affairs of the heart. After all, they had been to Oxford together.

A popular Drone, he has light hair, a Cheshire-cat grin and a high, squeaky voice like the tenor of a village choir failing to hit a high note. In build and appearance, he resembles a bulldog, with more lower jaw than was absolutely necessary and eyes a bit too keen and piercing from one who was neither an Empire builder or a traffic policeman.

His father was a research chemist who invented Runkle's Magic Midgets, a popular hangover cure among the Drones. However, it is the owner of the company, L. P. Runkle, who has made all the money, leaving Tuppy short of cash to marry Angela. However, Aunt Dahlia and Jeeves set about remedying that situation.

The Reverend Rupert 'Beefy' Bingham
A friend of Bertie's from Oxford, he runs a Lads' Club for local boys in Bermondsey East and puts on entertainments at the Oddfellows' Hall. Tuppy visits and plays backgammon there. The Reverend Bingham also has a life beyond Jeeves and Wooster. Elsewhere we learn that, at varsity, he was a Blood and Trials Eight man. He has a colossal frame and a face the colour of a side of salmon, and he is the nephew and heir to a shipping magnate.

Marmaduke 'Chuffy' Chuffnell
The fifth Baron Chuffnell of Chuffnell Hall, Chuffnell Regis, Somerset, Chuffy went to Eton and Oxford with Bertie. The local JP, he likes to ride, swim, shoot, chivvy foxes and generally bustle about. However, the family has fallen on hard times. He keeps Black Berkshire pigs to make money and he rarely gets up to London. To marry he must sell Chuffnell Hall. Before he meets Pauline Stoker, he has a reputation as a man of impulse and hot-blooded impetuosity – 'You find the girl, and he does the rest,' says Bertie.

Augustus 'Gussie' Fink-Nottle
Gussie was at school with Bertie who shared his last bar of milk chocolate with him. Despite stiff competition, Gussie

was known as 'Fat-head'. He then disappeared to a remote village in Lincolnshire where he studied newts, later carrying them around in glass tanks. He had not been up to London for over five years until he met Madeline Bassett out walking her dog. Removing a thorn from the dog's paw, he fell victim to the divine pash.

Despite being school friends, Bertie writes him off as one of those 'timid, obsequious, teacup-passing, thin-bread-and-butter-offering, yes-men who women of my Aunt Dahlia's type nearly always like at first sight'. Worse, the horn-rimmed-glass-wearing shrimp-like gargoyle is a teetotaller who drinks only orange juice. When he does taste liquor for the first time, he goes mad and proposes to Madeline Bassett and Angela Travers in quick succession.

With some tuition from Jeeves, he even stands up to Roderick Spode. Then he falls under the spell of Cora Pirbright. Everything seems back on track for him to marry Madeline Bassett when she tries to put him on a vegetarian diet and he is seduced by Emerald Stoker's steak-and-kidney pie.

Claude Cattermole 'Catsmeat' Potter-Pirbright

Brother of Cora Pirbright, Catsmeat is an actor. About the same build as Bertie, he is in demand for juvenile roles, though in society comedies he is often the 'Freddie' character – the light-hearted friend of the hero who carries the second love interest. He is also known for his imitation of Beatrice Lillie. He was famed at the Drones for hitting a game pie with six consecutive bread rolls from the far window and once livened things up with a police rattle. On another occasion, he had a hangover and, when he picked up his roll, it squeaked and rubber mouse ran out of it. He had to be revived with brandy.

He smokes cigars and is always on hand for a quick one at the Drones. In *The Mating Season*, sister Cora tells him off for getting pie-eyed and Bertie observes him closely to see which of the six varieties of hangover he has got. It transpires that, after a whisky and splash with Bertie, he drank two magnums of champagne before forcing Gussie Fink-Nottle into the fountain in Trafalgar Square.

At Malvern House, the Reverend Upjohn described him as 'brilliant but unsound'. Catsmeat and Bertie went on to Eton and Oxford together.

Catsmeat also has a life beyond Jeeves and Wooster stories, contributing an article for *Wee Tots* with Cyril 'Barmy' Fotheringay-Phipps called 'Some Little-Known Cocktails' and, eventually, heading for Hollywood.

The Reverend Harold 'Stinker' Pinker

At Magdalen with Bertie, Stinker is a large, lumbering, Newfoundland puppy of a man. He won his boxing Blue and played rugby for the university and England, and still turns out for the Harlequins. But off the field he is clumsy, always upsetting furniture. Bertie says he has two left feet and is constitutionally incapable of walking through the Gobi Desert without knocking something over. Despite being the curate at Totleigh-on-the-Wold he is prepared to steal a policeman's helmet for Stiffy Byng. His inability to maintain order at the school treat and taking on Roderick Spode does not endear him to Stiffy's guardian, Sir Watkyn Bassett. Even his private income of £500 a year does not help. Eventually it is his reputation as a prop forward that wins him a vicarage at Hockley-cum-Meston and allows them to marry.

D'Arcy 'Stilton' Cheesewright

Bertie's contemporary at school and university, Stilton was Bertie's rowing coach and continues to give him a hard time. He has a beefy frame, a face that looks like a slab of pink dough and a pumpkin-shaped head – though Bertie later concedes that it is shaped like the dome of St Paul's.

Despite having a wealthy uncle who wants him to stand for Parliament, he opts to become a policeman and moves to Steeple Bumpleigh to be near his beloved Florence Craye, to whom he gets engaged on three separate occasions. Nobby Hopwood thinks he opted for the constabulary because Florence made him read Karl Marx. He is very impressionable. Bertie agrees. At Oxford someone temporarily converted him to Buddhism.

He is uncontrollably jealous and threatens to break Bertie's spine in several places on several occasions. Despite it all, he is a member of the Drones.

Florence describes him as pigheaded, an uncouth Cossack and an obstinate, mulish, unimaginative, tyrannical jack-in-office. When he quits the police, they reconcile, but he eventually falls for Daphne Dolores Morehead.

George Webster 'Boko' Fittleworth

Purveyor of wholesome fiction to the masses, he has been headhunted by Hollywood. Both Florence Craye and Nobby Hopwood have fallen for him, despite the fact that he looks like a cross between a comedy juggler and a parrot that has been dragged through a hedge backwards. Like many of the younger literati, he dresses like a tramp cyclist who had been left out overnight in an ashcan. At the first sight of him, Jeeves winced visibly and went off to brace himself with the cooking sherry. While single, he shared a flat with Ginger Winship and employed Magnolia Glendennon as a stenographer.

Harold 'Beefy' Anstruther

Bertie's partner at rackets at Oxford, Beefy Anstruther goes on to get engaged to Hilda Gudgeon. It is not explained if he is related to the moth-eaten septuagenarian Mr Anstruther, a friend of Aunt Dahlia's late father in 'The Love that Purifies'.

Reginald 'Kipper' Herring

A lifelong friend of Bertie's, they were inmates of Malvern House together and Kipper went on to become a journalist on the *Thursday Review*. With a cauliflower ear and a nose that some hidden hand has knocked slightly out of the straight, he looks like Jack Dempsey after his first fight with Gene Tunney. It would be unsafe to back him in a beauty contest even if the other competitors were Boris Karloff, King Kong and Oofy Prosser from the Drones. Still, he manages to win the heart of Bobbie Wickham.

Harold 'Ginger' Winship

Aunt Dahlia was at school with Harold's mother and Bertie was at Oxford with him where he won a boxing Blue. From the moment he looked in on Bertie to borrow a soda siphon, they were like brothers. His body is still muscular and well knit, and he looks he could like fell an ox with a single blow. His eyes are clear, his cheeks tanned, his chin firm and his hair ginger. But Bingley, who had once been his valet, complains that he is the wrong size, which means he could not steal his shirts.

For a while, he was a prominent member of the Drones, but Florence disapproved. She decided that he should have a career in politics. But she does not know that he has a past – he was apt to get thrown out of restaurant for throwing eggs at the electric fan and seldom escaped unjugged on Boat Race night.

At his big speech at the Chamber of Commerce, all he could say was: 'Er, er, er!'

After that disaster, Magnolia rubs the back of his neck. Her soft fingers touch his skin like dainty butterflies and he knows he is in love.

Orlo J. Porter

Bertie and Orlo were on the same staircase at Oxford, but they did not really get to know each other as he was a prominent figure at the Union where he made fiery far-left speeches. Nor did Bertie share Orlo's hobby – bird-watching. Everybody predicted a hot political future for him. Instead, denied his inheritance until the age of thirty, he went to work for the London and Home Counties Insurance Company, which keeps him 'well nourished'.

Despite his left-wing leanings, Orlo wants his inheritance so he can have a flat in Mayfair, drink champagne with every meal and drive a Rolls-Royce. Bertie supposes that he will leave what he doesn't need for the hard-up proletariat; Orlo says that there won't be anything he doesn't need.

He has a beard like a Victorian novelist and claims to write for the *New Statesman* – the occasional letter to the editor and he rarely fails to enter the weekly competitions.

10

OLD HARDENED ARTERIES AND ROZZERS

Despite Bertie Wooster's almost unworldly innocence, he manages to make enemies. Something about him inflames the old generation – the Old Hardened Arteries, as Boko Fittleworth calls them in *Joy in the Morning*. These are the 'elderly gentlemen who snort like foghorns when I appear'. Bertie provokes much the same reaction, particularly among potential fathers-in-law. His adversaries are often JPs and they are aided and abetted by the constabulary, aka the rozzers.

Mr Blumenfeld
The New York impresario behind George Caffyn's *Ask Dad*, Blumenfeld becomes Blumenfeld when he arrives in London to scout for material, which involves a read-through of a play by Lady Wickham. He is large, round and fat – and admits it – with big spectacles and a hairless dome.

While overbearing and bossy, Blumenfeld relies on the

judgement of his son, reasoning that the child has the same level of intelligence as the average member of the general public. Caffyn calls the kid 'a pest, a wart, and a pot of poison' who should be strangled. Bertie calls him, ironically, Sidney the Sunbeam. He is a stoutish infant with a lot of freckles who, when Bertie first meets him, has a good deal of jam on his face and regards Bertie as if he were 'some sort of unnecessary product Cuthbert the Cat brought in after a ramble among the local ashcans'. His opinion of Lady Wickham's play appears to have been influenced by the presence of roly-poly pudding.

Ask Dad was the title of a musical comedy by Wodehouse, Guy Bolton and Louis A. Hirsch, which tried out in Toronto. It had changed its name to *Oh, My Dear!* by the time it reached New York.

Sir Roderick Glossop

An eminent brain specialist – or looney doctor – based at 6b Harley Street, Sir Roderick has been called in by every posh family in England at one time or another. He considers Bertie a looney, but himself has a phobia about cats and an inordinate fear of fire. He is president of the West London branch of the anti-gambling league, drinks no wine, taking only half a glass of lemon squash, strongly disapproves of smoking, eats only the simplest food due to impaired digestion and considers coffee the root of half the nerve trouble in the world.

A formidable figure, he is tall and broad, with bushy eyebrows and a hairless dome, which Bertie judges would take a size nine hat. We later learn that, as a small boy, he was praised for his skills at hunt-the-slipper and compared to a juvenile bloodhound. At prep school, he would steal down the headmaster's study at night to pinch his ginger-nut biscuits, making him Bertie's brother in crime.

While a penniless medical student, he would sing at smoking concerts, having a pleasant baritone voice. In his early twenties, he also aided the love affair between swimming instructor George Lanchester and his sweetheart Bertha Simmons by pushing her father into the river so that George could rescue him.

Master of Ditteridge Hall, he is the father of the soupy Honoria and the pestilential Oswald. Bertie calls him Oswald the Plague-Spot. Bingo tries to love him for the sake of Honoria, but finds it hard going. Lady Glossop is a friend of Aunt Agatha, but seems to have died.

By *Thank You, Jeeves*, the widowed Sir Roderick has fallen for Lady Chuffnell, though their romance is hampered by Seabury. Finding themselves in the same position – going around the countryside in blackface – Sir Roderick's attitude to Wooster mellows. By *Jeeves in the Offing*, they are calling one another Roddy and Bertie. And in 'Jeeves and the Greasy Bird', Bertie even attempts to smooth Roddy and Myrtle's path to marriage and casts his former adversary as Santa Claus at Aunt Dahlia's Christmas party.

His clinic in Chuffnell Regis is funded by J. Washburn Stoker.

Mr Waterbury

Sippy's former headmaster, Waterbury had a roar like a lion greeting early Christians and a cane with a bite like an adder. A large, authoritative man with a Roman nose, penetrating eyes and high cheekbones, he looks like a traffic cop and contributes articles on 'The Old School Cloisters' and 'Some Little-Known Aspects of Tacitus' to the *Mayfair Gazette*. He is shocked when his article on Elizabethan dramatists is rejected – Sippy suggests that he should submit a light-breezy piece on the latest fashion in lap dogs instead.

It is not recorded whether he is related to the actors' agent Jas Waterbury, his niece Trixie or the chauffeur at Brinkley Court in *Right Ho, Jeeves*.

A. B. Filmer

The Right Honourable A. B. Filmer is a Cabinet minister. President of the Anti-Tobacco League, he is a serious-minded man of high character and purpose. Worse, he advocates the abstinence from alcoholic stimulants. Even Jeeves suggests that he is scarcely a congenial companion for Bertie. Nor is he pleasing on the eye. Bertie says he is 'a tubby chap who looked as if he had been poured into his clothes and forgotten to say "When!"' Nevertheless he is agile enough to spring out of the way of a marauding swan.

It later transpires that he is a friend of Florence Craye and has pulled strings to get Ginger Winship adopted as the Conservative candidate for Market Snodsbury.

J. Washburn Stoker

Bertie's prospective father-in-law J. Washburn Stoker was born in Carterville, though his daughter cannot remember whether it was Carterville, Kentucky, or Carterville, Massachusetts. This is important. If he is a southerner he is more likely to shoot Bertie.

He inherited his wealth from his second cousin, George, who, after a lifetime of doing down widows and orphans, went crazy, but was certified sane by Sir Roderick Glossop. Stoker has a house on East Sixty-Seventh Street in New York and a large yacht.

When it comes to his daughters Pauline and Emerald, he is a stern Victorian father. He reminds Bertie of a pirate of the Spanish Main, a massive blighter with piercing eyes who chews broken glass and drives nails into the back of his neck instead of using collar studs, making Sir Roderick Glossop and even Aunt Agatha positively pale by comparison.

His young son Dwight takes after his old man. When, after seeing a gangster movie, Seabury asks Dwight for protection money, he finds he needs protection himself.

Sergeant Edward 'Ted' Voules and Constable Dobson

These two policemen are more puzzled by Bertie's behaviour than actively seeking to arrest him. Voules is built along the lines of the Albert Hall, round in the middle with not much above. Bertie says that it looked as if Nature had intended to make two police sergeants but had forgotten to split them up. He plays the harmonium, sells eggs and claims to have taken on ninety-six spiders single-handed out in India.

His nephew Constable Dobson is tall, lean and stringy, and in love with the red-headed parlourmaid, Mary. Both of these strong arms of the law are determined to keep Chuffnell Regis safe from marauders.

Sir Watkyn Bassett

Bertie first meets Sir Watkyn when he is the magistrate at Bosher Street Police Court. Soon after, Sir Watkyn inherits a pot of money from a distant relative and retires to Totleigh Towers, Totleigh-in-the-Wold, where he is a JP. Bertie thinks the money comes from the fines he has been pocketing. Bassett, for his part, believes that Bertie has appeared before him for bag-snatching and that he sent him to jail.

A small man, he compensates by wearing loud clothes, including a prismatic checked tweed suit in *The Code of the Woosters* and a purple dressing gown with yellow frogs on it that upsets Stiffy's dog Bartholomew in *Stiffy Upper Lip, Jeeves*. He is romantically involved with the widow of the late Colonel H. H. Wintergreen, who is also the aunt of Roderick Spode, who eventually becomes his son-in-law.

Bassett's hobby is collecting silverware and other antiques. He is ruthless in this pursuit, upsetting Tom Travers's delicate digestion with lobster so that he can claim a cow-creamer. He also attempts to use blackmail to obtain the services of Anatole and Jeeves and, callously, flushes Gussie Fink-Nottle's newts down the plughole. Prepared to allow Gussie

and Stinker Pinker into the family, he blanches at the thought
of Bertie.

Constable Eustace Oates

Aiding Sir Watkyn in his persecution of Bertie is Constable
Oates, who is large, stout and moon-faced. Stiffy calls him ugly.
Bertie concedes that she is technically correct, but he would win
a beauty contest if the other competitors were Sir Watkyn and
Oofy Prosser of the Drones. We learn had he has a wife and
children. When Stiffy asks after them, he makes a noise 'like a
hippopotamus taking its foot out of the mud on a river bank'.

He is officious. Robbed of his prize – the imprisonment of
Bertie – in *The Code of the Woosters*, he actually succeeds in
holding him overnight in *Stiff Upper Lip, Jeeves*, only to be
forced to release him again.

Roderick Spode, later Lord Sidcup

Leader of the Saviours of Britain, aka the Black Shorts, and a
would-be dictator, Spode has a powerful, square face, slightly
moustached towards the centre. His gaze is keen and piercing.
He starts at seven feet tall and, in Bertie's eyes, grows to nine
feet seven. Swathed in a plaid ulster, he looks about six feet
across. It was, Bertie says, as if Nature intended to make a
gorilla and had changed its mind at the last moment. And not
just an ordinary run-of-the-mill gorilla, but the large economy
size.

He is a violent man, always threatening to tear Bertie's head
off and make him eat it. However, he has a soft side, designing
ladies' underwear for his lingerie company, Eulalie Soeurs.
When his uncle dies, he becomes the seventh Earl of Sidcup –
one of the oldest titles in England, according to Pop Bassett.
He sells Eulalie Soeurs and disbands the Black Shorts so he can
make speeches in support of Ginger Winship as the Conservative candidate for Market Snodsbury.

Spode is a more or less permanent guest at Totleigh Towers and has known Madeline Bassett since she was a child. He is intensely protective towards her. Finally, he tells her how he feels and they marry.

Police Constable Ernest Dobbs

The local rozzer in King's Deverill, Constable Dobbs has been dragooned into playing Mike in the Pat-and-Mike routine in the village concert. Corky has it in for him and instructs Bertie not to pull his punches as Dobbs is an atheist and taunts her uncle, the local vicar, sneering at the story of Jonah and the Whale and asking where Cain's wife came from. However, finding he has no talent for the stage, Corky fires Dobbs from the role. In the process, her dog, Sam Goldwyn, bites him and he impounds the creature.

Dobbs is just under five feet nine, but built like a blacksmith and he has a moustache that bristles. Bertie also considers him 'a man of few words . . . but a good spitter.' His normal air, Bertie says, was that of a stuffed gorilla and a face carved out of hard wood by a sculptor who had taken a correspondence course and had only reached lesson three.

Dobbs is engaged to the parlourmaid Queenie Silversmith (Jeeves's cousin) at Deverill Hall. But she breaks off the engagement when he refuses to give up atheism, then gets engaged to Catsmeat after her father, the butler, finds them kissing. Bertie dismisses Dobbs as 'fatty' and 'not . . . one of Hampshire's brightest thinkers'. Esmond Haddock, the local justice of the peace, praises the constable for his devotion to duty. Nevertheless, Haddock discounts his evidence when he discovers that Catsmeat is Corky's brother, casting aspersions on his ability to distinguish between a man with a green beard in a check suit and a clean-shaven man in a plain blue suit.

Corky wants to exact her revenge for the confiscation of her dog and seconds Gussie who, at her father's suggestion, visits a plague of frogs on Dobbs's police cottage. She then dispatches Gussie to repossess Sam Goldwyn while Dobbs is watching the concert. But Dobbs does not enjoy the show and does not stay to watch the second half, so catches Gussie and gives chase. However his running is laboured and Gussie outpaces him, but then foolishly takes refuge up a tree. Jeeves coshes Dobbs, leading him to believe that he has been struck by a thunder bolt. He 'sees the light' and gives up atheism, allowing a reconciliation with Queenie. Bertie then claims that he has reunited eight sundered hearts.

Colonel Aubrey Wyvern

Chief Constable of Southmoltonshire (Northamptonshire), Colonel Wyvern is both an Old Hardened Artery and a rozzer. He is short and stout, while preferring to be tall and slender. A member of his club once told him that he looked like a retired member of Sanger's troop of midgets who, for years, had been piling on the starchy food. The master of Wyvern Hall, his patience is tried to the limit by his fifteen-year-old cook and sixteen-year-old butler.

The Reverend Aubrey Upjohn

Although Bertie frequently mentions the beatings he received at the hands of his old prep school headmaster, the Reverend Upjohn does not make an appearance until *How Right You Are, Jeeves (Jeeves in the Offing)*. When Bertie was at school, it seemed that Upjohn was eight feet six with burning eyes, foam-flecked lips and flames coming out of both nostrils. Bertie compares him to Captain Bligh. But when Bertie meets him again as an adult, he has shrunk to a modest five foot seven and even Bertie feels he 'could have felled him with a single blow'.

He has also grown a moustache, which softens his face, and, being of the walrus or soup-strainer variety, has the added advantage of hiding some of it. However, he suddenly decides to shave it off, almost causing Kipper to lose his nerve and abandon the plan to rescue him from the lake. The naked upper lip twitches when a look of smug satisfaction comes over his face.

Author of a tome on prep schools, he aims to be adopted as the Conservative candidate for Market Snodsbury. Plainly he fails and that honour falls to Ginger Winship.

Bingley

Bertie comes up against the matey villain Mr Bingley in *Much Obliged, Jeeves*. He appears in *Thank You, Jeeves* as the valet Brinkley who has a long, thin, pimply face with deep brooding eyes. Then he is taciturn and Bertie believes that he wants to see him sprinting down Park Lane chased by a mob wielding dripping knives. He does come after Bertie with a carving knife, but only because, with his black face, he thinks Bertie is the devil.

It is thought that he appears as Bingley, rather than Brinkley, in *Much Obliged, Jeeves* because Wodehouse did not realize that he was going to make Brinkley Court a major setting for the novels. By then, Bingley's uncle in the grocery business has died, leaving him a house in Market Snodsbury and a large sum of money, but not large enough apparently as he steals the famous book from the Junior Ganymede, which reveals secrets about Ginger Winship's past, and tries to profit from it during the Market Snodsbury by-election. Jeeves disapproves of Bingley, sensing from the off that he is dishonest and untrustworthy. He has worked for Ginger Winship and L. P. Runkle, and now has a butler of his own.

Major 'Barmy' Plank

Explorer and Empire builder, Major Plank has spent time in South America and Equatorial Africa, where he contracted malaria which has affected his memory. However, he does recall tales of the gruesome fate that befell contemporaries in far-flung parts of the world.

Scarred on the leg by the mother of an Honourable Mention in a competition for bonny babies in Peru, he developed an antipathy to marriage, once hitch-hiking from Johannesburg to Cape Town to avoid matrimony. On another occasion, he shot the chief of the 'Mgombis and changed his name to George Bernard Shaw to avoid capture.

Now elderly, but still tanned with a square face, he has inherited a large house in Hockley-cum-Meston from his godfather, which is decorated with the heads of African game. He breeds cocker spaniels, eats only non-fattening protein bread and indulges his passion for rugby, which he developed at school.

L. P. Runkle

With a large pink face and a double chin, the financier and amateur photographer L. P. Runkle has a Panama hat with a pink ribbon to match. He spends much of his time sleeping, but has a criminal past unearthed by Jeeves.

Mr Cook

Short, grey-haired and red-faced, Cook is father of Vanessa Cook and the owner of Eggesford Court and its stable of racehorses. These were acquired, according to Orlo Porter, by years of grinding the faces of widows and orphans. Bertie thinks it was by selling them pressed beef and potato chips at lower prices. Cook is the scourge of communists and Woosters alike. Even his daughter Vanessa describes him as 'a cross between Attila the Hun and a snapping-turtle'. When wielding his hunting crop, Bertie says he has the disposition of a dyspeptic rattlesnake.

11

STAGE AND SCREEN

Jeeves and Wooster first took to the screen in 1936 when Twentieth Century Fox made *Thank You, Jeeves!* with David Niven as Bertie and Arthur Treacher as Jeeves. But, apart from the title and the two main characters, it borrowed nothing from the book. Wodehouse complained: 'They didn't use a word of my story, substituting another written by some studio hack.' The screenwriters were Stephen Gross and Joseph Hoffman.

In it, an erudite manservant named Jeeves tries to keep his frivolous employer Bertie out of harrowing adventures, but a damsel in distress, who is trying to help her brother stop two spies from getting his mysterious plans, intrudes on their London flat one rainy night. Bertie follows her to a country hotel, Mooring Manor, where they end up doing battle with crooks who pose as detectives from Scotland Yard. During the fight, Bertie wields several medieval artefacts, while Jeeves reveals himself to be a former boxing champion. Niven plays a creditable Bertie. But although Arthur Treacher looks the part, instead of being helpful, he is irritable and petulant, which is hardly surprising, as in any good Hollywood movie, the hero, Bertie, gets the girls and Jeeves will have to move on. The movie, though dire, was one of David Niven's stepping stones to stardom.

Arthur Treacher took the role of Jeeves again the following year in *Step Lively, Jeeves!* This time Jeeves goes to the United States after being conned by two swindlers into believing that he is the heir to Sir Francis Drake, not a ruse that you would have thought Jeeves would have fallen for. Again, the film owes nothing to any Wodehouse story. Bertie does not appear because Sam Goldwyn only lent Niven to Twentieth Century Fox for one picture.

Guy Bolton borrowed Jeeves for the 1954 play *Come On, Jeeves*, which Wodehouse then turned into *Ring for Jeeves* (*The Return of Jeeves*).

The BBC TV series *The World of Wooster* ran in the UK in twenty thirty-minute episodes from 30 May 1965 until 17 November 1967. It starred Ian Carmichael, who plays Bertie with a lisp and a monocle, and Dennis Price as Jeeves.

The radio series *What Ho! Jeeves* ran on BBC Radio Four from 1972 to 1981. It starred Richard Briers as Bertie and Michael Hordern as Jeeves.

In 1975, with Wodehouse's blessing, Andrew Lloyd Webber wrote the musical *Jeeves* with playwright Alan Ayckbourn. The action takes place at the East London Club for Unmanageable Boys where Bertie is supposed to be playing the banjo. But the strings keep breaking and, while Jeeves goes out to buy new ones, Bertie tells stories using characters and plotlines from Wodehouse's work, notably *The Code of the Woosters*, to entertain the audience. It opened at Her Majesty's Theatre in London on 22 April 1975, starring David Hemmings as Bertie and Michael Aldridge as Jeeves. The notices were bad and it ran for just thirty-eight performances.

A one-man play, *Jeeves Takes Charge*, adapted by and starring Edward Duke, had a run in London in 1980 and then toured extensively in North America. Then, in his nineties, Wodehouse worked on a J&W musical titled *Betting on Bertie*, using the plot of the earlier Guy Bolton play *Come On, Jeeves*. It had lyrics by Wodehouse, book by Bolton and music by Robert Wright and George Forrest, but unfortunately no producers willing to put up the money to stage it. Within the last few years it has received a few amateur or semi-professional productions in Britain. Chicago's City Lit theatre also has a long history of producing plays based on Jeeves and Wooster novels and stories.

In 1996, Lloyd Webber and Ayckbourn revisited the muscial and completely reworked it. Now called *By Jeeves*, it opened at the Stephen Joseph Theatre in Scarborough on 1 May 1996. It then moved to London for a twelve-week season at the Duke of York's Theatre, opening on 2 July 1996. The run was extended and the show moved to the Lyric, Shaftesbury Avenue, where it ran for another twenty-one weeks. Steven Pacey, who played Bertie Wooster, was nominated for an Olivier Award for Best Actor in a Musical, and *By Jeeves* also received nominations for Outstanding New Production and Best Costume Designer.

The show had its US premiere on 12 November 1996 at the Goodspeed Opera House in East Haddam, Connecticut. American actor John Scherer took the part of Bertie and Richard Kline played Jeeves. The show was specially recorded and released on VHS and DVD with British actor Martin Jarvis taking over from Richard Kline as Jeeves. It also ran for seventy-three performances at the Helen Hayes Theatre on Broadway from 28 October 2001 to 30 December 2001. Directed by Ayckbourn, the cast retained John Scherer as Bertie and Martin Jarvis as Jeeves. Jarvis won the Theatre World Award.

The award-winning series *Jeeves and Wooster* starring Stephen Fry and Hugh Laurie ran on British commercial television from 22 April 1990 to 20 June 1993, though it has often been repeated since. DVDs of the complete series are available worldwide, with the US release preceding the sale in the UK.

A new dramatization of *The Code of the Woosters* came to BBC Radio Four in 2006, starring Andrew Sachs as Jeeves and Marcus Brigstocke as Bertie. Toodle-oo.

BIBLIOGRAPHY

Cazalet-Keir (ed.), Thelma, *Homage to P. G. Wodehouse* (London: Barrie & Jenkins, 1973).

Connolly, Joseph, *Wodehouse* (London: Haus, 2004).

Day, Barry and Tony Ring, *P. G. Wodehouse in His Own Words* (London: Hutchinson, 2001).

Donaldson, Frances, *P. G. Wodehouse: A Biography* (London: Prion, 2001).

Easdale, Roderick, *The Novel Life of P. G. Wodehouse* (Newtown: Cyhoeddwyr y Superscript, 2003).

Garrison, Daniel H., *Who's Who in Wodehouse* (New York: International Polgonics, 1989).

Hall, R. A., *The Comic Style of P. G. Wodehouse* (Hamden, CT: Archon Books, 1974).

Hichens, Mark, *The Inimitable Life of P. G. Wodehouse* (Brighton: Book Guild, 2009).

Jaggard, Geoffrey, *Wooster's World* (London: Macdonald, 1967).

Jasen, David A., *A Bibliography and Reader's Guide to the First Editions of P. G. Wodehouse* (London: Greenhill Books, 1970).

Jasen, David A., *P. G. Wodehouse: A Portrait of a Master* (New York: Continuum, 1981).

McCrum, Robert, *Wodehouse: A Life* (New York: W. W. Norton, 2006).

McIlvaine, Eileen, Louise S. Sherry and James H. Heineman, *P. G. Wodehouse: A Comprehensive Bibliography and Checklist* (New York: James H. Heineman, 1990).

Morris, J. H. C., *Thank You, Wodehouse* (London: Weidenfeld and Nicolson, 1981).

Murphy, N. T. P., *A Wodehouse Handbook: The World and Words of P. G. Wodehouse* (London: Popgood & Groolley, 2006).

Ring, Tony and Geoffrey Jaggard, *Wodehouse in Woostershire* (Maidenhead: Porpoise Books, 1999).

Sproat, Ian, *Wodehouse at War* (Bath: Chivers Press, 1981).

Taves, Brian, *P. G. Wodehouse and Hollywood* (Jefferson, NC: McFarland and Company, 2006).

Usborne, Richard, *Plum Sauce: A P. G. Wodehouse Companion* (London: Ebury Press, 2002).

Usborne, Richard, *Wodehouse at Work* (London: Herbert Jenkins, 1961).

von Bodenhausen, Baroness Reinhild, *P. G. Wodehouse: The Unknown Years* (Pannipitiya, Sri Lanka: Stamford Lake, 2009).

Wind, Herbert Warren, *The World of P. G. Wodehouse* (New York: Praeger, 1972).

Wodehouse, P. G., *America, I Like You* (New York: Simon and Schuster, 1956).

Wodehouse, P. G., *P. G. Wodehouse: A Life in Letters* (London: Hutchinson, 2011).

Wodehouse, P. G., *Over Seventy* (London: Herbert Jenkins, 1957).

Wodehouse, P. G., *Performing Flea* (London: Herbert Jenkins, 1953).

Wodehouse, P. G., *Plum Pie* (London: Everyman, 2007).

Wodehouse, P. G., *P. G. Wodehouse: The Jeeves Omnibus 1* (London: Random House, 1989).

Wodehouse, P. G., *P. G. Wodehouse: The Jeeves Omnibus 2* (London: Random House, 1990).

Wodehouse, P. G., *P. G. Wodehouse: The Jeeves Omnibus 3* (London: Random House, 1991).

Wodehouse, P. G., *P. G. Wodehouse: The Jeeves Omnibus 4* (London: Random House, 1992).

Wodehouse, P. G., *P. G. Wodehouse: The Jeeves Omnibus 5* (London: Random House, 1993).

Wodehouse, P. G., *The Pothunters* (London: A. & C. Black, 1902).

Wodehouse, P. G., *Something Fresh* (London: Herbert Jenkins, 1969).

Wodehouse, P. G., *Wodehouse on Wodehouse* (London: Penguin, 1981).

Wodehouse, P. G., *The World of Jeeves* (London: Barrie & Jenkins, 1967).

Wodehouse, P. G., *The World of Mr Mulliner* (London: Barrie & Jenkins, 1972).

INDEX

A. L. Burt Company 42
Adlon Hotel, Berlin 32, 34
After the Show (music-hall sketch) 13
Agatha, Aunt ix, 3, 16, 20, 156, 158, 165,
    177–8, 179, 182, 184, 186, 190,
    191–3, 200, 208, 211, 223
Aldridge, Michael 232
Alexander, Uncle 179–80
Allahakbarries cricket team 10
'All's Well' 30, 65, 66
America, I Like You 9, 39
American Magazine 23
Anatole 161, 183, 184, 195, 207, 213,
    225
ancestry (Bertie Wooster) 153
ancestry (P. G. Wodehouse) 1
Annie, Aunt 171
Anstruther, Harold 'Beefy' 158, 205–6,
    218
Answers 7
Anything Goes (Wodehouse, Bolton and
    Porter) 16–17, 26
Argosy magazine 87, 89
'The Artistic Career of Corky' 44–6, 164,
    171, 179, 189
Ask Dad 221, 222
Associated Press 31
'At Geisenheimer's' 15, 18
'Aunt Agatha Makes a Bloomer' 57–8

'Aunt Agatha Speaks Her Mind' 57
'Aunt Agatha Takes the Count' 19, 57–8,
    166, 176, 192–3
'The Aunt and Sluggard' 18, 46–7, 174
Aunts Aren't Gentlemen viii, 38, 40,
    147–52, 161, 165, 175
Ayckbourn, Alan 233

banking career (P. G. Wodehouse) 6–7
Banks, Rosie M. (later Little) 159, 172,
    182, 195, 200, 203, 212
Barlow 13
Barmy in Wonderland 37
Barnikov, Baron Raven von 32, 34
Barrie & Jenkins 143, 147
Barrie, J. M. 10
Barrymore, John 13
Bassett, Gertrude 187
Bassett, Madeline ix, 162, 164, 166, 187,
    203, 205, 206, 207, 216, 227
Bassett, Sir Watkyn 174, 193, 203–4, 207,
    213, 217, 225–6
Bassington-Bassington, Cyril 211
Bates, Reverand James 194
BBC 33, 40, 232, 234
Beach Thomas, William 5, 8
The Beauty of Bath 10
Bellinger, Cora 198–9, 201, 214
Berlin 32–3

'Bertie Changes His Mind' 19, 20, 63, 154, 155, 156, 170, 173
'Bertie Gets Even' 54
Bertie Wooster Sees it Through 38, 128–34, 154, 167
Betting on Bertie (musical) 173, 233
Bickersteth, Francis 'Bicky' 174, 181, 210–11
Biffen, Charles Edward 'Biffy' 155, 172, 212–13
Big Money 23
'The Big Push' 28
'Bill' (song for *Show Boat*) 17
Bill the Conqueror 20
Bingham, Reverend Rupert 'Beefy' 215
Bingley 170, 176, 229
'Bingo and the Little Woman' 19, 65–6, 159
'Bingo Bans the Bomb' 212
'Bingo Has a Bad Goodwood' 59, 60
Bittlesham, Lord *see* Mortimer, Uncle
Black Shorts ix, 25, 26, 226
Blandings Castle 14, 21, 24, 32, 37
Blandings Castle 23
Bleke, Roland 13
Blumenfeld, Mr 211, 221–2
Blumenfeld, Sidney 222
Bodenhausen, Baroness Anga von 34
Bolton, Guy viii, 16–17, 25, 37, 39, 123, 222, 232, 233
Bonzo, Cousin 184
'The Borrowed Dog' 77–8
Bovill, Charles 13
Bowes-Lyon family 8
Brady, 'Kid' 9
Brancaster, Lord 173–4
Braythwayt, Daphne 191, 212
Bridgeworth, Lord 174
Briers, Richard 232
Brigstocke, Marcus 234
Bring on the Girls! (Wodehouse and Bolton) 37, 38, 169
Brinkley 24–5, 229
Brinkley Manor 100, 172, 197
Briscoe, Angelica 165
Broadway 15, 16–17, 21, 37
Brock, H. M. 71

Brown, Arthur William 66
Bullivant, Freddie 214
Burgess, Mary 194, 212
'Buried Treasure' 28
Bush, Jack 71
Butter and Egg Man (Kaufman adapted by Wodehouse) 37
By Jeeves (Lloyd Webber musical) 233
'By the Way' column 8, 9
Byng, Stephanie 'Stiffy' 166, 203–4, 217, 225, 226

Caffyn, George 221, 222
Camp 30
Canada 71, 87, 117, 129
Canadian Home Journal 71
Candle-Light (Geyer adapted by Wodehouse) 23
Cannes, France 23–4
Captain 7, 11, 12
Carmichael, Ian 232
Carry On, Jeeves! 19, 20, 44, 45, 46, 47, 49, 50, 63, 67, 68, 69, 71, 164
The Cat-nappers 38, 40, 147–52
CBS 33
Chamberlain, Neville 27
Charmatz, Bill 89, 134, 138
Cheesewright, D'Arcy 'Stilton' 158, 167, 189, 190, 206, 217–18
Chiswick, Duke of 181, 210
Chuffnell, Dowager Lady Myrtle 185–6
Chuffnell, Lady 168, 223
Chuffnell, Lord Marmaduke 'Chuffy' 167, 173, 185, 202, 209, 215
Chuffnell, Seabury 185–6, 223, 224
Churchill, Winston 21–2, 35
Claude and Eustace 182, 194–5
Clive, Uncle 182
'Clustering Round Young Bingo' 20, 68–9, 165, 176, 213
Cocktail Time 39
The Code of the Woosters 26, 38, 104–11, 156–7, 166, 176, 178, 183, 204, 212, 225, 226, 232, 234
Collier's 11, 13
Come On, Jeeves (Wodehouse adapted by Bolton) 37, 123, 232, 233

communism 24
'Comrade Bingo' 19, 24, 59–60, 159, 193, 212
Conan Doyle, Sir Arthur 9, 10, 16
Connor, William 33, 38, 40
Constitutional Club, London (Wodehouse residence) 12
Cook, Mr 230
Cook, Vanessa 166, 208, 230
Cooper, John 87
Corbett, 'Gentleman Jim' 9
Corcoran, Bruce 'Corky' 179, 180, 189, 210
Cosmopolitan magazine vii, 12, 19, 20, 24, 32, 53, 54, 55, 57, 59, 60, 62, 63, 64–5, 66, 76, 77, 78, 80, 81, 83, 84, 85, 92
Craye, Edwin 186
Craye, Florence 159, 162, 163, 164, 166, 167, 168, 180, 186, 189–91, 204, 206, 207, 218, 219, 224
Craye, Percy *see* Worplesdon, Lord Percival
'Creature of Impulse' 169
Crombie, Charles 72, 73, 74, 76, 77, 78, 80, 81, 83, 84, 85
Cussen, Major 34, 35
Cyril, Uncle 172

Dahlia, Aunt (Mrs Travers) ix, 3, 156, 159, 161, 162, 164, 165, 173, 174, 176, 183–4, 185, 188, 189, 192, 195, 197, 198, 199, 206, 213, 215, 218, 219, 223
Daily Express 9
Daily Mail 11, 104
Daily Mirror 33
Damsel in Distress 22, 26
Danby, Joe 188, 210
Davies, Marion 21–2
Deane, Eleanor (later Wodehouse) *see* Wodehouse, Eleanor (mother)
Deane, Louise 'Looly' (aunt) 3
Deane, Mary (aunt) 2, 3
Deane, Mrs Bathurst (grandmother) 4
Deane, Reverent John Bathurst (grandfather) 2

'The Delayed Exit of Claude and Eustace,' 19, 64–6, 176
Denison, Ray 188–9, 210
Deval, Jacques 22
Dickens, Charles 35–6
Didier & Co. 117
Dobbs, Constable Ernest 175, 227–8
Dobson, Constable 225
'Doing Clarence a Bit of Good' 87–8
Donaldson, Frances 39
Donop, Colonel Pelham von 2
Dorchester Hotel, London (Wodehouse residence) 25
Double Jeopardy 129–34
Doubleday & Company 36, 38, 111
Doubleday, Doran & Company 72, 85, 104
D'Oyly Carte, Rupert 11
Drones Club 21, 71, 158, 159, 162, 163, 209, 212, 214, 216, 218, 219
Duke, Edward 233
Dulwich College 4–5
Durrell, Lawrence 17

education (P. G. Wodehouse) 3, 4–5
Edward I, King 1
Eggleston, Blair 168, 192
Eggs, Beans and Crumpets 28
Elizabeth College, Guernsey 4, 5–6
Elizabeth, Queen (Queen Mother) 8
Ellery Queen's Mystery Magazine 87
Emily, Aunt 171, 182–3
Encounter magazine 38
Enke, Max 30
'Episode of the Dog McIntosh' 77–8
'Exit of Claude and Eustace' 65
'Extricating Young Gussie' viii, 15–16, 42–4, 163, 177, 179, 188–9

Fairbanks Sr, Douglas 13
fascism 24 *see also* Nazis
Few Quick Ones, A 39, 71, 87
Filmer, A. B. 178, 224
films 22–3, 26, 231–2
Fink-Nottle, Gussie ix, 158, 162, 165, 166, 174, 201, 203, 207, 214, 215–16, 217, 225–6, 227–8

First World War 13, 14
Fittleworth, George Webster 'Boko' 189, 204, 218, 221
'Fixing it for Freddie' 20, 71–2, 171
Flagg, James Montgomery 76, 77, 78, 80, 81, 83, 85, 92
Forde-Rasche, Honourable Aubrey 13
Forrest, George 233
Fotheringay-Phipps, Cyril 'Barmy' 37, 217
France 19, 23–4, 25–6, 27–30, 34–5
Fred, Uncle 27, 34
French Leave 39
Fry, Stephen viii, 234
Full Moon 32, 34

Galahad at Blandings 39, 187
Galdone, Paul 111
Galsworthy, John 21
Garnet, Jeremy 10
Geisenheimers 18
Gentleman of Leisure, A 12, 13, 22
George H. Doran Company 47–9, 52
George Newnes publishers 44, 46, 49, 50
George, Uncle 185, 200–1
German Army 28–30, 31
Gershwin, George and Ira 16
Geyer, Siegfried 23
Gilbert, W. S. 9
Glendennon, Magnolia 207, 218, 219
Globe and Traveller 7, 8, 10, 11, 12
The Globe By the Way Book 11
Glossop, Hildebrand 'Tuppy' 159, 166, 198, 199, 201, 214–15
Glossop, Honoria 168, 191–2, 196, 212, 223
Glossop, Lady 191, 223
Glossop, Oswald 223
Glossop, Sir Roderick 185–6, 191, 192, 202, 214, 222–3, 224
Goldwyn, Sam 232
Gorringe, Percy 159, 189, 190
Grand Magazine 100
'Great Sermon Handicap' ix, 3, 19, 60–1, 154, 155–6, 212
Gregson, Spencer 177, 178
Gregson, Thomas 178, 184
Gross, Stephen 231

Gudgeon, Hilda 166, 205–6, 218

Haddock, Esmond 4, 187, 205, 227
Hagen, Jack 123
Harper & Row 112
Have a Heart (Wodehouse, Bolton and Kern) 16
health (P. G. Wodehouse) 6, 40–1
Hearst, William Randolph 21, 22
Heavy Weather (Brinkley Manor in US) 24, 25
'Helping Freddie' 71–2
Hemmings, David 232
Hemmingway, Aline 174, 192–3
Henry I, King 1
Her Cardboard Lover (Wodehouse adapted from Deval) 22
Herbert Jenkins publishers 35, 46, 47, 52, 72, 85, 87, 89, 92, 100, 104, 111–12, 117, 123, 128, 134, 138
'Hero's Reward' 54, 55
Herring, Reginald 'Kipper' 4, 168, 198, 219, 229
Hicks, Seymour 10
Hirsch, Louis A. 222
Hitler, Adolf 28
Hoffman, Joseph 231
Hogg, Nurse 157
Hollywood see films
Hollywood Cricket Club 22
homosexuality 163
Hong Kong 2–3
Hong Kong and Shanghai Banking Corporation 6
Hope, Philip 5
Hopwood, Roderick 186, 204
Hopwood, Zenobia 'Nobby' 186, 190, 191, 204, 218
Hordern, Michael 232
Hot Water 23, 26
Hôtel Bristol, Paris 35
Hotel Earle, New York (Wodehouse residence) 12
Hotel Impney, Droitwich (Wodehouse residence) 21
Hôtel Prince de Galles, Paris (Wodehouse residence) 25

Hôtel Royal, Picardie 25
How Right You Are, Jeeves 38, 134–8, 159, 161, 165, 168, 197, 198, 228
Hunstanton Hall, Norfolk 20, 25

Ice in the Bedroom 39
If I Were You 23
'Indian Summer of an Uncle' 20, 84–5, 185
'Inferiority Complex of Old Sippy' 20, 72–3, 175, 196
The Inimitable Jeeves (*Jeeves* in the US) 19, 38, 52, 53, 54, 55, 57, 59, 60, 62, 63, 65, 66
The Inside Stand 26
'Introducing Claude and Eustace' 55–6
The Intrusion of Jimmy 12
The Invasion (Le Queux) 11
Isabel, Aunt 180
ITV vii–viii

Jackson Junior 11
Jackson, Mike 16
James, Uncle 183
Jarvis, Martin 233
Jasen, David 7, 39
Jeeves viii, 16, 17, 63, 123, 153, 155, 156, 159, 160, 161, 162, 164, 180, 185, 186, 190, 192, 193, 195, 196, 197–8, 199, 201, 203, 210, 215, 216, 218, 224, 228, 229, 230
  appearance 175
  background and education 170–1, 173
  Bertie's clothes 176
  extended family 171–2
  Junior Ganymede club 173
  name 169–70
  nature of job and career 170, 173–4
  pastimes 173, 175
  violent acts 175–6
  Wodehouse's influences 169
  and women 172–3
  see also Wooster, Bertie; individual stories and novels by name
Jeeves (Lloyd Webber musical) 232
'Jeeves and Blighter' 55
'Jeeves and the Chump Cyril' 18, 51–3, 176

'Jeeves and the Dog McIntosh' 20, 77–8
Jeeves and the Feudal Spirit 38, 128–34, 154, 159, 167, 173, 183, 189, 190
'Jeeves and the Greasy Bird' 89–91, 186, 192, 223
'Jeeves and the Hard-Boiled Egg' 18, 50–1, 174
'Jeeves and the Impending Doom' 20, 73–4, 178, 195, 212
'Jeeves and the Kid Clementina' 20, 81–3, 153–4, 170, 176
'Jeeves and the Love that Purifies' 20, 78–80, 157, 163, 178, 197, 218
'Jeeves and the Old School Chum' 20, 83–4, 155
'Jeeves and the Song of Songs' 20, 76–7, 163, 198, 201
'Jeeves and the Spot of Art' 20, 80–1, 155, 159, 163
'Jeeves and the Stolen Venus' 87–8
'Jeeves and the Unbidden Guest' 18, 49–50, 160, 176, 180
'Jeeves and the Yuletide Spirit' 20, 74–6
Jeeves and Tie that Binds 38, 143–7, 154, 165, 170
Jeeves and Wooster (ITV) viii–viii, 234
'Jeeves Exerts the Old Cerebellum' 53
Jeeves in the Morning 111–17
Jeeves in the Offing 4, 38, 134–43, 159, 161, 165, 168, 197, 198, 223, 228
'Jeeves in the Springtime' 19, 53–4, 161, 165, 172, 182, 212
'Jeeves Makes an Omlette' 87–9, 183
Jeeves, Percy 169
'Jeeves Takes Charge' 18, 47, 154, 160, 175, 180, 189, 190, 233
Jerome, Jerome K. 10
John Bull magazine 134
Joy in the Morning 28, 29, 34, 36, 111–17, 154, 159, 163, 174, 189–90, 204, 221
Julia, Aunt 177, 179, 209, 210
Justice, Martin 42

Kaufman, George 37
Kern, Jerome viii, 10, 16
Kleine Komödie (Geyer) 23
Kline, Richard 233

knighthood (P. G. Wodehouse) 40

Ladies' Home Journal 123
Laughing Gas 23
Laurie, Hugh viii, 234
Le Queux, William 11
Le Touquet, France 19, 25, 26
'Leave it to Jeeves' 17, 44–6, 163–4, 171,
    189
Leave it to Psmith 11, 22–3, 38
Leete, Alfred 42, 44, 46, 49, 50, 51
'Letter of Introduction' 51–2
Liberty 20, 72, 73, 74
Lilliput magazine 87
'Lines and Business' 71–2
Little, Bown & Company 92–3, 100
Little, Mortimer 159, 172
The Little Nugget 13
Little, Richard P. 'Bingo' 159, 161,
    164–5, 172, 182, 191, 193, 194, 195,
    200, 211–12, 213, 223
Little, Rosie 165
Lorimer, George Horace 15, 26
Los Angeles Times 23
The Lost Lambs 11
Love Among the Chickens 10, 11, 20
'The Love that Purifies' 20, 78–80, 157,
    163, 178, 197, 218
Low Wood, Le Touquet (Wodehouse
    residence) 26, 27, 29
Luck of the Bodkins 25, 26
Lusitania, RMS 12–13
Lyon, Belinda 89

Mabel 155, 164–5, 172, 182, 192, 212
Mackail, Denis 17, 22
Madame Tussauds 40
Magdalen College, Bertie at 158
Mainwaring, Peggy 155
Malvern House, Kent 4
Malvern, Lady 180–1
Man of Means, A 13
'The Man Upstairs' 12, 22
The Man with Two Left Feet viii, 16, 18,
    42
Manhattan *see* New York
Mannering-Phipps, Cuthbert 179, 209

Mannering-Phipps, Gussie 177, 179, 188,
    209
Mannering-Phipps, Julia 177, 179, 209, 210
Markham Square, London (Wodehouse
    residence) 6
The Mating Season 4, 36, 37, 117–23, 161,
    163, 164, 165, 166, 173, 174, 175,
    178, 195, 216–17
Maudie 185, 200–1
Maxwell-Fyfe, Sir David 39
McClure's Magazine 13
McIntosh, Hal 117
'Men Who Have Missed Their Own
    Wedding' 7
Methuen publishers 42
'The Metropolitan Touch' 19, 63–4, 160,
    212
MGM 22–3, 26, 232
MI5 34, 35
MI6 34–5
Mike 11
Mills, Phyllis 168, 206–7
Milne, A. A. 10
Miss Springtime (Wodehouse, Bolton and
    Kern) 16
Money in the Bank 30, 31, 35
Moon, Gwendolen 196–7, 214
Morehead, Daphne Dolores 206, 218
Morgan, Wallace 72, 73, 74, 104
Mortimer, Uncle 182, 195, 211
Mosley, Oswald 25
Motague-Todd, Mr 173
Mowat, H. J. 68
Mrs Tickell's 9–10
Much Obliged, Jeeves 38, 143–7, 154,
    155, 165, 170, 173, 175, 189, 201,
    204, 213, 229
Muggeridge, Malcolm 34–5, 36, 38
Mulliner, Mr 21, 23, 28, 197
mumps 9
Munsey's Magazine 13
Muriel, Aunt 180
musical comedies 10, 16–17, 18, 22, 25,
    26, 173, 233
Mussolini, Benito 25
My Man Jeeves 18, 20, 44, 45, 46, 49, 50,
    163

Nazis 28–34
Needham KC, Raymond 25
New York vii, 9, 11–13, 17, 19, 36
New York Times 31, 40
New Yorker 39, 40
Niven, David 231, 232
Nixon, Richard 40
No Nudes is Good Nudes 38
'No Wedding Bells for Bingo' 53–4
Norfolk Street, London (Wodehouse
    residence) 21, 169
Norman Conquest 1
Nuts and Wine 13

Oates, Constable Eustace 226
Observer 36
O'Casey, Sean 37–8
Oh, Boy! (Wodehouse, Bolton and Kern)
    16, 17, 21, 22
Oh, Kay! (Wodehouse, Bolton and the
    Gershwins) 16
Oh, Lady! Lady! 22
'Oh, Mr Chamerlain!' 10
'The Ordeal of Young Tuppy' 20, 85–7,
    163
Orwell, George 36, 38
Over Seventy (America, I Like You in the
    US) 3–4, 7, 9, 11, 17, 22
Oxford English Dictionary 170
Oxford University, Bertie at 158, 162
Oxford University honours (P. G.
    Wodehouse) 21, 27

P. G. Wodehouse: Portrait of a Master
    (Jasen) 39
Pacey, Steven 233
Paris 34–5
'The Parrot' 9
'Pearls Mean Tears' 57, 58
Pearson's Weekly 7
Pelican at Blandings, A 38
Pendlebury, Gwladys 155, 159, 199
Penguin 38
Pepper, Reggie 13, 18, 20, 71, 87
Percy, Uncle see Worplesdon, Lord
    Percival
Performing Flea 5, 37–8

Pershore, Lord 'Wilmot' 180, 181
Piccadilly Jim 18
Pictorial Review 13, 71, 87
Pigott, Mrs P. B. 171
Pigs Have Wings 37, 38
Pim, Lucius 199
Pinker, Harold 'Stinker' 166, 204, 217,
    226
Pinker, J. B. 10
Pirbright, Cora 'Corky' 157–8, 164, 165,
    204–5, 216, 227–8
Plack, Werner 32, 34
Plank, Major 'Barmy' 229–30
Platt, Rhoda 185, 200–1
Playboy 89, 134, 138
Plum Pie 39, 89, 212
poetry 9
politics 24–5, 27
    see also Second World War
Porter, Cole 16–17, 25, 26
Porter, Orlo J. 208, 220, 230
Post, A Damsel in Distress 18
The Pothunters 8
Potter-Pirbright, Claude Cattermole
    'Catsmeat' 204, 205, 216–17, 227
Price, Dennis 232
'Pride of the Woosters is Wounded' 54,
    57, 211, 212
The Prince and Betty 12
Prince, Cissie and Florrie 3
Prince for Hire, A 23
Pringle, Heloise 195–6
prisoner of war, P. G. Wodehouse as a
    29–32, 33, 34, 39
propaganda, Nazi see radio broadcasts,
    German
Psmith in the City 6, 11
Psmith, Journalist 11, 12
Psmith, Ronald Eustace (earlier Rupert)
    11, 16
Public School Magazine 6, 8
Punch 9, 28, 38
Punch XI cricket team 10
'The Purity of the Turf' 19, 62
Purkiss, P. P. 212
Pyke, Laura 199–200

quarantine, animal 25, 28
Quick Service 27, 28

radio broadcasts, German 32–3, 34, 35, 38, 39
radio shows, Jeeves and Wooster 232, 234
Raleigh, Henry 47, 49, 50, 100
'Rallying Round Clarence' 87
Ranelagh, Lord Frederick 174
rascism 93
Redmond, Alex 129
The Return of Jeeves 123–8, 156, 161, 174, 175, 176, 232
Reynard, Grant T. 51
Right Ho, Jeeves 25, 38, 100–4, 172, 175, 184, 197, 201, 223
Ring for Jeeves 37, 38, 123–8, 156, 161, 174, 175, 176, 232
RKO Pictures 26
Robinson, Eugene 169
Rockmetteller, Isabel 180
Rogate Lodge, Petersfield (Wodehouse residence) 21
Roper, Miss 3
Rosalie 26
Rose, Richard O. 134
Rowbotham, Charlotte Corday 193–4, 212
Rowcester, Lord 174
Royal Society of Literature 21
'The Rummy Affair of Old Biffy' 20, 66–7, 172, 183, 192
Runkle, L. P. 215, 229, 230

Sachs, Andrew 234
Sally (Wodehouse, Bolton and Kern) 16
Sarg, Tony 44, 46
Saturday Evening Post vii, 9, 11, 14, 15, 17, 18, 20, 26, 28, 31, 32, 33, 34, 42, 44, 46, 47, 49, 50, 51, 66, 68, 69, 100, 104
Scherer, John 233
Scholfield, Mrs 154
Schwed, Peter 38
'Scoring off Jeeves' 19, 25, 54–5, 192, 211
Screen Playwrights 26
Screen Writers Guild 26

Second World War 27–34
Sergeant Brue 10
Service with a Smile 39
Sevier, Gerry 134
Show Boat 17
Sidcup, Lord *see* Spode, Sir Roderick
Silversmith, Charlie 172
Silversmith, Queenie 172, 227, 228
Simon & Schuster 38, 87, 89, 123, 129, 134, 138, 143, 147
Simpkins, James 87
Singer, Muriel 179–80, 189
Sipperley of the Paddock, Miss 184–5
Sipperley, Oliver 'Sippy' 162, 163, 175, 184–5, 195–7, 213–14, 223
'Sir Roderick Comes to Lunch' 55–7
Sitting Pretty (Wodehouse, Bolton and Kern) 16
Skidmore, T. D. 53, 54, 55, 57, 59, 60, 62, 63, 65, 66
Smith, Charles Aubrey 22
'Society Whispers from the States' 9
'Some Aspects of Game Captaincy' 6
Something Fishy 39
Something Fresh (*Something New* in US) viii, 14, 15
'Song of Songs' 76–7
song writing *see* musical comedies
Soviet Union 33, 34
Spenser, Uncle 179
Spode, Sir Roderick ix, 25, 26, 155, 168, 173, 183, 203, 207, 216, 217, 225, 226–7
'The Spot of Art' 80–1
Spring Fever 34
SS *America* 36
Star Weekly 71, 87, 117, 123, 129, 134
Starr, Cora 178
'Startling Dressiness of a Lift Attendant' 51–3
Step Lively, Jeeves! (film) 232
Stiff Upper Lip, Jeeves 39, 138–43, 170, 171, 174, 176, 202, 204, 225, 226
Stoker, Dwight 224
Stoker, Emerald 203, 207, 216, 224
Stoker, Pauline 156, 166–7, 174, 201–2, 215, 224

Strand Magazine vii, 12, 13, 15, 16, 18, 19, 20, 24, 42, 44, 46, 47, 49, 50, 51, 53, 54, 55, 57, 59, 60, 62, 63, 64, 65, 67, 68, 69, 71, 72, 73, 74, 76, 77, 78, 80, 81, 83, 84, 85, 87, 92, 169
Sullivan, Frank 39
Summer Moonshine 26
Sunset at Blandings 40–1
The Swoop 11

tax issues (P. G. Wodehouse) 18, 23, 25, 26, 34, 36
television adaptations vii–viii, 40, 232, 234
Thalberg, Irving 22–3, 26
Thank You, Jeeves 23, 24–5, 92–100, 165, 167, 170, 173, 209, 223, 229, 231–2
'The Love-r-ly Silver Cup' 15
theatre 10, 16–17, 18, 25, 26, 232–3
Theif in the Night, A (play) 13
Theosophical Movement 6
Those Three French Girls 22
Tickell, Mrs 9–10
Tit-Bits 7
Todd, Rockmetteller 'Rocky' 210
Todds, Rocky 174, 180
Tom, Uncle 158, 183, 184, 225
Toronto Star 87
Tost PoW camp 30–2, 33
Tost Times 30
Townend, Bill 5, 9, 17, 21, 22, 24, 27, 37, 39
Travers, Angela 166, 184, 199, 201, 214, 216
Travers, Dahlia *see* Dahlia, Aunt
Travers, Thomas Portarlington *see* Tom, Uncle
Treacher, Arthur 231–2
'Tuppy Changes his Mind' 85–7, 163
Twentieth Century Fox 23, 232
Twistleton, Pongo 162

Uckridge 20
Uffenham, Lord 30
Ukridge, Stanley Featherstonehaugh 6, 10, 16
Uncle Dynamite 34, 35

'Uncle Fred Flits By' 27
Uncle Fred in Springtime 27
Uneasy Money 14, 15
United States of America, P. G. Wodehouse and the vii, viii, 9, 11–14, 15–19, 21–3, 25, 29, 30, 31–3, 34, 36–7, 38–9, 40
see also Saturday Evening Post
'Unpleasantness at Kozy Kot' 71
Upjohn, Reverend Aubrey 157, 158, 161, 206, 217, 228–9
Usborne, Richard 39
Vanity Fair 14, 16
VC Magazine 9
Vera, Aunt 184–5
Very Good, Jeeves 20, 72, 73, 74, 76, 78, 80, 81, 83, 84, 85, 92
Voules, Sergeant Edward 'Ted' 225

Wallis Mills, A. 47, 53, 54, 55, 57, 59, 60, 62, 63, 64, 65, 67, 68, 69
Walpole Street, London (Wodehouse residence) 8
Ward, Phillips 71
Wardour, Marion 182, 194–5
Washburn Stoker, J. 174, 201, 207, 223, 224
Waterbury, Jas 183, 223
Waterbury, Mr 223
Watson, Jane 172, 182
Waugh, Evelyn viii, 40
Wayman, Ethel *see* Wodehouse, Ethel
Wayman, Leonora *see* Wodehouse, Leonora
Webber, Andrew Lloyd 232, 233
Wells, H. G. 23–4
West End, London 18
Westbrook, Herbert 9, 10, 11
What Ho!, Jeeves 232
'Whither Wodehouse?' 31–2
Wickham, Roberta 'Bobbie' 159, 165, 176, 197–8, 219
Wickhammersley, Lady Cynthia 155–6, 164, 194, 212
Wickhammersley, Lord 154, 194
Widgeon, Freddie 164
Wilkinson, Gilbert 92

William the Conqueror 1

Willoughby, Uncle 154, 160, 180, 186

Wingham, Reverend Hubert 194

Winkworth, Dame Daphne 187

Winkworth, Huxley 187

Winship, Harold 'Ginger' 155, 189, 207, 218, 219, 224, 226, 229

'Without the Option' 20, 69–70, 162, 184–5, 195–6, 213–14

Wodehouse at Work (Usborne) 39

Wodehouse, Eleanor (mother) 2–3

Wodehouse, Ernest Armine 2, 6

Wodehouse, Ethel (wife) 13–14, 19, 21, 27, 28, 33, 34, 35

Wodehouse, Henry (father) 1–2, 3

'Wodehouse in Wonderland' 34, 35

Wodehouse, Leonora (step-daughter) 14, 19, 33, 35

Wodehouse, P. G. (Pelham Grenville) viii
  ancestors 1
  banking career 6–7
  birth and childhood 2–6
  education 3, 4–5
  films 22–3, 26, 231–2
  in France 19, 23–4, 25–6, 27–30, 34–5
  German radio broadcasts 32–3, 34, 35, 38, 39
  health and death 6, 40–1
  knighthood 40
  and MI5 34, 35
  musical comedies 10, 16–17, 18, 22, 25, 26, 173, 233
  Nazi propaganda 32–3
  Oxford University honours 21, 27
  as Prisoner of War 29–32, 33, 34, 39
  Second World War 27–34
  sport 4, 5, 7, 9, 10, 14, 22
  tax issues 18, 23, 25, 26, 34, 36
  in the US 9, 11–14, 15–19, 21–3, 25, 36–7, 38–40

Wodehouse, Philip Peveril 2, 4, 5–6

Wodehouse, Richard Lancelot 2

Wodehouse, Sir Bertram de 1

Wodehouse, Sir Constantine de 1

Wodehouse Society viii

Wolkenstein, Count and Countess von 34

Wooster, Algernon 14

Wooster, Bertie viii–ix, 3, 4, 10, 15–16, 17, 24–5, 30, 170, 171, 172, 173, 174, 175, 177–8, 179, 180, 181, 182, 183–4, 185, 211, 212–13, 214, 215, 216–17, 218, 219, 220, 221, 222, 223, 224, 225, 226, 227, 228, 229, 230
  age of 160–1
  ancestry 153
  appearance 159
  cars 155
  childhood and education 153–4, 157–8, 165, 183–4, 186
  clothing 176
  finances 154–5
  food and drink 161–3
  intelligence and character 156–7, 164
  parents and sister 153–4
  reading preferences 159–60
  sport 158–9
  university 158, 162
  and women 163–8, 188–208
  work 155–6
  see also Jeeves; individual stories and novels by name

Wooster, Sir George (Uncle George) 185, 200–1

The World of Jeeves 16

The World of Wooster (BBC) 40, 232

Worple, Alexander 179–80, 210

Worplesdon, Lord Percival 158, 160, 173, 174, 179, 180, 186, 190, 204

Wright, George 69

Wright, Robert 233

Wyvern, Colonel Aubrey 228

Yaxley, Lord (Uncle George) 185, 200–1

Ziegfeld, Florenz 17